FRACTURING OPPORTUNITY

Studies in the Postmodern Theory of Education

Shirley R. Steinberg
General Editor

Vol. 362

PETER LANG
New York • Washington, D.C./Baltimore • Bern
Frankfurt • Berlin • Brussels • Vienna • Oxford

R. EVELY GILDERSLEEVE

FRACTURING OPPORTUNITY

Mexican Migrant Students & College-going Literacy

PETER LANG
New York • Washington, D.C./Baltimore • Bern
Frankfurt • Berlin • Brussels • Vienna • Oxford

Library of Congress Cataloging-in-Publication Data

Gildersleeve, R. Evely.
Fracturing opportunity: Mexican migrant students
and college-going literacy / R. Evely Gildersleeve.
p. cm. — (Counterpoints: studies in the postmodern
theory of education; v. 362)
Includes bibliographical references.
1. Mexican American college students—California.
2. Mexican Americans—Education—California.
3. Mexicans—Education—California.
4. People with social disabilities—Education—California.
5. Mexico—Emigration and immigration.
6. United States—Emigration and immigration. I. Title.
LC3732.C2G44   378.1'98296872073—dc22   2009014921
ISBN 978-1-4331-0553-1 (hardcover)
ISBN 978-1-4331-0554-8 (paperback)
ISSN 1058-1634

Bibliographic information published by **Die Deutsche Nationalbibliothek**.
Die Deutsche Nationalbibliothek lists this publication in the "Deutsche
Nationalbibliografie"; detailed bibliographic data is available
on the Internet at http://dnb.d-nb.de/.

Cover photograph by Nana Osei-Kofi.

The paper in this book meets the guidelines for permanence and durability
of the Committee on Production Guidelines for Book Longevity
of the Council of Library Resources.

© 2010 Peter Lang Publishing, Inc., New York
29 Broadway, 18th floor, New York, NY 10006
www.peterlang.com

All rights reserved.
Reprint or reproduction, even partially, in all forms such as microfilm,
xerography, microfiche, microcard, and offset strictly prohibited.

Printed in the United States of America

Para estudiantes migrantes, especial de revolucionarios:
Alex, a caretaker,
Antonio, a political scientist,
Armando, an el shorty,
Butterfly, a people changer,
Carlitos, a fighter,
Cristina, a singer,
Eduardo, a funny guy,
Jesus, a scholar–athlete,
Lorena, a helper,
Nené, a poet,
Renaldo, a cheerleader,
and Yaneth, a believer,
and all so much more.
¡Viva la revolución de educación para hermanos todos!

Table of Contents

List of Tables and Figures ... ix

Foreword, *Patricia M. McDonough* ... xi

Acknowledgements ... xiii

1. Introduction ... 1

2. Mapping Migrant Students' College-going Literacy Development ... 23

3. Reading and Writing Migrant Students as Subjects ... 61

4. Mapping Tools and Rules: Mediating and Regulating College-going ... 89

5. (im)Migration as Tools for College-going ... 105

6. *¡Confianza!* ... 119

7. Mapping the Community's Division of Labor: Who Does What in Migrant Students' College-going? ... 143

8. Toward a College-going Pedagogy: Implications of Mapping a Fracture ... 183

Afterword: On Method and Coming to Know ... 207

Bibliography ... 227

List of Tables and Figures

Table 1: Family division of *mechanical* labor	152
Table 2: Family division of *organic* labor	157
Table 3: Schooling division of *mechanical* labor	159
Table 4: Schooling division of *organic* labor	165
Table 5: Higher education division of *mechanical* labor	166
Table 6: Higher education division of *organic* labor	169
Table 7: Outreach division of *mechanical* labor	173
Table 8: Outreach division of *organic* labor	175
Figure 1: Higher education opportunity as activity	40
Figure 2: Migrant students' college-going activity	190

Foreword

Patricia M. McDonough
University of California, Los Angeles

Fracturing opportunity: Mexican migrant students and college-going literacy is an engaging, compelling and intellectually robust piece of research that speaks to scholars, practitioners, and advocates interested in improving Latino migrant students' post-secondary opportunities and in transforming high school guidance and college admissions practices.

At its core, this book documents the sociocultural dimensions of college-going in the lives of Mexican migrant students. Starting from a place of documenting the multiple underrepresentations of race and class combined with marginalized conditions of language, geography, and the contested social stigma of immigration, Gildersleeve presents a critical ethnography of 12 Mexican migrant students in California. He shows how college going is missing from, and yet must be institutionalized into, the everyday lives of students in order to systematically affect college enrollment rates for this population of Latino students.

Professor Gildersleeve's research sits at the intersection of two bodies of scholarship, notably critical literacy studies and college access. Critical literacy studies assert that all learning is culturally-mediated, historically bound, and is ultimately a meaning-making process. Also, literacy development leads to increasing participation, which in turn leads to transformation. College access research uses a variety of interdisciplinary lenses to understand the psychological, organizational, economic and cultural processes that help or hinder students' college opportunities and choices and focuses on persistent inequalities. Gildersleeve uses an interdisciplinary approach to reframe college access as a social practice by using sociocultural theories of learning and development and positioning college access as literacy development. The result was what Dr. Gildersleeve calls a college-going literacy development model of understanding college access.

Gildersleeve's positioning of college access as a question of literacy strengthens the study of college access and college choice by privileging and emphasizing the ways that students succeed in getting to college, critiquing deficit views of students from marginalized social and cultural conditions. In doing this, Gildersleeve presents the study of college access with a new unit of analysis, cultural practices, and documents how these micro-level practices are connected to macro-level policies and structures. Thus, by focusing on how students and families navigate and negotiate their everyday lives in culturally mediated ways, his analysis illuminates the sense-making around college-going that gets embedded in daily routines. His analysis then connects these insights to broader social practices (e.g. how high schools structure course-taking and advise students as well as how colleges administer financial aid and admissions) at the institutional and field levels.

Gildersleeve shows how these migrant students begin to understand college, their opportunities, and the ways in which they will need to integrate college preparation activities into their daily lives. Through this analysis, Gildersleeve shows us that *preparing to access college* is more than college course preparation and more than college application preparation. Instead, Gildersleeve demonstrates that *learning* college access means that students come to understand the inequalities in higher education opportunities and how their changing practices will enable them to attend college. These students can and do tranform their lives and thus create wider educational opportunities for themselves than their schools normatively offer them.

Gildersleeve's meticulous data collection and analysis irrefutably shows the malignant neglect of migrant students' college access needs by their schools and that these students succeed primarily because of a mix of serendipitous individual interventions (e.g., a counselor takes special interest) and student determination or family assistance (e.g., extreme sacrifices made for educational purposes). His implications for schools, higher education, family, and outreach, point to specific ways that each can help support and assist students in college

Foreword

access. These implications stem from findings about important and consequential relationships between students and adults, the specific ways that immigration influences the discourse through which families make sense of education, and the construction of tacit knowledge around the process of college-going in coming to know and actualizing college access. All of this analysis is done within a vibrant and compelling narrative.

Gildersleeve's attention to the intertwined influences of family, schools, colleges and outreach programs deftly and subtly shows both the moments of inequality as well as moments of transformative learning that empower students. Moreover, his nuanced analyses of college access for migrant students is put forth in actionable terms that will effect real social change, while providing a framework from which future research can help explain and work to ameliorate inequity in higher education opportunity. His contributions to the field of higher education have the potential to leave a lasting imprint on the study of higher education opportunities and what those opportunities mean for the relationship between higher education and society.

Acknowledgments

I would like to extend my gratitude to the *Counterpoints* series editor, Shirley Steinberg for her enthusiasm for this manuscript. I wish to recognize Joe Kincheloe's contributions to the *Counterpoints* series. Losing Joe before his time marks a critical void in the educational community today. I thank also Chris Myers, Sophie Appel and everyone at Peter Lang Publishing who helped usher this volume into existence, made important edits, and suggested revisions that strengthened the manuscript. Nana Osei-Kofi graciously shared her talents for the cover art, and graduate assistants Susana Hernandez and Rodolfo "Rudy" Mondragón provided indispensible support in the final days of editing and typesetting.

I have been privileged with a number of critically engaged colleagues, all of whom have had some influence in the culmination of this project. Shannon Calderone had the (mis)fortune of sharing desk space with me during most of the early stages of this project. Five key groups from my time at UCLA contributed to making me the scholar I strive to be today. I thank the Triangle, Rozana Carducci and Casandra Harper, with whom the room is always full. I thank the DaWGs, Jevon Hunter, Nathalia Jaramillo, and Althea Nixon who were there all along the way. I thank the UCLA/Inglewood GEAR UP crew (O-G), Tracy Lachica Buenavista, Ifeoma Amah, Tyson E. J. Marsh, Peter Kim, Minerva Avila, and our fearless leader, Jennifer Obidah. The opportunity to work with them fostered my early interests in educational equity and college access. I thank Daniel G. Solórzano and the UCLA Critical Race Theory Research Apprenticeship Crew, in particular Lindsay Perez-Huber, Maria Malagon, Veronica Velez, Rebecca Burciaga, Dolores Calderone, and Martha Rivas. I share big love with my fellow staff members from the 2005 and 2006 Migrant Student Leadership Institutes. Collectively, we've managed to come a little closer to the world as it could be and armor ourselves for the world as it is. Some have already been mentioned, but also I especially thank Benji Chang, Julie Cortez, Arash Davari, Rodrigo "Brother Bear" Díaz, Octavio Estrella, Emily Grijalva, Jennifer Guzman, First Captain Ramon Martinez, Kimberly Nao, Anne-Marie Nuñez, Gloria Sanchez, Shirin Vossoughi, and Miguel Zavala. Also from my days at UCLA, I thank Jolynn Asato, Leobald Estrada, and Patricia Perez.

The Disruptive Dialogue Project has been a constant source of inspiration and motivation. Founding members Rozana Carducci, Aaron Kuntz, and Penny Pasque have held me accountable to the praxis I preach and pushed me to be as precise as possible with the arguments I craft. Much of this research was funded by fellowships sponsored by the Spencer Foundation's Research Training Grant at UCLA, the UCLA Graduate Division, and the Association for the Study of Higher Education-Lumina Foundation for Education. As a Lumina Fellow, I was introduced to Angela Bell, Stella Flores, and Kristan Venegas, all of whom encouraged me to complete this book.

Academics do not exist in isolation, and I am thankful for the ongoing support of my friends and family. A number of people extended their support, and quite often their sofa-beds, while I was driving across California during fieldwork: Deborah Baraka, Clark Dawood, Amy Kampmeyer, Laura Kampmeyer Jaeggi, Jill and Ray Osofsky, Rachel and Rouzbeh Rotabi, and Corie, Matt, Emilia, and Landon Wightlin. Back home in West Hollywood, Nathan Austin Jacroux and BigBoyBrandon Wirth provided me unwavering support. Marisa Singer, Kirsten Emilie Norbu Westby, and Phill Bartell each hold a special place in the constellation of friendships that sustain me.

Finally, I recognize my family. They never falter in their support for me and my work. Most especially, I thank my husband, Rodolfo Mayubay Bugarin, Jr. and my mother, Jan Evely Gildersleeve, who was my first, and remains my favorite teacher.

Chapter One
Introduction

A master narrative exists in the contemporary United States that operates to disallow a college education for Mexican migrant students. This master narrative precludes Mexican migrant students from educational opportunity and is founded on assumptions about Mexican migrant students including, but not limited to: 1) They do not deserve college admission; because 2) they do not care about education; 3) they do not have the intellectual ability for college admission; and 4) they are criminals. These assumptions stem from deficit-oriented interpretations of the sociocultural (including educational) contexts through which Mexican migrant students participate in U.S. society. Cumulatively, the master narrative results in the chronic and persistent under-representation and marginalization of Mexican migrant students in higher education.

This book fractures that master narrative and opens up pedagogical possibilities within the hostile and deficit-laden discourse through which Mexican migrant students struggle to persist toward college access. This book seeks to map that fracture—to map Mexican migrant students' processes of coming to know educational opportunity—by re-presenting a critical ethnographic inquiry of the learning and development of 12 Mexican migrant students from across the state of California. This inquiry sought to answer the question: How do Mexican migrant students come to know college access? In this mapping process, I document disruptions in the master narrative across the lives of students: who they are, how they practice college-going, and how their practices rely on, intersect with, and challenge the hegemonic practices of other social actors, social practices, and social institutions.

By mapping this fracture, I come to know and share that Mexican migrant students' college-going can be understood as a complex and dynamic meaning-making system negotiated across their culturally mediated worlds; in short—a college-going literacy. Further, as a question of literacy, college-going can therefore be understood as pedagogically produced—a *learned social practice co-constructed by multiple agencies that interact with various social structures*. Moreover, Mexican migrant students' college-going is shown to be almost completely serendipitous. Institutionalized practices are rarely among the effective interventions. By mapping this fracture, I hope to show not only the moments in which Mexican migrant students contest the hegemonic practices that produce the master narrative, but also the transformative pedagogical moments wherein Mexican migrant students' develop a college-going literacy and direct their educational opportunity toward college access. Indeed, the mapping of the fracture works toward a radical pedagogy of hope, possibility, and transformation. Founded on critical and sociocultural theories of learning and development, and empirically anchored in the findings that emerged from my ethnographic inquiry as re-presented in this fracturing of the master narrative, I put forward a call for a critical college-going pedagogy. Outlined in the final chapter of this book, college-going pedagogy serves to assist critical educators concerned with the democratic and social justice ethics of increasing educational opportunity for historically marginalized cultural communities.

Mexican migrant students' experiences are generally ignored in educational research literature, and nearly vacant from scholarship on college access (see Gildersleeve, 2009; Nuñez, 2009; Salinas & Reyes, 2004; and Zallaquett et al., 2007). Among groups that face under-representation in American higher education today, Mexican migrant students often experience a nexus of marginalizing barriers to college. Generally, Mexican migrant students who participate in K–12 schooling are from low-income families with lower-educational attainment and non-dominant language practices (Gibson, 2003; Gildersleeve, 2009; Gutiérrez, 2008a, 2008b; Lopez, 2001, 2004; López et al., 2001; Salinas & Franquiz, 2004; Zallaquett et al., 2007). Structural barriers that Mexican migrant students face might at times interact differentially with each other, and with individual Mexican migrant student understandings of educational opportunity.

From this brief background and the aforementioned purposes, I came to the following research questions, which frame the inquiry re-presented as the mapping of the fracture:

1. How do Mexican migrant students come to know college access?
   a. What experiences help shape students' understanding of college access?
   b. How do barriers (structural or otherwise) shape students' understanding of access to college?
2. How do Mexican migrant students engage in college choice processes?
   a. What understandings of access help shape students' experiences?
   b. How does students' understanding of access to college shape their participation in college-going practices?
   c. How does students' understanding of access to college shape their participation in family/community cultural practices?
3. In what ways are Mexican migrant students constituted as subjects in college-going?
   a. What are the effects of social identifications on the project of increasing representation for historically under-represented and traditionally marginalized students?
   b. How can research more holistically capture the meaning-making influence of macro-level processes on micro-level practices in order to effect change in policy and practice that can increase the representation of historically under-represented and traditionally marginalized students?

The first and second questions illustrate how Mexican migrant students develop a college-going literacy and what it might look like. They work in tandem, each informing the other in the nexus of sense-making between macro-processes of college access, and micro-practices of college choice, each operating across the mezzo-market of educational opportunity in the contemporary United States. The third question derives from a pragmatic need to understand the construction of the "subjects" under inquiry—Mexican migrant students. It is a methodological consideration that will yield knowledge immediately applicable within this study, and furthermore, inform the greater field of educational research. Question three interrogates the constructs used in scholarship, reflexively informing the discourse of the inquiry. Answering these three questions will create an understanding of what it means for Mexican migrant students to come to know college access. The fracture within the master narrative represented within this book as a mapping of Mexican migrant students' college-going provides these answers and shows how the 12 Mexican migrant students included in this study came to know college access.

Significance of Migrant Students' Educational Opportunity

Studying Mexican migrant students' participation in college-going is one of the most important lines of inquiry in social research today, because Mexican migrant students' college-going raises important fundamental questions about social life, social justice, and the democratic role of education in the twenty-first-century United States. An interest in Mexican migrant student college-going requires concerted attention be paid to many of global society's preeminent dilemmas today, including neocolonial empire, human migration, poverty, racism, and the primary concern in this book, education. As post-industrialized nations continue to move toward information-based economies where the power of the consumer reigns supreme and non-dominant nations continue to struggle within the imperial relations of neoliberal and neoconservative transnational and global economic policies, questions of democracy and social opportunity inherently rely on questions of education—for whom, by whom, of what kind and toward what purpose?

Furthermore, the construction and (re)production of social opportunity has historically taken root and been refracted by educational institutions. For example, social movements such as desegregation (e.g., *Brown v. Board of Education of Topeka, Kansas; Mendez v. State of California*) and affirmative action (e.g., *Gratz v. University of Michigan; Grutter v. University of Michigan; Bakke v. Regents of the University of California*; see for example, Rhoads, Saenz, & Carducci, 2005), as well as cultural battles over language (e.g., California Proposition 187) ethnic studies (see for example, Rhoads, 1998), and racial injustice have each manifest within educational contexts. In short, education has been the stomping ground for securing, testing, and demonstrating the power of social opportunity in mediating (whether improving or constraining) the way of life for disenfranchised communities.

Pragmatically, the study of college access provides an operationalization of social opportunity that few other lines of inquiry can provide. College access—where, why, and how someone benefits from increased educational attainment—affords a certain security and potential entrance to privileged spheres of influence in society. Obtaining a college education has been shown to increase gross earning potential across all races/ethnicities, social class, and across the lifespan. According to The College Board's annual report, *Education Pays*, a typical full-time year-round employee earns 62% more income with a four-year degree than those who have a high school diploma only (Baum & Ma, 2007). Furthermore, lifetime earnings of those with some college are 19% higher than those with none, while the cumulative lifetime earnings of four-year degree holders is $800,000 more than expected earnings of high school graduates. Also calculated by Baum and Ma for The College Board, the increased earnings from college attendance surpass the loss of income from full-time work *and* the added expenditures of tuition and fees while attending college. According to the same report, Hispanic [sic] workers with a four-year degree between the ages of 25 and 34 earn 57% and 86% higher incomes for women and men, respectively, as compared to high school graduates. That makes a difference of over $13,000 and $22,000 in gross dollars for women and men respectively.[1]

Furthermore, workers with a college education are more likely to find employment with employer-provided pension plans, making retirement planning and achievement easier and most likely for those with at least a bachelor's degree (U.S. Census Bureau, as calculated by Baum & Ma, 2007). Concerning the U.S.'s historic levels of uninsured and high costs of health care generally in the United States, it is noteworthy that private-sector workers covered by employer-provided health care programs are more often bachelor's degree holders by 16 percentage points higher than those with only a high school diploma (Mishel, Bernstein, & Allegretto as quoted in Baum & Ma, 2007). Cumulatively, the increased security of higher earnings, pension plans, and health care associated with a college education lead to overall declines in unemployment (Bureau of Labor Statistics, 2007), poverty (U.S. Census Bureau, 2006), and participation in public assistance programs (U.S. Census Bureau) as compared to high school graduates. All of these benefits increase significantly with four-year degree attainment and rise even further when compared to individuals without a high school diploma.

The benefits of higher education are not limited to income and employment. According to Baum & Ma (2007), college-educated adults over the age of 25 reported better perceptions of health (National Center for Health Statistics, 2005), reduced rates of smoking (DeWelque, 2004), and increased levels of exercise (National Center for Health Statistics, 2005) across the lifespan, income-level, and race/ethnicity. Beyond health, college graduates participate in volunteerism at higher rates, more often and more regularly (Bureau of Labor Statistics, 2007). Finally, college graduates are more likely to vote in presidential elections, especially in early adult years between 18 and 24 (U.S. Census Bureau, 2004). Clearly, access to college has ramifications for social opportunity with consequences for the shape of U.S. democracy. Participating in society as healthy, socially engaged, and deliberative subjects currently is a privilege reserved for the elite of U.S. society—the college-educated elite. Being precluded from these privileges, which in some discourse are considered fundamental rights, is part of the dehumanizing effect of the master narrative that precludes Mexican migrant students from participating in higher education.

Significance of the Mexican Migrant Student Subject

Migrant education in the United States is a multimillion dollar enterprise. The federal government allocates nearly $400 million a year to special migrant education funds as provided in Title I, Part C of the Elementary and Secondary Education Act (U.S. Department of Education, 2005). In 2005, California alone expended just over $93 million of this federal money to serve over 300,000 migrant students (CA Department of Education, 2005, 2007). The initiatives under the U.S. Migrant Education Program vary by state and by region. In California, migrant education is administered by two comprehensive assistance centers and 21 regional offices. Most of the work done by these initiatives focuses on K–12 participation and assistance.

Migrant students in California could potentially be located in many categories that might indicate ways they are (under)represented in (higher) education: Latino, English-language-learners, first-generation college students, and by geography, gender, and socioeconomic status. Although a college-going literacy could be investigated via any student group, I deliberately choose migrant students because of their multiple-(under)representations in higher education. These students are, by many accounts, not expected to attend, and in some ways, undesired, in higher education. "Migrant student" is a way of demarcating multiple social, cultural, and individual forces to which the participants in my study are subjected.

I choose the term *migrant* in order to capture the fluid yet sustainable nature of these subjective experiences. Migrant can be understood as a cultural community in California. In sociocultural theory, cultural communities are co-constructed by the bodies and practices that are familiar to subjects who organize themselves around these practices (Cole, 1996; Gutiérrez, 2002; Nicolopolou & Cole, 1993). They are constituted by these practices that some subjects may or may not participate in.

Migrant also indicates a specific cultural tie and relationship to place and history. As described by Tejeda (2000):

> ... the dominant discourses through which the spaces of Southern California are lived by their inhabitants are the white supremacist discourses that yesterday rationalized the Anglo conquest and colonization of the region (see Alaguer, 1994) and today signify Anglos (white bodies) as a natural extension of those spaces, as entitled to the geography and its resources, while signifying Mexicano immigrants (brown bodies) as alien and un-natural to those spaces, as un-entitled. ... discourses which, inscribed on the very flesh of body/subjects, frame struggles that are essentially about social spaces (the academy, the workplace, the nation-state) and racialized body/subjects' access and entitlement to those spaces. (p 52–53)

Contemporary migrant students in California confront a neo-colonial context tied to the material places and social spaces they inhabit as well as those spaces to which they seek access. As Gonzalez and Fernandez's (2003) *A Century of Chicano History* demonstrates, the U.S. government continues a colonial relationship over Mexico and its descendents, using primarily economic and educational tools, rather than military conquest. Part of this neocolonial relationship relies on the persistent ebb and flow of Mexican labor in the agricultural industries that Mexican migrant farm-working families support. As Gonzalez and Fernandez's analysis shows, U.S. immigration, economic, and educational policies over time have both restricted and encouraged Mexican participation in migrant farm-working labor when it has been most advantageous to U.S. capitalist interests. Yet, historically, Chicana/os, Mexicans, and Indigenous communities have organized in the lands of California and the greater American southwest for longer periods of time than the dominant social classes. Paradoxically to contemporary nativist discourses around education and immigration, Mexican migrant students could arguably hold a stronger native claim of control to the foundations of education in California, yet they do not.

Particular to migrant students' participation in higher education, Salinas and Reyes (2004) outlined a myriad of challenges that students face, including access to curriculum, support for college preparation, and family involvement. The Zallaquett et al. (2007) study of successful migrant students at a metropolitan university confirmed these challenges and suggested that families are the paramount influence in migrant students' educational achievement. There are no accurate numbers to indicate how many migrant students actually attend college; however, the high dropout rates and persistently lower high school achievement indicate that migrant students are safely assumed to be under-represented in higher education. Moreover, considering that 86% of migrants are Latina/o (Salinas & Franquiz, 2004), and understanding that the majority of Latina/o students in higher education do not attend top-tier institutions, but rather are over-represented in community colleges (Horn, Flores, & Orfield, 2006), it is also safe to assume that Mexican migrant students are stratified in inequitable ways within higher education. Indeed, Nuñez's (2009) study of the college outcomes of migrant students from the Migrant Student Leadership Institute[2] confirms that migrant students who did *not* participate in the outreach program were most likely to attend community colleges or noncompetitive four-year institutions, if they attended college at all.

Beyond Under-representation and Acknowledging Marginalization

Alas, establishing the under-representation and stratification of Mexican migrant students in American higher education and briefly describing the ways that Mexican migrant students constitute significant subjects in questions of educational equity does *not* adequately provide the context for the importance of this study, nor its underlying ontological and epistemological assumptions. Rather, as a critical ethnographer, I must acknowledge and demonstrate the consequences of the historic traditions of marginalization against Mexican migrant students. Put simply, saying Mexican migrant students are "under-represented" does not cut it. Mexican migrant students are *marginalized* in U.S. educational opportunity, and this marginalization has longstanding historical traditions supporting it. Hence, I use the master narrative to frame the knowledge constructed in this text.

Master narratives operate to normalize the oppressive conditions within society by telling stories from the perspective of the dominant social group, in order to sustain their racial and class privilege (Dixson & Rousseau, 2007). According to Yosso, stories from the dominant voices in society "perpetuate myths that darker skin and poverty correlate with bad neighborhoods and bad schools" (2006, p. 9). These discursive configurations render the perspectives and experiences of non-dominant groups illegitimate and deficient in reference to the dominant group. The master narrative that precludes Mexican migrant students from educational opportunity is founded on assumptions about Mexican migrant students such as: 1) They do not deserve college admission; because 2) They do not care about education; 3) They do not have the intellectual ability for college admission; and 4) They are criminals. These assumptions stem from deficit-oriented interpretations of the social and cultural (including educational) contexts through which Mexican migrant students participate in U.S. society.

This master narrative has been well documented by scholars working within LatCrit and Critical Race theoretical frameworks (Solórzano & Delgado Bernal, 2001; Solórzano & Ornelas, 2002; Solórzano & Yosso, 2001; Valencia & Black, 2002; Yosso, 2006), as well as by sociocultural theorists engaged with Latino, specifically Mexican, and most particularly Mexican migrant communities (Faustich-

Orellana, 2001; Gutiérrez, 2006; Gutiérrez & Jaramillo, 2006). Yet, the master narrative and the sting of its dehumanizing power persist. The master narrative's longevity can be explained, in part, by examining the social and educational contexts in which Mexican migrant students participate in college-going. These contexts are not specific to a subaltern identity of "Mexican migrant student," but rather emerge from the myriad of social and cultural identifiers to which Mexican migrant students are subject. Specifically, racialized identifiers such as Latino, classed identifiers such as poor, geographic identifiers such as rural or urban, and nationalistic identifiers such as "illegal" or undocumented interact with socio-educational identifiers such as English language learner, first-generation student, and under-represented. Mexican migrant students' college-going contexts emerge from differential intersections of these (and undoubtedly other) social constructs.

In education, these intersections often are accompanied by specific material inequities. For example, the schools that Mexican migrant students typically attend are associated with lower rates of available college-preparatory courses, adequately qualified teachers, and available counselors to guide the application process (McDonough, 2005; Nuñez, 2009; Oakes, Rogers, Lipton, & Morrell, 2002; Oakes, Rogers, Silver, Valladares, Terriquez, McDonough, Renee, & Lipton, 2006). Furthermore, the mobility, poverty, and lower parental education levels that Mexican migrant students and their families face have been shown to be associated with more challenging pathways to college (McDonough, 1997; Ream, 2005; Cabrera & LaNasa, 2000; Gildersleeve, 2006; St. John, 2003; Price, 2004; Long, 2003). Finally, as most Mexican migrant students are either immigrants themselves or the first generation of children of immigrants, ties to the global phenomenon of human migration subject students to a litany of socially repressive and culturally *ir*relevant expectations for modes and forms of family participation in education (Auerbach, 2004; Gildersleeve, 2006; Suarez-Orozco & Suarez-Orozco, 2001; Tierney & Auerbach, 2005).

These contexts have been produced and recursively aggressively appropriated as cannon fodder for social and educational policies that have fostered a hostile political climate for Mexican migrant students.

Introduction

This hostility is evident in anti-immigrant legislation such as California Proposition 187, which tried to refute the state's responsibility for educating and protecting the public health of Mexican immigrants and effectively barred bilingual education programs. Anti-affirmative action movements, such as California's Proposition 209, have been shown to discourage under-represented students from applying to public universities (Brown & Hirschman, 2006; McDonough, 1999). Enrollments of Latino and African American students have been shown to decline in light of these policies, especially at state flagship universities (Contreras, 2005). Furthermore, educational policies that encourage magnet schools, charter schools, and advanced placement tracks within schools serve to further (de)track under-represented students out of college preparatory curricula (McDonough, 1997, 2004; Oakes, 1985). The hostility that Mexican migrant students face as they struggle to come to know college access perhaps can be seen most clearly in the contemporary controversies over the once-bipartisan-supported DREAM Act.[3] In its earliest and most supported versions, the DREAM Act would have allowed states to extend in-state tuition benefits to undocumented students and provided a pathway to citizenship for all immigrant students. Following the hotly contested and failed immigration reform efforts of the U.S. Congress, such as the dehumanizing U.S. House Resolution 4437,[4] the DREAM Act has been revised into a military recruitment technology, which has served to further polarize social and political views of immigration.[5]

Ultimately, the master narrative, as constituted in part by neoliberal and neoconservative maligned interpretations and appropriation of the social contexts of Mexican migrant students' college-going, has produced the tragic outcome of Mexican migrant students being among the *most* under-represented communities in higher education (Nuñez, 2009; Nuñez & Jaramillo, 2005; Salinas & Reyes, 2004; Zallaquett et al., 2007). In order to address this historic under-representation, many educators turn to college outreach programs (Tierney, Corwin, & Colyar, 2005). Unfortunately, most college outreach programs function from frameworks that re-inscribe the master narrative (Gildersleeve, 2009; Villalpando & Solórzano, 2005). Typical college outreach programs, despite their good intentions, position their students as deficient in academic ability, college knowledge, and/or the cultural and social capital necessary to get into college (Tierney et al., 2005; McDonough, 2005; Villalpando & Solórzano, 2005). Typical programs reduce outreach to remedial education and basic learning skills. These deficit-oriented programs continue to populate the educational landscape, despite calls for culturally relevant and academically rigorous college-preparatory experiences, especially in programs geared toward Latino students (Conchas, 2006; Gandara, 2002; Gibson & Bejínez, 2002; Perna, 2005a, 2005b; Villalpando & Solórzano, 2005).

Coming to Know and Mapping the Fracture in the Master Narrative of Mexican Migrant Students' College-going

Studying Mexican migrant student college-going requires a robust yet pragmatic framework for understanding the complex multidimensional field or activity through which Mexican migrant students struggle for educational opportunity. Dominant frameworks for understanding college access have led to a consensus of the primary barriers facing historically under-represented student populations (McDonough & Gildersleeve, 2006). These barriers are captured in six domains: financial barriers (Heller, 2002; King, 1999; St. John, 2002), K–12 mission and advising services (Gandara & Bial, 1999; King, 1996; McDonough, 2004; Tierney & Hagedorn, 2002), information on postsecondary education and financial aid (Hossler, Schmit, & Vesper, 1999; Kirst & Venezia, 2004), admissions practices and policies (Avery, Fairbanks, & Zeckhauser, 2003; Breland, Maxey, Gernand, Cumming, & Trapani, 2002; Tienda, Cortes, and Niu, 2003), college preparation in K–12 institutions (Gladieux & Swail, 1999; Oakes, 2004; Perna, 2005a), and family involvement (Choy, 2002; Flint, 1992; Hossler, Braxton, & Coopersmith, 1989; Tierney & Auerbach, 2005).

These common findings stem from a subset of fields dealing with students' transitions to higher education. As an area of study, college access has grown into four main divisions of inquiry. *College access research* is a macro-level orientation that views the problem of educational opportunity as primarily structural. This division often focuses on state- and federal-level policies regarding eligibility, financial aid, and enrollment shifts (Berkener & Chavez, 1997; Ikenberry & Hartle, 1998; King, 1996; Tienda et al., 2003). *College admissions research* is generally large-scale, quantitative analysis of institutional concerns, such as recruitment and the impact of tuition on individual behaviors (Jackson, 1982; King, 1996; Litten, 1979; Olson & Rosenfeld, 1984). *Student college choice* is a division that addresses the micro-level processes of individual decision making. Studies in this area focus on social-psychological, economic, sociological status attainment, organizationally analytic, and/or culturally analytic concerns at the individual level (Fann, 2005; Hossler et al., 1999; McDonough, 1997; Oakes, 2003). Finally, *academic preparation and college advising* studies focus at a macro-level on K–12 institutions, addressing issues such as college preparation, planning, and the entrepreneurial admissions sector (Adelman, 1999; McDonough, 2005; McDonough, Ventresca, & Outcalt, 2000; Perna, 2005a, 2005b; Tierney et al., 2004).

Generally, studies that have sought to explain the persistent under-representation of subaltern or marginalized groups have relied on a set of three primary analytical models for understanding college access: econometric, Hossler's three-phase model of college choice, and Bourdieuian sociological models of reproduction. I thoroughly critique these models individually in chapter two, but for the purposes of this introduction, I put forward a cumulative critique of these dominant models. Despite their contributions in establishing the field of college access, they cumulatively fail to substantively address scholars' increasing calls for more systemic, integrative, and culturally analytic modes and models for inquiry that address the increasingly complex and dynamic forces constituting the unequal educational opportunity structures present today (McDonough & Gildersleeve, 2006; Kirst & Venezia, 2004; Villalpando & Solórzano, 2005). Hence, the fracture re-presented in this book puts forward and works from a field corrective for the study of college access—the college-going literacy development model of college access.

College Access as College-going Literacy

My work views college access as a question of literacy of sense-making via cultural practices that co-construct students' participation in the social practice of college-going (Gildersleeve, 2009). Thinking of college-going as literacy development allows researchers to focus on how various social actors *participate* in students' college-going. It emphasizes the teaching and learning of the social text, therefore, framing college-going as literacy development affords the opportunity to document how other agents and structures support and/or constrain students' learning (and practicing). The college-going literacy model is grounded in sociocultural theories of learning and development, particularly in cultural-historical activity theory (see for example, Gutiérrez, 1995, 2007a, 2007b, 2008a, 2008b; Roth & Lee, 2007), as well as the complementary theories of multiliteracies and New Literacy Studies (Barton & Hamilton, 1998; Barton, Hamilton, & Ivanic, 2000; Gee, 1991; New London Group, 1996; Street, 1995). These collected theories share a commitment to a neo-Vygotskian perspective on learning, literacy and development. Each assumes that all learning is culturally mediated and historically bound, hinging on the participation of multiple actors governed by a common set of explicit and implicit rules (Cole, 1996; Roth & Lee, 2007; Vygotsky, 1978). Development is understood as the change in participation over time that leads to transformation (Rogoff, 2003; Engeström, 1987, 1993, 2006). Literacy is understood as a meaning-making process within and across multiple modalities of design (New London Group, 1996).

Applied to college access, the activity of going to college is both a latent and active practice of any and all students. Yet, far fewer students' participation in this activity is directed toward attaining actual higher education opportunity. Students perform college-going over the life-course of their educations, taking cues and making sense of various artifacts (e.g., teachers' expectations, available curricula, tuition prices, family labor practices). Their opportunities and choices are delimited by the participation of others within their college-going *and* the meaning-making that happens in the intersections of these activities. Thus, the college-going literacy model seeks to understand how post-secondary opportunities are mediated in students' lives as they participate in the social practice of college-going. This model, its theoretical underpinnings, and its relation to the methods I used to understand college-going are explained in much greater detail in chapter two.

Introduction

Methodological Choices

The evidence marshaled in this book comes from data and analyses from a critical ethnographic project with 12 Mexican migrant students and their families in California (see Gildersleeve, 2006, 2009). The project was simultaneously a critical research project and an extension of a critical pedagogical project—the Migrant Student Leadership Institute (MSLI)—that was a pre-college, summer outreach program based in the Vygotskian pedagogical principles of CHAT and New Literacy Studies (see Gildersleeve, 2009; Gutiérrez, 2008a; Gutiérrez et al., 2009). MSLI was the context in which the student participants and I first met. As a pedagogical project, the study reported here was organized to be congruent with the principles of its theoretical framework, paralleling the framework for learning and development in the MSLI. Writing specifically about developing a critical ethnography for the study of immigrants, Trueba and McLaren (2000) state, "a critical pedagogy of hope based on Vygotskian principles establishes the relationship among culture, language, and cognition as the foundation to understand the role of culture in mediating the transmission of knowledge and intellectual growth" (p. 59). Thus, critical ethnography was chosen as the guiding methodology for the project. As Trueba and McLaren continue:

> In spite of the inherent challenges and difficulties faced by ethnographers, critical ethnography with a Vygotskian perspective continues to be one of the most promising fields in the hands of educational researchers committed to sound pedagogy and the full development of immigrant children, for they are new avenues to create a pedagogy of hope." (60)

Also, critical ethnography focuses on practices and formations of power and power relations (Kincheloe & McLaren, 2005; Noblit, Flores, & Murillo, 2004). As demonstrated by the context of migrant educational opportunity briefly described above, the marginalization of migrant students in college access is clearly a power-laden phenomenon.

Conceptualizing an ethnographic project as pedagogical in its core purpose, function, and practice calls into question the role of the ethnographer. Within the pedagogical project of critical ethnography, I as ethnographer became a primary pedagogical instrument. Rather than positioning myself as the knower or truth-teller, I participated in the project as learner and co-conspirator in the struggle to make sense of Mexican migrant student college-going. Here is a moment in the inquiry that New Literacy Studies, CHAT, and critical ethnography transcended the theory, methodology, and practice divides and became central as theory-methodology-practice. I consistently vacillated between expert and novice. I continually sought new tools from which I could examine, break, and re-create new rules for the ethnographic endeavor that students had agreed to engage with me. The argument I extend in the following chapter gets into greater detail about how I (dis)organized a critical ethnographic project in order to serve as a transformative instrument within a broader pedagogical project.

The goals of this inquiry never sought to alleviate all marginalization related to college access, but rather to learn about such marginalization and configure ways that different social actors, institutions, and practices might be reconceived in order to support college-going—as a commitment to the broader social struggle to end oppression and marginalization. This learning activity borrowed shapes (e.g., interviews) and forms (e.g., field notes) from ethnography proper, but importantly reflected the material and symbolic realities it came to be known through. That is, as a learning activity, my critical pedagogical ethnographic project appropriated new tools (e.g., co-writing with participants) and rules (e.g., developing radically committed relationships with participants) in order to learn about inequality in the college-going lives of Mexican migrant students. I have sought to make my meaning-making as apparent as possible throughout the process of inquiry and the production of this text so as to engage readers in assessing my learning and participating in their own.

A Brief Introduction to *Los Estudiantes Migrantes*

The 12 Mexican migrant students who participated in the study came from across the state of California. Students lived as far southeast as the Imperial Valley in the California-Arizona-Mexico borderlands, as far northwest as East San Francisco Bay, as far southwest as San Diego County, and as far northeast as the upper Central Valley. The

Introduction

average family income ranged from roughly $15,000/year for a family of seven to $45,000/year for a family of four. Students' families all relied on migrant agricultural labor for employment. All of the students had held responsibility for contributing to the family economy in some way during their high school years. All but two of the students had been enrolled, at some point, in English language development courses while attending California public schools. Of the 12 students, four were female and eight were male. Four of the male students were undocumented migrants from Mexico. All 12 students' parents had migrated from Mexico.

All of the students' families worked in migrant farm-working agricultural industries (e.g., harvesting fruits and vegetables and/or canneries). Some families moved around often, while others established a more permanent or fixed home base while one or more family members would travel for work. Migrant farm-working labor, and the families who perform it, has been documented as the most impoverished occupation in the United States (Rothenberg, 1998; Salinas & Franquiz, 2004). As laborers, they are some of the most vulnerable to employer abuse, workplace health and safety risks, and employment insecurity. Their lives are marked by poverty, mobility, and low levels of education. The students in this study struggled for social opportunity through these contexts. Each of these students and the worlds they inhabited in relation to their college-going will be introduced and described more fully in chapter three.

Map of the Book

This book maps a fracture in the master narrative—a mapping of Mexican migrant students' processes of coming to know educational opportunity. These processes were conceived in theory and analysis as literacy development. As such, chapter two goes into further depth about the theoretical and methodological frameworks developed for this inquiry. It reviews literature from New Literacy Studies (Barton & Hamilton, 1998; New London Group, 1996) and sociocultural theories of learning and development in order to explain how educational opportunity, specifically college access, can be operationalized as college-going literacy development. Major theoretical concepts are explained and methodological implications are described. For the reader who is less interested in abstract discussion of strategies for coming to know the fracture mapped in this book, chapter two could be read with less scrutiny. However, I require such a reader to understand broadly that the fracture and its potential for pedagogical possibility that emerge in this book rely on an analytical framework asserting that educational opportunity can be read and written as social text.

Chapter three introduces the 12 primary participants in the study within the contexts of their home environments, documenting through literature and fieldwork the social contexts of Mexican migrant college-going. In this chapter, I analyze ways by which students' identities get constructed from the social forces to which they are subject—specifically, the external forces of racialization and class versus the internal forces of motivation and dedication. The chapter concludes with a discussion of how migrant families served as a resource for students' self-promotions as college-going subjects.

After mapping the primary subjects that constitute the fracture, I turn to mapping the ways that their college-going was regulated as well as the cultural artifacts students used to carve out their space within college-going. In chapter four, I investigate the beliefs about college opportunities that guided students' college-going practices, and the development of these beliefs over time. This chapter discusses findings related to the ways in which students' college-going was mediated and regulated by explicit and implicit rules about higher education opportunity, and their relation to the cultural tools that students used to make sense of college-going.

Chapters five and six describe and analyze in detail the ways in which students used two of the most salient cultural tools available in their college-going toolkit: immigration and *confianza*. Immigration mediated students' college-going in different, yet related ways. As a social and cultural artifact, it became an organizing tool for understanding how undocumented immigrant children, the documented children (U.S. citizens) of undocumented immigrants, and the children of documented immigrants each produced a subjective (im)migrant lens through which to participate and make sense of their college-going lives. *Confianza* signifies a particular organization of relations between students and more-expert-others that served to afford the students transformative learning experiences. An empirically derived theoretical concept, *confianza* is discussed to explain the production of relationships that enabled students to extend their practices in new ways toward the goal of college-going. Adding detail to the fracture, the ecologies from which these relationships emerged are documented in order to draw the lines to potential pedagogical implications for future research and practice.

Chapter seven asks and answers the question: Who does what in migrant students' college-going? I map four groups of institutions, organizations and individuals that make up the community of migrant students' college-going spaces. These groups are family, schools, higher education, and outreach. I also document the various tasks that students must complete in order to perform college-going as a social practice. I organize this schema of the community and the list of tasks into a conceptual model of the community's division of labor—a map of who does what in migrant students' college-going. Using the community's division of labor model, I discuss how families, schools, higher education, and outreach programs each participate in migrant students' college-going. This chapter illustrates the serendipity of migrant students' college-going, ethnographically documenting and re-presenting how none of the enabling practices are institutionalized, yet most of the deterring processes emerge directly from schools or higher education.

In the final chapter, I summarize the findings presented in chapters three through seven. I explain how college-going literacy was developed by the 12 students who participated in this inquiry; this summary provides a holistic (yet still tentative and partial) description of the fracture in the master narrative that I found. I make two fundamental arguments: college access needs to be understood as college-going literacy development in order to cut across the somewhat fixed categories that oftentimes constrain representations of educational opportunity, and Mexican migrant students' college access is primarily a serendipitous journey without any enabling processes institutionalized in either K–12 or higher education. To address this racist marginalization of Mexican migrant students, I call for a college-going pedagogy by drawing on the exceptional interventions documented by this book and illuminated by mapping the fracture of the master narrative. I discuss the pedagogical possibilities provided by this fracture as I put forward implications for research, practice, and policy that emerge from a college-going pedagogy.

Finally, I provide a reflexive afterword that documents my personal insights from participating in the inquiry with the 12 migrant students. This afterword situates the book in my personal-political perspective, arguing for critical and grassroots ways and means of understanding and studying educational problems with historically marginalized students.

Mapping the Fracture

Before proceeding into the mapping activity, I hope to clarify the fracturing undertaken in this book. A fracture in the literal sense is a break in something. In a metaphoric-analytic sense, I borrow the term from Weis and Fine (2005), who deployed the term to indicate a disruption of normative and expected social behavior as represented in micro-, macro-, and mezzo-levels of analysis. According to Weis and Fine, fractures are provided by, "designs that fracture ideological coherence and designs that document those spaces, relations, and/or practices in which possibility flourishes or critique gets heard" (p. xxi). Furthermore researchers that seek to establish these fractures work ethically from "… an obligation not simply to dislodge the dominant discourse, but to help readers and audiences imagine where the spaces for resistance, agency, and possibility lie" (p. xxi). Hence, critical fractures not only describe the world as it is, but document an imagined world as it could be. I build on Weis and Fine's fracture, applying it to the case of Mexican migrant students' college-going, and recognize its potential to serve as a transformative pedagogical space, what Gutiérrez might describe as a "third space—a transformative space where the potential for an expanded form of learning the development of new knowledge are heightened" (2008a, p. 152). My emphasis on the learning and teaching potential of this fracture underscores the pedagogical nature of the project re-presented in the rest of this text.

This book fractures the master narrative by re-presenting an additive process of coming to know educational opportunity for migrant students. This fracture is multidimensional. It siphons the racist and hegemonic practices that structure college-going for Mexican migrant students and opens up pedagogical possibilities from migrant students' everyday lives. From another vantage point, theorizing access as a pedagogical project, as literacy development, fractures the organization of educational opportunity as it is known within the confines of the master narrative. This dimension of the fracture is buttressed by the innovative and hopefully transparent re-presentation of practices that I employed in coming to know the fracture. This dimension disrupts the master narrative's insistence on a unified truth put forth by a detached, objective observer-as-researcher. In fracturing the master narrative of Mexican migrant college-going, I hope to illustrate the transformation of social relations between the student participants and myself.

Finally, the writing and (re)/presentation of my process of coming to know Mexican migrant students' college-going from a sociocultural perspective fractures the master narrative in the multiple and multi-vocal genres employed. Specifically, the text herein will read at times as a traditional qualitative inquiry, while in other moments, I blur genres of representation in order to make the most compelling and disruptive argument for the fracture's pedagogical potential. Some chapters will be filled with students' verbatim narrative, others with tables and text, still others will show analysis in creative forms, such as a political speech generated from the experiences of students' sense-making around their complex and dynamic social locations.

I invite readers to engage, indulge, inhabit, and most importantly, call into question the fracture mapped throughout this book. As a pedagogical text, I mean it to inform, but to co-construct the informative experience. Moreover, I invite readers to come to know the marginalization experienced by the 12 Mexican migrant students whose college-going is re-presented in construction of this fracture. I extend this invitation in hopes that the pedagogical possibilities I suggest will be extended, built upon, revised, and refined so that we might re-imagine the world as it is into the world as it could be, and Mexican migrant students' marginalization will be reconfigured into Mexican migrant students' radically democratic participation in society.

Notes

[1] All income-based statistics reported herein from The College Board's *Education Pays 2007* report are based on median incomes for the respective groups.

[2] For more information about the Migrant Student Leadership Institute, see Gutiérrez, 2008a, Gutiérrez, Hunter, & Arzubiagga, 2009, and Gildersleeve, 2009.

[3] 2001, U.S. Senate Bill 1545, The Development, Relief, and Education for Alien Minors (DREAM) Act was drafted federal legislation that sought to afford states the opportunity to extend in-state tuition benefits to undocumented students. It was originally introduced in the U.S. House of Representatives as HR 1918, The Student Adjustment Bill.

[4] 2005, U.S. House Resolution 4437 was drafted federal legislation that sought to revise current immigration law and further restrict the rights of undocumented immigrants in the United States.

[5] One current version of the DREAM Act has been offered as an amendment to U.S. Senate Bill 1547, The Department of Defense authorization bill. In this amendment, undocumented immigrants could gain legal residency by participating in the U.S. Armed Forces (Justice for Immigrants, 2007).

Chapter Two
Mapping Migrant Students' College-going Literacy Development

Scholars have repeatedly documented the importance of understanding higher education opportunity and college access/choice from a three-pronged argument that focuses on the economic interests of the nation-state, societal benefits for others, and personal benefits from participating in higher education (Baum, 2007; Gándara, Orfield, & Horn, 2006; Perna, 2006; Tierney & Hagedorn, 2002). The argument goes that educating more people is more socially just, because it serves a national interest by increasing economic prosperity at personal and social levels, increasing health in both public and personal realms, and decreasing social ills for both communities and individuals. This is the primary motivating logic and rationale for the development of the dominant frameworks for understanding college access/choice. The national interest, based primarily in economic prosperity, is the foundation for increasing access to higher education, and therefore it has shaped the ways by which scholars have sought to understand issues related to college access/choice. These are all excellent reasons to support the broadening of higher education.

However, the national interest arguments ignore something even more fundamental to American society, and indeed to social justice broadly—democracy. Drawing on the national interest primarily defined as economic prosperity, ignores, or at best minimizes, the role that higher education can play in supporting democratic structures, practices, and infrastructure in society. The national interest argument, which undergirds the dominant framework for understanding access/choice, does not allow for the consideration of college access as a means to redress past discriminations, nor as a means to combat and confront racism in society. The irony here is that without equal opportunity to participate in society's institutions, such as higher education, democracy fails and the master narrative remains rampantly in control of people's opportunity to contribute meaningfully to society.

In this chapter, I outline the theoretical and methodological choices that made it possible to engage in the mapping activity this text attempts to represent. I present an extended definition of college-going literacy, explain my critique of dominant college access frameworks and ground my new conceptual model in critical sociocultural theory. I then explain my methodological choices, arguing that critical ethnography is the most relevant mode of inquiry for exposing the fracture I sought to uncover and re-present (Trueba & McLaren, 2000). I discuss two dominating frameworks that have shaped higher education opportunity. My discussion is not exhaustive of conceptual organizations of the field, but rather addresses two of the most influential. These dominating frameworks are known as the three-phase model of college choice (Hossler & Gallagher, 1987) and Bourdieuian theories of reproduction. The former framework is located in the college choice category of higher education opportunity research, while the latter has been used across categories, at times making important connections between macro- and micro-concerns, as well as between structural and cultural barriers. After introducing these frameworks, I then put forth my critique of how their explanatory power is limited. Following my critique of these two influential frameworks, I discuss how financial aid, as a topic that cuts across multiple categories and barriers, has been limited in its explanations of sociocultural understanding related to higher education opportunity. I then present a critique of Conley's (2005) college knowledge framework, which is a newer appropriation of the term, *college knowledge,* and falls short of capturing the complexity of inequities across higher education opportunity. Finally, I suggest a field corrective (McDonough & Gildersleeve, 2006), that seeks a more integrated, culturally analytic, and systemic framework for understanding college access. I put forward the college-going literacy development model of college access, which takes a critical perspective and illustrates the ways that inequities in educational opportunity manifest over time in the social practice of college-going. I conclude this chapter by describing the methodological choices I made in order to design a critical sociocultural inquiry (Lewis, Enciso, & Moje, 2007) appropriate for this college-going literacy project with Mexican migrant students.

Dominating Frameworks—Three-phase Model of College Choice

Research on college choice focuses on micro-processes of individual agents (students) as they decide upon post-secondary plans. College choice has been conceptualized as a developmental process in three stages: predisposition, search, and choice. This model was championed by Hossler and Gallagher (1987), expanded on by Hossler, Braxton, and Coopersmith (1989), and reinvigorated by Hossler, Schmit, and Vesper (1999). It has emerged as the preeminent model of the college choice process (Gildersleeve, 2003). In brief, it addresses both individual and organizational influences at each of the three phases.

As a linear and predictive model, students confront specific factors in each phase and consequently achieve specific outcomes—advancement to the next phase or departure from the pathway to post-secondary education. Predisposition is the phase in which students develop aspiration for higher education. Search is the phase in which students gather information about colleges and universities, participate in appropriate college-going activities (e.g., taking the SAT), and develop a tentative list of post-secondary educational plans (or names of specific institutions). Choice is the final phase in which students solidify their post-secondary educational plans. The choice phase is a twofold process: first, students definitively choose to participate in higher education; second, students decide which specific higher education institution they will attend.

The three-phase model points researchers to topics that look at individual and/or organizational influences. For example, within the predisposition phase, scholars deploying this model have focused on the influence of: specific student characteristics, such as gender or socioeconomic status; significant others, such as family; and school characteristics, such as the academic track (Cabrera & La Nasa, 2000; Freeman, 1997; Hamrick & Stage, 1998; Hossler & Stage, 1992; Perna,

2000). This pattern of attending to organizational and individual influences as topics of research continues across the three phases of the model (Hossler, Braxton, & Coopersmith, 1989).

However, recent scholarship has identified a need for the three-phase model to be made more responsive to different cultural communities. For example, some scholars have observed that the parental influence in African American families is qualitatively different than that of white families (Smith & Fleming, 2006; Freeman, 2005; Smith, 2002). Smith and Fleming (2006) specifically found that African American mothers encourage their sons to make decisions in order to survive, while encouraging their daughters to make decisions in order to develop and sustain independence. These findings added nuance to cultural understandings of the three-phase model, which originally posited parental encouragement as simply setting high expectations for students at an early age. Freeman (2005) further complicated the three-phase model, explicitly addressing the need for the three-phase model to take cultural differences into account when assessing the predisposition, search, and choice practices of African Americans. Through her longitudinal and nationwide qualitative study, she found that African American students came to be predisposed to higher education through context-specific influences of family and kinship as well as school characteristics that informed individual cultural characteristics in the formation of post-secondary educational aspirations.

Dominating Frameworks—Bourdieuian Studies of Reproduction

In efforts to understand the nuances between structural barriers and individual agency in college access, some scholars have appropriated the sociology of Pierre Bourdieu and his analysis of education as reproduction (Fann, 2005; Lareau & Horvat, 1999; McDonough, 1997; Smith, 2001). These studies invoke a framework based on three core concepts in Bourdieu's work: cultural capital, habitus, and the field. Cultural capital are the practices and artifacts (primary, secondary, and tertiary) that families possess that provide advantages in reaching an objective goal (Harker, Mahar, & Wilkes, 1990; Lareau & Horvat, 1999; McDonough, 1997). Habitus is a set of goals, values, and strategies that form a framework for understanding and taking action in the social world (McDonough, 1997). Fields, as put forth by McDonough, Ventresca, and Outcalt (2000), summarizing Bourdieu, "are definable areas in which people struggle because capital is at stake" (p. 373). These three concepts are contingent upon each other. Capital is valued based on its field and can only exists in its exercise, which must be employed from a specific habitus (Harker, Mahar, & Wilkes, 1990; Lareau & Horvat, 1999).

Bourdieuian-oriented studies of college access can locate themselves within or without the Hossler and Gallagher model of college choice. They address the persistence of inequality in schooling and opportunity at individual, organizational, and/or field levels of analyses. In general, these studies direct research to topics based on the idea of capital—how it is exercised, how it is transmitted over generations, and how it promotes some groups over others. Specifically, studies have investigated how individual cultural characteristics (e.g., socioeconomic status, racialization, and physical geography) interplay with structural barriers (e.g., schooling, admissions tests, and counseling) to affect college-going (Fann, 2005; McDonough, 1997, 1999, 2004; Terenishi et al., 2004).

Critique of Dominating Frameworks

Both the three-phase model of college choice and Bourdieuian reproduction frameworks have advanced the study of higher education opportunity and helped scholars better understand the problem of inequality. However, each of these frameworks has limitations. In this section, I discuss the applicability of the two frameworks across three categories of students: rural, poor, and students of color. These categories are not mutually exclusive, but serve to organize my analysis of the limitations in applying the Hossler and Gallagher model and Bourdieuian framework. I offer this critique in order to further describe how higher education opportunity has been theorized and organized. These categories of applicability are therefore offered as tropes in order to demonstrate my critique.

In an empirical study of rural students' college choice, McGrath, et al. (2001) employed both the three-phase model and a Bourdieuian framework. I use this case to illustrate how these dominant theories both benefit and constrain research on rural students. Part of the study addressed how student ability, an influence derived from the canon of work associated with the three-phase model, could be used to examine how students' skills at planning and decision-making interacted with their development of college aspirations. The model provided a conceptual framework for McGrath et al. to organize and analyze their study, which found that professional-managerial families in rural areas held high levels of human and social capital, which placed their students on a direct trajectory to higher education. However, the model restricted their understanding of how and why students from farm families, who did not exercise similar capital, still succeeded in sending students to college. The model suggested a deficit perspective of these students, and McGrath's implementation of Bourdieuian reproduction fed into deficit ideology. McGrath et al. suggested that farm students who appropriated behaviors similar to those of professional-managerial families approximated the cultural capital necessary to matriculate into post-secondary education. Thus, one of the limits of both models is that social constructs, such as socioeconomic status, can be constructed differently across cultural communities and is not as universally applicable as some authors' use of these frameworks might suggest.

Bourdieuian theories of reproduction serve analyses across social class extremely well. McDonough's (1997) study of four high schools across the strata of social class in California, found that individuals' social class and the schools' organizational habitus were defining mechanisms in structuring educational opportunity. Her analysis revealed that where students attend high school greatly determines what post-secondary opportunities will be available to them, and this was tied closely to the cultural capital of individual students. Complicating this strength of the framework, however is that, increasingly, social class is diversified across fields of racialization and ethnicity. McDonough's study held these constructs constant, focusing on white women's experiences. Other researchers (Gomez, 2005; McDonough, Nuñez, Ceja, & Solórzano, 2003) have turned to critical race theory in order to compensate for some of the ways in which Bourdieuian sociology makes it difficult to understand the diversity of populations within a common category. Regarding the three-phase model's applicability to lower-income students, a major problem is the tendency to view students in deficit perspectives when they do not achieve the objective outcomes of each phase. For lower-income students, as documented by Oakes (2004), these outcomes are often inaccessible due to limitations of local schools to provide the basic resources required for educating students for college.

The clearest example of the limitations of the three-phase model's applicability to students of color can be found in Freeman's (2005) study of African American student college choice, which I briefly discussed near the beginning of this chapter. Freeman used the three-phase model while simultaneously critiquing and revising it. Through her use of the model, she documented a key missing link in explaining African American under-representation in higher education. The model does not account for cultural influences on the individual and organizational influences encompassed within it.

Freeman (2005) found that the influences of "significant others," and "school contexts" as described by the three-phase model do not acknowledge nor allow for analysis to account for how different cultural influences shape experiences differentially across populations in these influences. Freeman's insistence on incorporating cultural influences leaves space open for Bourdieuian frameworks to be employed, but again, as articulated earlier, these frameworks have been used most productively by work in homogenous analyses. As American demography gets more diverse, it will continue to be a challenge to analyze influences across racialized and social class constructed categories.

In her recent review of college choice literature since 1990, Perna (2006) recognized that most scholarship on higher education opportunity falls into one of two broad paradigm frameworks: economic human capital investment or sociological status attainment. Although organized differently from the critique I lay out above, Perna's goal was similar—to build upon the strengths of the dominant ways that access/choice has been understood in the research literature. Perna put forward a new conceptual model herself. Perna's proposed conceptual model sought to address two main limitations in the literature on college access/choice: it did not integrate influences across human capital investment and sociological frameworks and it ignored the influence of contexts at the higher education, social, economic, and policy levels. In sum, for Perna, the main problem with existing explanations of college access/choice was that of integration.

Perna's (2006) proposed conceptual model for college choice advances the dominant framework for understanding higher education opportunity by nesting individual, school, higher education, and social, economic, and policy contexts. Through nesting these contexts, Perna's proposed conceptual model integrates the varying contexts through which students' college choice processes and outcomes manifest. Importantly, Perna draws attention to the social, economic and policy contexts in which college-going occurs, which, as she points out, have been largely ignored in the research literature and cannot be adequately addressed when working within either the human capital investment or sociological frameworks alone.

Perna succeeds in integrating scholarship. However, Perna's model remains a normative explanation of college choice processes. Her model does not explicitly engage with exercises of power that operate to reproduce inequality. Her conceptualization of college choice relies upon Hossler's and others' understanding that college choice is a series of decisions. In particular, Perna discusses her proposed conceptual model within the broader framework of Hossler and colleagues' predisposition, search, and choice phases of college choice.

Financial Aid and the Ability to Pay

Research on financial aid and the ability to pay for higher education focuses on macro-policies and structural inequalities across schooling and individual contexts. For example, many studies about financial aid have addressed the impact that various policies have on different socioeconomic categories of students (Heller, 2002; Price, 2004; St. John, 2003). These studies highlight how financial aid policies have differential impacts and thus enable and/or constrain college opportunities structurally for different groups. Heller (2002), for example, found that the transition to merit-based financial aid that occurred over the previous 20 years has led to a decline in the affordability of college for lower-income students, while benefiting middle- and higher-income families.

Additionally, some studies have observed family attitudes toward certain types of aid. For example, Price (2004) observed that students of color and their families are more averse to accepting loans than white students. Often these findings are linked to the specific choices that under-represented students make. For example, some students might limit their range of post-secondary options to schools they can afford more readily, and as a consequence they will have less need for loans. Scholars have pointed out that a pattern of loan-based financial aid policies have not increased the representation of lower-income students, and they have also suggested that the ruling ideas behind financial aid policies are in competition with the economic realities of lower-income students' families (Price, 2004; Swail, 2004).

However, there is a lack of scholarship that ties the local understandings and meanings made by families regarding these macro-policies to individual students' participation in schooling and other college choice activities (e.g., gathering information about individual colleges) (see for example, McDonough & Calderone, 2006). Research has not considered how these macro-policies influence students' understanding of post-secondary opportunities, while, by extension, influencing how they participate in schooling and other college choice processes based on that understanding. There is a nebulous sense-making space that scholarship has left unattended. That sense-making space is shaped by forces that are structural and cultural as well as external and internal to individual subjects.

College Knowledge

Some scholarship has sought to understand the problem of representation in college by studying how students get to college. This approach conceptualizes the problem of unequal access to college as one of information and agency. Conley (2005) organizes college access as a developmental process in which students need to follow specific practices, in specific ways in order to get to college. Conley uses the term *college knowledge* to describe the toolkit needed to complete this developmental process. Some practices of college knowledge include taking the PSAT exam as a sophomore in high school and writing letters to college admissions offices requesting information about their campuses. In his book, *College Knowledge,* Conley (2005) goes as far as standardizing practices that each student needs to perform in order to get to college. Although this kind of approach can be helpful for outreach and preparation programs, it is limited in its ability to explain the persistent disparities between different groups' participation in higher education.

The college knowledge framework assumes that students understand post-secondary opportunities similarly across their subjective social positions. It relies on students having similar goals and practices available to them in order to meet those goals. "Availability" in this sense covers both the accessibility of resources, and the cultural congruence to students' ecocultural niche. If a student's cultural community requires her/him to contribute to the family economy in income-producing ways, then she/he might not be available to participate in certain practices (campus visits) that could lower the income she/he generates for the home, even if she/he has the funding and time resources to participate in such practices. Positioning college access as the development of a college-going literacy refocuses the acquisition of skills and how students deploy them from a replacement model, where students' cultural values and practices are seen as needing to be replaced by normative college-going behaviors (college knowledge), to an extension of their already present repertoires of practice (Gutiérrez & Rogoff, 2003; Rogoff, 2003) where students' cultural values and practices are extended to address the structural and cultural barriers to the object of their activity—access to college.

College Access as Literacy Development—A Field Corrective

The corpus of research within the field of higher education opportunity has contributed significantly to general understanding of equal educational opportunity at the post-secondary level. However, missing from the analyses in these four domains (college access, college admissions, college choice, and academic preparation and college counseling) are considerations of how students' participation changes over time and how that development informs and is informed by their understanding of higher education opportunity. Research has yet to focus its analysis on how students participate in the project of college choice, based on an understanding of the post-secondary opportunities as informed by the broader projects of college access and college admissions. Furthermore, the participation in college choice practices, as structured by academic preparation and college advising, also informs students' understanding of post-secondary opportunities. In this sense, individual practices toward the specific goal of college choice relate to individual understanding of the broader project of college access, dialogically. The processes are mutually informing of each other.

I suggest a field corrective that integrates the four domains and examines higher education opportunity across the six identified barriers (financial barriers, K–12 mission and advising services, information on post-secondary education and financial aid, admissions practices and policies, college preparation in K–12 institutions, and family involvement) that were mentioned in chapter one. I seek to complicate the ways that the field of higher education opportunity is understood. I argue that it can be represented and analyzed as a project of literacy. Literacy, in this sense, can be understood as the critical reading of social texts and the writing of social action in strategic response to that reading. As a project of literacy, then, higher education opportunity encompasses not only the local habits, practices, and values, but also the contexts of those cultural artifacts and the structural conditions by which they are bound. In order to capture this new conceptualization of higher education opportunity, I deploy the term, *college-going literacy*.

Toward a College-going Literacy

Thinking of higher education opportunity as a question of literacy fundamentally challenges the existing literature on college access/choice. Whereas previous studies and reviews work from an overriding assumption that college choice is best understood as a series of choices (e.g., predisposition, search, and choice), the college-going literacy development model argues that college choice/access is a learned social practice. For sure, choices are made, and they have consequences. However, these choices are by no means the primary mode of movement as students navigate and negotiate their educational lives. Rather, students' opportunities are expressions of the racist, nativist, sexist, and classist practice of education that society has developed over time. In short, college access/choice is a power-laden social practice where exercises of power stemming from institutions, organizations, communities, families, and individuals are organized to sustain and contest the dominant social order. Put simply, college access/choice is *not* a rational exercise in investment, nor a rational exercise in status attainment, and further, it is more than the cultural and social contexts shaping students' decisions about it. Rather, college access is a learned activity. Achieving it can best be accomplished by the development of college-going literacies, which afford students the opportunity to respond to, navigate, and negotiate the complex, power-laden processes that interact across college-going activity.

The emphasis of dominant frameworks on students' choices makes primary the student role and responsibility in whether, if, and where she/he enters college. Emphasizing the students' agency, although important in order to acknowledge the role of agency in college access/choice, too easily succumbs to analyses that lend themselves to deficit understandings and representations of historically marginalized communities. These deficit representations foster and perpetuate the master narrative that works to keep Mexican migrant (and other marginalized cultural communities) out of higher education. Thus, a primary emphasis on the series of choices students make ignores fundamental considerations and the power-laden organization of American schooling and education more broadly. Ignoring these considerations undermines any kind of real democratic reform of college access.

Similar to the ways in which criticalists like Michael Apple (1990; 2006) have shown curriculum to be a collection of processes that result from concerted exercises of power from dominant forces that seek to perpetuate inequality, I am arguing that college-going is a practice reflected by society's racist, nativist, sexist, and classist organization. As Peter McLaren (1995; 1998) and other critical pedagogues have sought to explain, engaging in the struggle to understand, subvert, and promote democratic structures, a critical pedagogy must be enacted popularly, so that individuals and communities can come, via pedagogical transformation, to interrogate the ideological formations in society and take action toward a more equitable re-imagining of the very social structures that preclude democratic participation. Thus, I am arguing that as a social practice, college access/choice, is a learned activity and therefore can be taught. If it is to be taught for a re-imagined and equitable society, it should be taught from a critical pedagogical standpoint.

On Literacy

When constructing a college-going literacy framework, I am drawing from an expansive model of literacy—an ideological model of literacy advanced by new literacy studies (Gee, 1991; New London Group, 1995; Street, 1984, 2003). As described by Gutiérrez, Morales, & Martinez (2009), the ideological model:

> reflect[s] a culturally sensitive account of literacy that rejects static and homogeneous views of the literacy practices of cultural communities ... an ideological model posits that literacy is always embedded in social practices, where the consequences of learning a literacy are dependent on its context of development. (p. 213)

As such, literacy can be understood as a coherent understanding of signs, symbols, and practices, combined with the ability to execute, or deploy those understandings strategically toward an objective. Whereas traditional notions of literacy worked from an autonomous model of literacy, wherein literacy was thought to affect other social and cognitive practices, the ideological model asserts literacy *as social practice*. This shift opens up the previously restrictive notion that literacy could only mean one kind of reading and writing—leading to particular knowledges of written text. The ideological model affords scholars engaged in new literacy studies to expand literacy as social practice to include multiple, hybrid, and pluralistic meanings of social texts, such as video games and political action (Barton and Hamilton, 2000; Gutiérrez, 2002; Kress, 1997; New London Group, 1995; Street, 1993). For example, Gee (2003) has explored the semiotic dimensions of literacy in video games, while Davis (2004) has explored the authorship of identity as literacy development in digital storytelling, an activity of constructing a story in a digital medium. In his investigations of the social construction of literacy, Luke (2002) examined literacy as policy, through a sociocultural framework.

It is in the vein of these new literacy scholars that I appropriate the concept of literacy as an analytic tool for understanding and operationalizing higher education opportunity. Essentially, I put forth that a college-going literacy is one in which students' understanding of the messages they receive about post-secondary opportunities is put into action by their own repertoires of practice (Gutiérrez & Rogoff, 2003; Gutiérrez, 2002) that stem from their personal backgrounds and experiences toward the object of higher education opportunity and a desired outcome of college attendance.

Practicing a college-going literacy might include participating in a college-awareness day assembly at school. The student might then follow-up on the information shared in the assembly by investigating the specific admission requirements for an institution. Based on this information, the student may then seek an appointment with a school counselor and demand enrollment in a congruent course schedule.

In this example, not only does the student recognize that the social texts of the assembly have specific meaning (reading), but the student is able to decipher what further steps could benefit her personal objective of college admission (critical reading), and finally, she can take action toward that objective (writing). It is important to acknowledge that although my hypothetical example has been laid out in a linear fashion, the real-world experiences of students engaging in college-going literacy development will be much more fluid. Students read and write their educational opportunities simultaneously. As Freire and Macedo (1987) discuss, reading the social world requires writing in the blank spaces, and human beings can only write based on their sociocultural understandings of the world.

This model is a theoretical depiction of college-going literacy based on New Literacy Studies concepts of what literacy means. This model does not assert that all students' literacy will yield an outcome that brings them to college matriculation. The activity of college-going literacy development will yield differential outcomes across subjects (e.g., community college, four-year college, military enlistment, and/or full-time workforce employment).

It is at this turn that cultural-historical activity theory becomes helpful in explaining how college access might be understood as literacy development.

Cultural Historical Activity Theory

With its origins in the social-psychological works of Vygotsky (1978), which were built upon by Cole and Griffin (1978), and combined with the activity theory of Engeström (1987), cultural-historical activity theory has emerged in contemporary scholars' work to help explain learning and development (Cole, 1996; Gutiérrez, 2002; Moll, 2000; Rogoff, 2003). Cultural-historical activity theory (CHAT) assumes that learning is socially organized, culturally mediated, and historically bound. That is to say, we learn things in and amongst other people, while doing the things that we do with those people, and this all happens in a specific space/time. Development is evidenced by changes in participation over time (Rogoff, 2003; Vygotsky, 1978). However, CHAT is far less reductive than the picture I just painted. Using CHAT as a framework asserts that college choice processes can be understood as socially acquired, culturally mediated, and historically bound instantiations of learning.

The Role(s) of Culture

Taking a CHAT approach to exploring the issues faced by migrant students provides for rich description of their educational experience as it frames and informs their educational opportunity. CHAT also positions cultural practices, rather than cultural identity, in order to unpack the artifacts, beliefs, values, and normative routines that mediate the choice processes of students. These elements of culture cannot be analyzed directly; rather, the everyday mediations of how people participate in cultural practice must be the focus of analysis (Gutiérrez, 2002). Using cultural practices as a unit of analysis allows the myriad of variables at play in college choice and college access to receive attention as dictated by the subjects' experience and participation over time. Cultural practice analysis seeks a holistic understanding of how migrant students make sense of higher education opportunities and the salient influences shaping those understandings.

Positioning cultural practices as the central unit of analysis in understanding migrant students' college access changes the role that culture plays in higher education opportunity research. Conceiving culture as a category of identity often promotes deficit perspectives of cultures, perpetuating the devaluing of traditionally marginalized students' experiences (Mehan, 1997; Nieto, 2005). Culture in this concept is often equated with race or ethnicity, and socioeconomic status, and is often used as a proxy for these demographic variables. Reductive and categorical notions of culture fail to adequately address the structural formation of educational opportunity in schools (Deyhle, 1995). Thus, much of college access research can, at times, promote praxis that puts the onus of change on the individual student and/or students' cultural communities (Freeman, 1997). College and/or university responsiveness in addressing the needs of students is ignored.

Repositioning cultural practices as the central concern in investigating students' higher education opportunity challenges the traditional view of culture in the literature. Instead of deficit perspectives or concepts of culture as an independent agent, identifying cultural practices as the units of analysis provides for a rich exploration of how post-secondary opportunities are viewed, understood, and represented through educational efforts. Culture is redefined as the mutually constituted experiences of individuals and their communities (Rogoff, 2003). Put another way, it is "the artifact-saturated medium of human life" (Cole, 1998, p. 294) that comes into being as how we know culture. Students' culture is the meaning made from their experiences within their communities—experiences that have acquired value over time. In this case, meaning can be found in the ways that students navigate educational pathways leading to college attendance or non-attendance through their cultural practices. Culture must be conceived as pluralistic and dynamic; the individual and the community constantly negotiate and re-define "culture."

College Access as Activity, Learning and Literacy

CHAT serves as a framework that rethinks how this redefinition of culture is used in understanding educational opportunity processes. It positions college choice processes as an activity system—one with an internal and external logic to its operations, yet always in contest with the agency of its practitioners (e.g., students, parents, admissions officers, teachers, counselors, etc.). Participation in higher education (i.e., access to college) might serve as an object of the activity. Examining the mediation of social and personal values and expectations related to higher education highlights how cultural tools construct the learning processes that yield various outcomes in educational opportunity. Engeström's (1987, 1993) framework of activity supports repositioning educational opportunity as activity systems. In Engeström's framework, activity is historically conditioned systemic relations among individuals and communities. The concept of community, as used in this framework, indicates shared practices of a culturally organized environment, proximal to the individual. For this study, the community includes all individual bodies (subjects) that mediate behavior and therefore influence higher education opportunity. Thus, as argued by Gutiérrez (2002), "educational practices must be understood in terms of the activities that constitute them and in relation to the institutional contexts they constitute" (p. 314). Therefore, looking at college access as systems of activity fosters analysis of the reciprocal influences co-constructed by education, community, and individuals. Methodologically, activity analysis allows a robust understanding of the complex interplay between structural and individual influences inherent in higher education opportunity.

For example, as shown by the illustration below (*fig. 1*), a migrant student (subject) comes to know college access (object) through specific cultural practices (mediating tools). These practices might include learning about post-secondary options during conversation with family members over dinner. They might also include writing a personal statement as an assignment in a high school English class. Each of these practices involves the participation (or lack thereof) of other members of the community. In educational opportunity (activity), the community might include parents, high school personnel, peers, higher education admission officers, military recruiters, and supplemental academic preparation providers. The labor of the greater activity is divided into specific responsibilities among these individuals. Since the subjects (migrant students) in this activity (educational opportunity) have been historically marginalized, it makes sense to expect that not all members of the community work in accord to produce a similar outcome. In other words, the way that the labor is divided between parents, school personnel, and higher education admission officers does not necessarily lead to an understanding of college access (the object) that produces an outcome of higher education participation.

Figure 1: Higher Education Opportunity as Activity

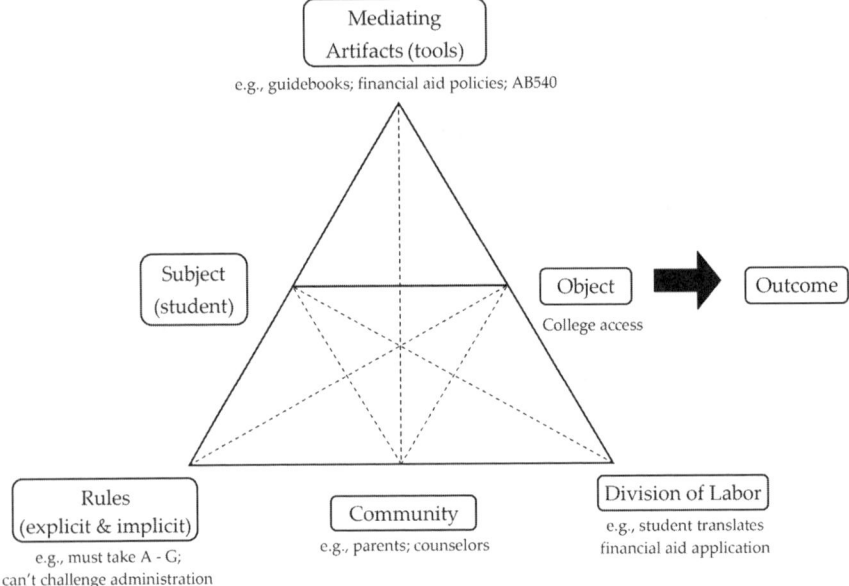

Figure 1 above shows how an activity system of higher education *might* be constituted from the subjective position of an individual migrant student. The activity is educational opportunity, and coming to know college access, as an idea and reality, serves as the object of the activity. The bold titles represent the elements of Engeström's activity system: subject, mediating tools, object, division of labor, community, and rules. In brief, the subject comes to understand the object as mediated by certain tools. However, the subject is bound by the rules of the activity, which is co-constructed by the community. The community is a set of individuals engaged in the activity of the object (college access) within a specific division of labor.

This shift in understanding higher education opportunity as a cultural learning activity can also be understood as literacy development. The shift allows me to investigate how students "read" educational opportunity, similar to ways in which other critical scholars investigate the "reading" of cultural texts toward other objects of activity (Davis, 2004; Gee, 2003; Kellner, 2004; King & O'Brien, 2002; Kress, 1988a, 1988b; Moje, 2000; Morrell & Duncan-Andrade, 2004; Street, 1993). Extending this definition requires that literacy be understood as learning that is socially constructed and mediated through historically bound cultural activity. In this sense, understanding and expressing ideas requires people to read and to write simultaneously. A number of scholars have used CHAT to study various literacy developments (see for example, Gutiérrez, Baquedano-Lopez, & Asato, 2000; Gutiérrez, 2002; Gonzalez, Moll, Floyd-Tenery, Rivera, Rendon, Gonzalez, & Amanti, 2003; Moll, 1997) across contexts. Each of these scholars operationalized ideological models of literacy—literacy as social practice—through Engeström's activity theory and sociocultural (i.e., Vygotskyian) understandings of learning and development.

I am importing this framework to college access studies, situating college access as literacy development. This shift eschews conceptual arguments that posit college choice as questions of predisposition, search, and choice (Hossler & Gallagher, 1987) and college access more generally as questions of aspiration, academic preparation, or the ability to pay (Thomas & Perna, 2004), but rather affirms a differently fluid and dynamic understanding of higher education opportunity as processes interpolated through subjective forces and exercises of power. By studying the literacy development of migrant students, I come to understand how the constitutive practices embedded within traditional higher education opportunity categories interact and manifest in the knowing of higher education opportunity for the 12 Mexican migrant students engaged in this project. This knowing is a knowing in the cognitive, affective, and behavioral dimensions of human activity.

CHAT, however, provides only a skeleton of a framework for understanding college access as college-going literacy development. There are other key concepts from sociocultural theory that help to fashion a more productive, integrative, and culturally analytic lens for understanding college-going. Chief among these are Vygotsky's (1978, 1986) "zone of proximal development" and its contemporary theorizations as "Zoped" (Griffin & Cole, 1984) and "third space" (Gutiérrez, 1995). Put plainly, the zone of proximal development is the space between what a student can readily do, or achieve, on her own and what a student can do or achieve with the assistance of more-expert-others. The Zoped is the moment in which such learning can occur—wherein current understandings can be transformed. Third space recognizes the social space through which learning happens—dissolving the learning activity from any fixed material place, but rather emphasizing that there are moments in students' development ripe with opportunities to transform current understandings into more critical, more powerful, and more meaningful understandings that might serve students better in achieving particular (academic) outcomes. Third spaces, according to Gutiérrez, emerge when official discourse and unofficial discourse merge into hybrid spaces where new possibilities for meaning and learning become available. Throughout this text, I refer to *transformative learning opportunities* in students' college-going literacy development. These are moments when and where students' repertoires of practice were extended in productive ways toward the object of college access, reconstituting their college-going literacy development. Transformative learning opportunities, in this sense, are instantiations of the zone of proximal development that I analyzed in the social space of college-going for Mexican migrant students. They might come about from third spaces, or the Zoped, or other yet-to-be-theorized neo-Vygotskyian manifestations.

The central tenet that all learning is culturally mediated lies at the core of Vygotskian thought on learning and development. From this perspective, Trueba (1990) has documented ways that Latino immigrant students' failures in school should rightfully be attributed to schooling itself, rather than to the individual students. As Trueba noted:

> Failure is not individual, so much as it is a failure of the sociocultural system which denies the child an opportunity for social intercourse, and thus for cognitive development. "Academic failure" is a sociocultural phenomenon fully understandable only in its macro-historical, economic, and political contexts. (p. 5)

Trueba shows how the logic of the system produces failure, rather than any individual trait of the student. In applying Trueba's findings to Mexican migrant college-going, I sought to uncover the transformative learning opportunities that afforded migrant students "an opportunity for social intercourse" with the social practice of college-going.

Understanding that college-going is a social and cultural activity, it is important to recognize that "activities can be viewed as social practices situated within communities invested with particular norms and values"(Lewis, Enciso, & Moje, 2007, p. 5). These communities organize around particular practices. As such, communities of practice (Lave, 1996; Lave & Wenger, 1991; Wenger, 1998) emerge over time. Communities of practice are collections of individuals sharing in cultural practices that make life meaningful to them. Communities of practice shape and are shaped by their social circumstances as well as their continuously developing cultural practices.

Similarly, a community of learners (Rogoff, 1995) can develop over time, wherein individuals collectively engage in learning and development, as organized by mediating artifacts and governed by rules. Thinking about Mexican migrant students as belonging to and participating in a community of learners, while stemming from, interacting with, and returning to various communities of practice (e.g., migrant farm-working families, educators, etc.), underscores the notion that social practices are learned in situated contexts. Theories of situated learning highlight that all learning happens in shifting contexts of broader social conditions and cultural practices (Rogoff, 2003).

Different communities of practice emerge from different histories of participation within particular social practices. In college-going, some communities of practice (e.g., upper-middle class whites) have longstanding and well-established histories of participation that have secured certain values as congruent with the process of achieving college access, whereas other communities' histories of participation have been based on exclusion and marginalization (e.g., Mexican migrant communities), thus disenfranchising these communities from sharing the cultural norms, values, and practices most congruent with achieving college access. To be clear, a community's history of marginalization is not a reflection of any sort of deficit in their cultural ways of knowing the world. Rather, it is a reflection of how the social practice of college-going itself has evolved over time to ensure that some communities are brought in while others are left out.

Rogoff's (2008) ideas around "intent community participation" are helpful in explaining this tension. Rogoff contrasts traditional, factory-model or banking models of education with more collaborative and community-driven models. She and her colleagues have documented how students can learn more and more productively when an entire community of learners invests itself in the success of any given student. It is given that Mexican migrant families' history with higher education is marked by under-representation and marginalization. It also is given that upper-middle-class white families' history with higher education is marked with over-representation, increased access to a broader range of post-secondary choices, and greater ease of affordability. Putting the onus of this inequity on the activity system of college access itself—the social practice of college-going—then can show how students from one community (the white one) benefits from an entire array of individuals working to secure their access to college. Parents, siblings, extended family, school personnel and higher education admission officers all work *intently* on getting upper-middle-class white kids into college. These are normative expectations. However, efforts to increase Mexican migrant students in higher education remain exceptional. Mexican migrant students, as will be shown in chapter seven, do *not* benefit from intent community participation, but rather achieve college access from serendipitous relations with caring individuals and interventional programs.

In order to recognize the normative versus the exceptional in learning and development, socioculturalists can draw from the metaphor of design, specifically designing learning environments and processes (New London Group, 2000; Rogers & Fuller, 2007). In this metaphor, teachers, counselors, parents, admission officers, policy-makers, and anyone else implicated in students' college-going engage in the design of college-going learning environments. As cultural workers, these individuals use tools (e.g., the SAT exam or policies that track students into and out of college-preparatory curricula) to design an ecology that enables college access for some students, while constraining opportunity for others.

The New London Group (2000) instructed:

> To treat any semiotic activity, including using language to produce or consume texts, as a matter of design involving three elements: Available designs, designing, and redesigning. Together, these three elements emphasize the fact that meaning-making is an active and dynamic process, and not something governed by static rules. (p. 20, as cited in Rogers & Fuller, 2007)

There are innumerable available designs. These are the designs readily available based on community members' cultural practices that are brought into the co-constructed social space of college-going. Over time, these designs become hybridized as cultural practices shift, often in response to different exercises of power in any given activity. In the case of college admissions, the design of college-going has changed as federal financial aid policy has moved from a grants-based to a loans-based orientation in assisting low-income families to pay for college. Thus, the financing of higher education, which can play a major role in the mediation of college choice outcomes (who can go where), has changed the ways that some students learn college-going. The learning ecology has been redesigned, and college-going emerges with new meanings. Rogers and Fuller (2007) put it this way:

> This redesigning may occur in terms of ways of interacting, ways of representing, ways of being as well as in terms of the overall goal or agenda. Every act of available design, designing, and redesigning involves a chain of meaning that is historically shaped. (p. 81).

Design, as a sociocultural metaphor for the construction of learning opportunities that shape how students' understand and practice college-going, affords educators (broadly conceived) the opportunity to assess how they organize students' college access. Are the available designs operating to preclude some while privileging others? The most flexible designs, designs that encourage hybridity, most likely transform the histories of participation in college-going more readily for non-dominant groups (e.g., Mexican migrant students) than more predictable, rigid, and standardized designs. At this point on the college-going literacy map, it is important to turn to the explicit political dimensions of this project—the moments that make it a *critical* sociocultural inquiry.

Critical Sociocultural Inquiry

This study operates on multiple levels. At its most generic, the study was designed to re-theorize college access as college-going using a cultural-historical activity theory perspective. This required a systems-level analysis, based on the normative practices embedded in migrant students' college-going lives. At a more generative and particular level, the study was designed to understand how migrant students' disrupt normative notions of college-going in their development of college-going literacies. This required individual-level analyses of students' everyday practices and the institutionalized as well as interventional educational forces that shaped them. Institutionalized forces are those practices and policies officially sanctioned and made normative for students in their schooling and higher education experiences. Interventional forces are those practices that transcend institutional authority, seeking to disrupt the normative college-going experiences for migrant students. From a tangential perspective, and as an artifact of the genesis of my relationships with the student participants (i.e., MSLI), this study provides a follow-up assessment of how students engaged socio-critical literacies after working to develop them in the summer program.

I want to be clear that the study reported herein was not evaluative. I did not set out to design a project that sought to evaluate the 2005 MSLI. Rather, I sought to engage MSLI participants in a critical inquiry of their college-going, the inequalities that mark that social practice, and the exercises of power/agency/resistance that disrupt the hegemonic systems of oppression on which college access is based.

In my critical orientation, I participated in inquiry as a pedagogical practice. As such, my methodological choices were informed as much by critical pedagogy as by critical ethnography. Each strives to transform the social world, while unabashedly making clear what that transformation might look like. For me, I imagine a radically transformed public education that educates all students for college—not just in state standards of content and official curricula, but in the ability for students to read the world and the word, and take strategic action to increase and equalize social opportunities.

In order to engage Mexican migrant students in an investigation of their college-going literacy development, I designed a *critical sociocultural inquiry*, operationalizing sociocultural theories of learning and development into a methodology imbued with concerns about power and power relations (Moje & Lewis, 2007). Sociocultural theory generates robust analysis, in part, because of the wide range of mediators in learning and development for which it tries to account. However, socioculturalists have themselves pointed to a need for a theoretical heteroglossia in order to more fully understand the power embedded in culture and learning (Gutiérrez & Larson, 1994; Lewis, Enciso, & Moje, 2007). Lewis, Enciso, and Moje (2007) comment on the timeliness of such a critical component to sociocultural theory:

> Making issues of identity, agency, and power visible is essential at this historical moment ... with political discourse about "scientific" research having persuaded the public that literacy is a neutral skill and that "achievement gaps" can be addressed without attention to histories of power relations or group and individual struggles for identity. (p. 3).

From a political perspective, most college access projects concern themselves with leveling the playing field. As a socioculturalist, I sought to uncover ways to redesign the playing field (Lewis, Encisco, & Moje, 2007), by paying attention to the ways that power circulates in higher education opportunity, the ways that identities are generated, crafted, exchanged, and mutable in becoming a college-going student, and the ways that Mexican migrant students exercise agency in their development of college-going literacies. Inherent in these goals are theories of power as something exercised in a field of relations, rather than held in a dominating position. Identity is understood as dynamic social production, and agency as strategic constructions of selves that seek particular goals (Lewis, Enciso, & Moje, 2007). Cumulatively, these critical perspectives co-construct the fracture that I re-present throughout the rest of this book.

College-going literacies, then, are the sense-making processes that students develop throughout their life spans, enabling them to access college opportunities and succeed in college. College-going literacy is formed by the cumulative meaning-making events in students' lives. These events are constituted by the cultural practices that students engage in their daily lives—their ways of being and knowing. College-going literacy is mediated by the cultural artifacts, or tools, that assist students in making sense of college access—the required preparation, the politics and hidden curriculum of admissions, the construction of merit, and the economics of paying for college. College-going literacy is mediated also by the formal and informal rules of college access—how and why different students gain access to and succeed in college. Furthermore, college-going literacies take form and are shaped by the other people implicated in the use of these tools, the generation and practice of these rules, and by the different roles and responsibilities that these other people take on in the broader system of college-going. College-going literacies are the coding and de-coding skills that students use in order to navigate college pathways. Most importantly, college-going literacy development is a site of struggle and contest, marked by shifts in identities, exercises of agency, and circulations of power.

Studying Mexican Migrant College-going Literacy

As cultural practices become central to activity analysis and the interactions within and across activity settings are always situated in particular yet dynamic relations of power, I drew from critical ethnography and critical pedagogy, each characterized as inquiry concerned with empowerment and emancipation, interrogation of power and culture, and a commitment of linking theory to practice (Kellner, 1989; Kincheloe & McLaren, 2000; Jaramillo & McLaren, 2008). These methodological ideals are by no means neutral. This project assumed that migrant educational inequities stem from oppressive social relations and explicitly sought to engage in the struggle to uproot, disrupt, and transform them. Deeply concerned with my own unwitting participation in the marginalization of Mexican migrant students, and fueled by my conviction that theory/method and inquiry are pedagogical encounters, I sought to design a "(post)critical ethnography" (Noblit, Flores, & Murillo, 2004, p. 21) that engaged explicitly with issues that critical ethnography, in its now classical sense, continues to grapple with: positionality, reflexivity, objectivity, and representation.

As this book is not a methods textbook, nor a volume dedicated to theorizing (post)critical ethnography, I will speak to each of these concerns only briefly enough to provide a sense of how they came to matter in the project that generated the fracture that I re-present herein. I sought to make my positionality explicit throughout this project—from my initial engagement with the participants to the prose that sits on the page here. I am deeply implicated in this project, and I have made no attempt to hide my participation in the ethnographic depictions, descriptions, narratives, and other forms of representation that I deploy throughout the text. My objectivity, as will be discussed later in this chapter, was not neutral, but rather generated from my explicit subjectivities that I try to lay bare. I do this not through any self-reflective position statement, but rather by providing reflexive commentary throughout the re-presentation of my ethnographic engagement with students. In short, the fracture in the master narrative about Mexican migrant college-going that I put forth in this volume is in many ways a presentation of how *I* learned about Mexican migrant college access. I do not pretend to speak with authority that claims a scientific assuredness, an absolute truth, nor an unwavering demonstration of how the world works. Rather, I speak with an authority based on my process of coming to know, as documented in my epistemological, theoretical, methodological, analytical, relational, and representational choices that were made across the tenure of this project.

Research Design

To these ends, I participated in the lives of 12 Mexican migrant students whom I had met and forged deeply invested relationships with during the 2005 Migrant Student Leadership Institute (MSLI) at UCLA. The institute served self-identified migrant students from across the state of California. MSLI sought to develop critical consciousness and academic literacy that each of the 99 participants could take back to their communities and continue to effect change while preparing for post-secondary education (Nuñez & Jaramillo, 2005). The 2005 MSLI participants included rising sophomores, juniors, and seniors with varying grade point averages (2.0–4.0). Additionally, hybrid language practices were valued as legitimate means of expression and therefore, no student was prevented from participating because of primary or secondary language ability. All but a few of the participants were first-generation college students from lower-socioeconomic status backgrounds. Most self-identified as Latino, predominantly Mexican American. All students were either immigrants themselves, or the first-generation child of immigrant parents.

As an instructor, I had daily, structured, direct contact over a one-month period with approximately 45 of the 99 students. This contact took place in either structured classroom settings or during structured tutoring sessions. It is from this sub-population of the greater MSLI that I solicited participation. I extended invitations to all 45 students to participate in the study. As I am a limited-to-English speaker, I solicited participants with the caveat that respondents must be comfortable interviewing in English.

I did not discriminate based on any other subjective identifiers (e.g., age, racialization, academic achievement, or immigration status). By drawing on critical ethnography and critical pedagogy, social constructs such as these could be accounted for in my analysis, and therefore, I was not concerned about them in design. One possible critique of these recruitment practices is that I did not discriminate based on student grade level. The critique could argue that school and college choice processes are structured in such a way that students are subject to different developmental experiences by grade level, and as such need to be captured in similar space/time in order to generate robust and accurate findings. This critique would definitely be true if I were conceiving of college access/choice as a unidirectional and linear process, or even as a more complex process in a zero-sum game. However, in situating college access as a project of literacy—as an activity system—not only *could* I include multiple grade levels, but indeed, this inclusion proved helpful to my analysis.

The individual's activity of coming to know college is situated in a larger community system of college-going. It is impossible to talk about just one grade level, because each grade level is situated in a larger system that has a certain logic dictating what things/activities must occur at particular developmental levels (Rogoff, 1994; 2003). What sophomores do with regard to college is always configured within a larger logic of what the community system of college-going deems as appropriate for that year with the assumption that students will continue within the larger system of college-going. This logic holds true whether students are identified as college-preparatory students or not, as the same logic of the activity system applies to both privileged and marginalized individuals. What happens at one level is dependent to a certain extent on what happens at other levels. It is imperative to conceive of all students' experiences as occurring within this larger cultural system. While each individual student's grade level matters, it does not make sense to close off and isolate their experiences from others allotted different roles in what is essentially the same cultural system.

Also, previous qualitative work in educational opportunity has been based in heterogeneous populations. Prominent in the field of college access is educator Kassie Freeman's study of African American college choice (2005), in which she interviewed 10th, 11th, and 12th graders individually and in focus groups across different geographies and socioeconomic status. Although her findings were derived from some class-based and geographically based considerations, she did not disaggregate her data based on grade level. This was appropriate for her study, similar to mine, in that her research questions were not bound to a specific task or developmental level in the activity of college-going. Another example comes from sociologist, Julie Bettie's (2003) ethnography of Mexican American girls in California's Central Valley. Although Bettie's primary concern is the construction of class for Mexican American girls, she draws a number of conclusions about educational opportunity, including some directly related to postsecondary opportunity. For example, Bettie argued for a holistic curriculum that prepared all students for university eligibility requirements and exposed them to baccalaureate options after high school. Bettie did not limit her sample or her analysis by grade level. She too was looking at cultural practices within the larger logic of a cultural system.

My recruitment plan led me to work with 12 students over the course of the study. These students came from seven migrant regions across the state of California. There were four female and eight male participants. Six participants graduated from high school during data collection. Four participants, all of whom were male, were undocumented immigrants.

Students' experiences were rich with opportunities for substantive critical and conscientious inquiry. As Nuñez and Jaramillo (2005) point out, students from MSLI begin to investigate their social worlds in critical ways as they develop post-secondary plans. They cut across multiple subjective positions that have been traditionally marginalized by educational institutions, and they have a vested interest in promoting college access for migrant students. Finally, my prior personal relationship with students helped foster the trust and intimacy that any critical engagement demands.

Fieldwork took form as monthly visits to students and their families in their home communities. Some formal interviewing occurred, but more often I simply tried to spend time with students, deepening our relationships with each other. We talked about our experiences in schools and in our families. We discussed current events and shared our past histories. We imagined new futures and explained our goals with each other. I took a radical subjectivist approach to fieldwork, informed by feminist sentiment about the relational nature of fieldwork (Bloom, 1998). Again, stressing the pedagogical nature of the project, our mutual sense-making, both students and my own, were integral to the project. As much as students involved me in their lives, I involved them in mine. These relationships strengthened the sense-making I sought to understand from students. Because students knew me, knew what I was about, knew what I was hoping to achieve with this project, I could freely and directly ask questions that other more traditional researchers might need to "cloak" or mediate in a vernacular that lost some of the deeper conceptual meaning. For example, if I wanted to learn about how students' financial practices were mediated by their parents' labor and income, I did not necessarily frame my questions in a discourse similar to "Do you get an allowance?" which preemptively embeds a Euro-normative expectation of how money and decisions might be organized in a family. Rather, because of our relationships with each other, and our shared histories in the 2005 MSLI, I could share a research article about the financial aid practices of Latino families, introduce the sociocultural concept of mediation, and then embark in a critical discussion of students' financial practices and their parents' labor, income, values, and expectations.

I do not wish to give a false impression that all of my time with students was spent in deep, analytical, and reflective think-tanks. Rather, these sense-making moments happened while we were hanging out at bowling alleys, coffee shops, living rooms, graduation parties, city parks, playing tennis, watching television, or sharing a meal together. Our interactions were exceptional in many ways, but they were embedded in students' everyday practices. As such, we kept our relationships alive and vibrant even when I was away from students' home communities. Social networking sites like MySpace, instant-messaging programs like AOL Instant Messenger, e-mail, text messages, and voice mails were all critical communicative acts in sustaining our engagement across time and space.

Data Analysis

As stated by Merriam (2001), "data collection and analysis is a simultaneous activity in qualitative research" (p. 178). Qualitative data analysis of my respondents' cultural practices provided a sociocultural-historical interpretation of the data. My first moment of analysis focused on establishing how individual students understood college access, as an idea/process. I analyzed the data from codes associated with activity theory that identify the mediating tools (e.g., college fairs), members of the community (e.g., counselors), rules of the activity (e.g., deadlines for applications), and divisions of labor (e.g., translating school correspondence to parents) that constituted learning *the idea/process* of college access. Additionally, emergent codes associated with the subject (student), and her/his positionality in relation to the object were used to help explain the meanings associated with each of these activity codes. The specific concepts that I examined in this phase are the constructs in Engeström's activity theory, as discussed and illustrated previously in this chapter.

My second moment of analysis looked at the practices that students reported, across cases and the meanings that students ascribed to these practices. This analysis showed not only how practices made sense to students as they worked toward college access, within their understanding of college access, but how that understanding was informed by their practices. Again, the specific concepts that I examined in this phase came from Engeström's activity theory, but as informed by the case-based analysis from moment one. Understanding the dialogic meaning-making process in a college-going literacy makes my study a first step to understanding new dimensions of how macro-processes of college access and micro-processes of college choice work together. This need was previously identified by the field-level analysis of college access provided by McDonough, Ventresca, and Outcalt (2000). It is necessary to understand this unexplored space of meaning-making to create an understanding of college access for migrant students.

From my critical perspective, constructions of reliability and validity in social research are transformed. Reliability in social research has historically suggested that researchers need to insure the accuracy of their data. Verification practices, such as triangulation and member-checking emerged to insure the truthfulness of data (Maxwell, 2004; Cresswell, 2008). My critical ethnographic praxis eschews this verification process as hegemonic and positivistic. In order to verify something as truthful, especially using practices of triangulation and member-checking, one inherently assumes that there is a unitary truth against which the data will be judged. If enough sources (triangulation) confirm that the data are what they appear to be, then the data are deemed reliable. If respondents confirm (member-checking) that they shared what they shared, then the data are deemed reliable. Each practice assumes that there is a single truth that will remain constant across the contexts of the meaning-making that generated the data in the first place.

As a critical pedagogical project straddling the borderlands around radical constructionist and subjectivist epistemologies, and based in sociocultural understandings of learning and development, data are to be treated as partial, in-process, contested, and always (im)possible. I do not structure triangulation practices into my inquiry in order to verify students' realities, nor do I do formal member-checks with students in order to double-check their original accuracy in the recounting of their experiences. Rather, I rely on

Freire's (1970) advice in working against "false generosity" and toward "true generosity" in the struggle for humanizing education. I sought to support students in unleashing their own power so that we could more deeply understand the ways that power circulated in their college-going lives and put our "human hands which work, and, working, transform the world" (Freire, 1970/2004, p. 45).

Freire wrote, "trusting people is the indispensible precondition for revolutionary change" (p. 95). I trust the expertise, the intelligence, and the analysis of the student participants who engaged in this inquiry with me. As such, I respect that any data we generated together can be truthful, understanding truth in the radical constructionist tradition as co-constructed and in the subjectivist tradition as always contingent upon the lens to which we subject human experience in order to make sense of it. In these ways, all truths are representations of imagined realities—in the past, present, or future. Data remain as truthful as they can be whether verified using positivistic methods or not. They represent imagined truths—possible ways of understanding the social world and one's participation in it.

Validity, from critical perspectives has been theorized in multiple constructions as well. Patti Lather argues for *catalytic validity* in critical research, wherein the goodness of research is evaluated by the social change it can effect (1986; 1993). If conclusions seem reasonable based on the marshaled evidence, and if they address the social problem under inquiry in ways that work toward positive social change, then the research has catalytic validity. Complementing Lather's catalytic validity is Sandra Harding's (1995) construction of *strong objectivity*, which holds that objectivity is not synonymous with neutrality, nor should it be. Rather, strong objectivity draws from Feminist standpoint theories and values the explication of social locations embodied by the researcher in order to achieve an objectivity that might be useful in social analysis. These (post)critical theorizations about the integrity of social research support the pedagogical function of my critical ethnographic inquiry. They are each relational and contribute to my critical goal of transforming the social world to eliminate human suffering.

An Introduction to Analyzing and Mapping College-going Literacy Development

From field notes after a visit with students in the California Central Valley:

> Sitting on the edge of a double bed, I scanned an eight-foot by seven-foot bedroom. Carlitos had run to the kitchen to grab a soda for each of us. I took the opportunity to absorb the space as best I could, documenting the impressions and observations I made in my notebook. There was a double bed. Behind the bed was a small closet. There was a wooden floor. An old desk and wooden folding chair leaned against a bookshelf. There were books and folders on the shelves. A window with white mini-blinds let some light into the room. If I took half a step in any direction, I could reach out and touch any of these furnishings.
>
> The room was simple.
>
> The room was complex.
>
> My first notes did an injustice to the space. Carlitos and his ten-year-old brother shared the double bed every night. It was a mattress without a bedspring on a drooping frame with a combination of what appeared to me to be store-bought sheets and homemade blankets. The small closet housed all of their clothes, which they shared, in a meticulously adhered to organization. Despite the sneaking of light between the mini-blinds, the room was fairly dark, with at least one of the bulbs in the overhead light fixture burned out. The wood floor was unfinished in places and some planks were in desperate need of repair.
>
> These additional descriptors might signify something about the standard of living that Carlitos knew. Some might use the word poverty to sum up his habitat. That word is a correct descriptor. Yet, it still leaves out much of the complexity in his simple 8' x 7' room.
>
> The room was spotlessly clean. Despite its lack of accoutrements, it was evident that the materials Carlitos and his

family did have meant a lot to them. They were well cared for. This space was important, as were the people living in it.

Still deeper in my first notes, I found an "X" to mark yet another spot to dig—the books and folders on the shelves. Besides being neatly cluttered across the shelves and desk space, almost like a Crate & Barrel advertisement for "shabby chic" décor. Some of the folders wore labels indicating their function. One of these said "MEDICAL." Carlitos, being the oldest of the children that could speak English in the family, was responsible for keeping track of the family medical records and bills. Most recent of these were his and his mother's diagnoses and treatments for "yellow fever," a commonly diagnosed, yet little-understood ailment of many fieldworkers in the San Joaquin Valley.

There were also used textbooks that Carlitos had collected. Some of these textbooks were never used in classes he had taken. He just wanted to learn more, so he took them when the opportunity presented itself. There was also an encyclopedia set from the mid-1990s. Carlitos explained that his father had found the set and brought it home to help him and his siblings with their schoolwork.

Carlitos' simple 8' x 7' bedroom was the family office.

There were two other bedrooms for six other people in the house. It was the homework den for him and his siblings. It was a refuge for him and his brother. It was the space where Carlitos glided over, between, amidst, and across being his ten-year-old brother's best friend and mentor, his parents' broker to the bureaucratic English-speaking world, a nearly straight-A student, and a 16-year old developing adolescent.

Carlitos returned with the soda. He said to me, "Tell me again why you're doing this study?"

I replied, "Well, to be simple about it, hopefully so that we can get more students like you into college. To make it more fair."

Carlitos smiled, "That doesn't sound so simple."

He was right. He knew that his learning was not simple. It never had been. Like the journey to college, Carlitos' life was scattered over complicated constellations of borders, responsibilities, desires, people, and goals. Even his migration northward to the San Joaquin Valley could not be mapped in a straight line.

Understanding college access is not simple. Understanding how subjects traverse land and become college students is complex work. It is easy to get lost when seeking understanding, and so, Carlitos' room serves as the canvas to be painted with a map to help guide the way. Maps help to decipher the space/time they represent. Carlitos' complicatedly simple room is a reminder to "never complicate what is simple, nor simplify what is complex" (Roy, 2003). College-going is a complex social practice that draws on some of the simplest of human needs. It is imperative to account for both.

The following chapters present the primary analyses that have been made on data collected from this inquiry. They bring an empirical notion to the theoretical and conceptual representations of college-going in these early chapters. Taken together, they provide summarized, simple answers to the research questions under study, and subsequently, they individually provide extended explanations of the development of migrant students' college-going literacy. I constructed these answers using a mixture of students' own voices and my first-hand observations to exemplify the patterns of experiences that were ethnographically documented in this inquiry.

I invoke the metaphor of a map, that of mapping, in order to balance between the complexity of college-going and the pragmatic determinism of written text. I treat college-going literacy development—learning college access—reading and writing higher education opportunity, as a dynamic geography. This map is not fixed, but rather a malleable guide to understanding how migrant students develop college-going literacy. Furthermore, this mapping depicts the practice of college-going as a site of social, cultural, physical, and cognitive intersection—a site of struggle. Reading and writing are sites within an activity that intersect at transformative moments, where new readings and writings are made possible. My mapping explains college-going as a social practice that is performed amidst structural and cultural constraints and affordances.

Thinking of college access as a learning activity means that instead of thinking about the influence that various factors or variables might play in a student's life while structuring their higher education opportunity, I think about how participation in the activity of higher education opportunity is organized, and how the goal(s) of that activity—college access—is mediated for students. To this end, Engeström's activity theory is helpful in providing a conceptual framework in which to organize discussion. Learning can be understood in the dynamic interplay between a subject (student) and the object of learning (college access), as mediated by artifacts, or tools (e.g., college fairs). There are rules that regulate students' learning of college access—regulating their development of college-going literacy. There are many other actors involved in the activity (community), and their participation can be documented (division of labor) in reference to or from the perspective of the student (subject). The following chapters describe how the activity of college access is constructed for the migrant students in this study.

Chapter Three
Reading and Writing Migrant Students as Subjects

The students to whom this book is dedicated came from seven different migrant regions in California.[1] From as far south as the Mexico-U.S. border to as far north as the San Francisco Bay area to as far west as the Pacific Coast Highway and as far east as the foothills of the Sierra Nevada Mountains, these students represent a wide array of geographic contexts. They also represent the same geography—that of the 2005 Migrant Student Leadership Institute (MSLI). What follows are brief analytic descriptions of each of the 12 students who participated in this study, and the geographic area in which they live.[2] These descriptions in no way attempt to summarize any of these students' experiences. Rather, I hope to provide an illustration of how I came to know each of these students and some background information about some of the most salient characteristics in their lives in relation to their college-going. I present the following portraits in an effort to begin a textual narrative about the constitution of the migrant student subject in college-going.

Introducing *Los Estudiantes Migrantes para* College-going Literacy

In addition to their common experience in the Migrant Student Leadership Institute, all of the students in this study are what Suárez-Orozco and Suárez-Orozco (2001) call "children of immigrants." One-third of the students migrated to the U.S. from Mexico themselves. Each come from working-class families, or families who might be considered members of the working poor. The annual family income ranges from $15,000 to $43,000. Nine of the 12 participants grew up in two-parent homes where both parents worked at least part-time.

Most of the students attended predominantly Latino schools. There were three exceptions to this, one of whom attended a private Catholic high school. Every student had at least some experience in English Language Development (ELD) instruction (or some derivation) during some part of their K–12 education in the United States. All but one participant will be the first college-educated student in their families. All of the students participated in some sort of outreach or supplemental academic preparation program(s) in addition to MSLI. Finally, all 12 of the participants in this study aspired to a four-year college degree.

As Suarez-Orozco and Suarez-Orozco (2001) point out, immigrant destinations—that is, neighborhoods—play large roles in determining their families' futures. Students' physical locations within the state of California shaped their experiences in decisive ways. As such, I present the following individual portraits of each participant in geographic groupings, with a brief description of the geographic area preceding the student portraits.

East San Francisco Bay Area

The San Francisco Bay area has a long history as a destination for families migrating to the United States. In recent decades, the East Bay has emerged as a more affordable and economically viable location than the region's cornerstone city of San Francisco. Like many California areas in demographic transition, the East Bay is increasingly populated by first- and second-generation Latino and Asian/Asian American families. As such, the schools in the area are largely segregated along racialized lines. Students of color overwhelmingly attend more poorly funded schools with lower achievement indicators, while white and middle/upper-middle class families have relocated into the hills, or further inland where schools appear more suburban. The immediate East Bay is an urban environment with a strong history of political activism, especially around issues of race and race relations. There are both University of California and California State University campuses within commuting distance via car, bus, or rail to serve residents of the East Bay.

Armando—El Shorty

Armando's family subsists as part of the East Bay's working poor. Having come to the United States during middle school, he has persisted through various ELD programs since entering the California public education system. He is the second oldest child in his immediate family, and their rented modular house serves as home for his aunt and nephew, while at least two other extended families live in close proximity. Armando maintains a strong social network with other students from the 2005 MSLI. He is an avid contributor to his MySpace page, where he stays in contact with friends that he has met through his school, MSLI, and other outreach programs.

Inside Armando's family home, the pride his parents feel for him is abundantly clear. There are framed certificates from his achievements in school hanging on the living room walls. His parents also display certificates of their own involvement in education. The centerpiece of one wall collage is the certificate from participating in the Migrant Parent Leadership Institute, a "sister" program to the MSLI. Armando's parents work long, hard hours. His father works two jobs to earn enough money for the family to get by. Armando and his older brother share duties of looking after younger siblings. Often when I would visit Armando at his home, I would first see his siblings and cousins playing baseball or soccer on the street of their neighborhood. Armando's political status as an undocumented immigrant is a palpable influence on his life. He is hyper-aware of the fact that his opportunities are shaped differently than peers of his who can produce a two and a half by three inch piece of paper documenting their presence in the U.S. Although he would entertain my questions that asked about his experiences directly related to migration, he was always a bit guarded and happy to change the subject. Armando aspires to attend a four-year university, and he is looking into the matriculation agreements between various UC campuses and his local community college, as well as private colleges in California that might offer financial aid, despite his political status.

Armando gained attention and notoriety in the 2005 MSLI alongside his friend, Alex, because the pair was almost inseparable after the first couple of days. Standing next to each other, they looked like a photograph that could not be planned any better. Alex happened to be the tallest student in MSLI that summer, standing a proud 6 feet, 2 inches. Armando happened to be the shortest, standing an equally proud 5 feet flat. Armando welcomed the adoration that this juxtaposition brought him, and he emerged as one of the most charming and goal-oriented students of the program. For me, I remember vividly the day that I felt Armando and I reached a point of honesty and mutual admiration. I asked him what was hard in school, and he said "English." I asked him if it was hard speaking with me, and he said, "No, because I know that you won't get upset with me if I don't use the right words. I know that you'll help me." Ten minutes later, he was giving me Spanish lessons before inviting me to stay later and participate in his cousin's first birthday party. Armando and I exchanged e-mails throughout the study. Our correspondence was dominated by him sharing the development of his goals, and me sharing new resources I found for undocumented students seeking a college education. We are friends, but we are not confidants.

Monterey Bay Area

Just minutes from the Pacific Ocean lies a quiet city filled with family-owned shops and restaurants competing with the encroaching corporate influence of suburban strip-malls each seeking to serve and benefit from the working-class and working-poor families that constitute the labor force for the agricultural industry driving the economy of nearby Pajaro and Salinas Valleys. Located just east of the Monterey Bay along the central California coast, this predominantly Latino, bilingual community is surrounded by coastal cities populated by predominantly white, limited-to-English families in households making over six-figure incomes to sustain their multi million-dollar homes. Many of the community's working-poor families work in the fields of strawberries, artichokes, or garlic for which the area is known. This particular Latino migrant community also provides the workforce for the vast cannery sector of the agricultural industry. There are both University of California and California State University campuses within an hour's drive. Each of these campuses is nestled within the predominantly white and affluent neighborhoods closest to the ocean.

Nené, the Poet

Born of parents who migrated to the United States from Mexico and found work in the agricultural economy of California's central coast, Nené grew up as the middle child in his family and claimed himself to suffer from "that whole middle kid never getting the attention thing." With an older sister, as the only girl in the family and the oldest child by at least four years before Nené's older brother, and a younger brother following three years behind, Nené's middle-ness came from being sandwiched between his brothers. His siblings played important roles in his college-going. Both his older sister and brother went to California State Universities. His younger brother was regarded as "the smart one," because he excelled early in school, especially in math. Nené, however, made his mark in school in different ways. He was easily liked, and liked by many. His popularity was not of the "too cool" crowd type, but rather that he was cool with anybody. He participated in track and field and cross-country sports, and was elected homecoming king in his senior year. As Nené proudly proclaimed, his high school's "first Mexican homecoming king, ever."

Nené attended a different high school than any of his siblings. His was in the more affluent and predominantly white neighboring city. The high school population reflected this difference, which added to the significance of Nené's involvement in the immigrant rights movement. As will be discussed in further detail in chapters five and six, Nené organized a public forum to discuss student involvement in the marches, walk-outs, rallies, and protests around HR4437 in the spring of 2006.[3] His budding activism was reminiscent of the immigrant rights movement's actions during the early 1990s when migrant workers collectively protested the employment practices of the local canneries, achieving greater gender equity and better working conditions. Nené's mother had worked in the canneries when he was a child, and she remembered the protests vividly. Most currently, Nené's mother works on an assembly line for a local manufacturer. His father initially found employment as a fieldworker, but later secured employment with a local produce stand. His parents worked hard for a long time to secure residency and a safe home to raise their children. They each participated in migrant education programs throughout their children's schooling. Primarily a Spanish-speaker, Nené's father had insisted that Nené attend a special bilingual charter school for his elementary education. Although accepted into the California State University, Nené opted to begin his post-secondary studies at the local community college, with the goal of transferring to the University of California.

When I first met Nené, I did not think we were going to get along. I remember thinking to myself, "This kid is trying hard to be cool. He ain't gonna get along with me. I am going to be an issue for him." I was judging his general confidence and dress as similar to those of my own peers when I was in high school—the kids who made me feel insecure. Much of these early impressions were also part of my regular and predictable process of coming in and out to a classroom as a queer body. Luckily, Nené and I each realized that there was a greater goal at stake. We challenged ourselves to get to know each other. I made an effort to partner with Nené during an early icebreaker in the earliest days of MSLI. He made an effort to answer questions honestly and challenged me to be as forthright with my own answers. A week later we were looking for each other in the cafeteria, eager to share stories from our lives outside of the institute. Intellectually, Nené hooked me as a lifelong fan when he brought in some of his poetry, read some verses aloud in class, then asked me to read some verses privately and tell him what I thought. Nené is a writer, with a clear point of view, and an excellent grasp of metaphor. Our relationship since MSLI became friendship, and throughout this study it continued to gain strength into something indescribable in the English language, *confianza*, which will be detailed more analytically in chapter six. Through his unabashed curiosity and commitment to being cool with anybody, Nené has taught me not to be afraid of what I don't know, but rather, trust that I'm cool enough to ask for help in figuring it out.

Greater Central Valley

The greater Central Valley, also known as the San Joaquin Valley, is California's agricultural megalopolis. Two major highways run its length, Interstate 5 and California 99, each of which transport enough produce, meat, and cheeses each year to feed the rest of the United

States. The agricultural industry in the Central Valley operates year-round. More migrant workers live and work in the Central Valley than any other single location in California. There are a few large cities that serve as hubs of metropolitan areas and dozens of small towns scattered throughout the large farms and acreages surrounding them. One-third of the participants in this study lived in the greater Central Valley. Two of them in small towns, and one in each of two major cities. The public schools they attended were predominantly Latino, with higher representations of whites and Asian/Asian Americans in the larger cities. There are three California State Universities and one brand-new University of California campus in the Central Valley, each of which is within two or three hours drive from any participant's home in the area. However, there is not an integrative public transportation system throughout the Valley.

Eduardo, the Funny Guy

Eduardo is the oldest sibling in his family. His home is marked by a tumultuous relationship between him and his father. One week they are best friends. The next week, Eduardo's mom has moved him and his younger sister to their aunt's house. One month later, the family reunites, and Eduardo and his father pretend that nothing ever happened. Eduardo related this relationship to his post-secondary planning. He said, "I don't know is like, how I know. I should go to college, but why and what will I study? Kind of like, I should get along with my dad, but I don't know why we don't or even why it matters." Eduardo struggled with motivation throughout schooling. He went through periods where school was his favorite place to be, and he excelled in classes. He also went through periods where school seemed like an obligatory six hours out of his day. He felt like he was in constant struggle between his schooling and his family.

Eduardo's father worked in the fields for a long time while he was growing up. He became a truck driver when Eduardo was in middle school, which sheltered his younger sister from ever fully realizing what the fieldwork meant in their father's life. Eduardo's mother did some post-secondary education as an adult and full-time working mother. The primary lesson that Eduardo learned from her about college was that he needed to do it as quickly as possible after high school. He did not want to struggle through school while trying to support a family. Over the course of this study, Eduardo graduated from high school and was accepted to the closest California State University campus.

Eduardo and I were not especially close during the 2005 MSLI. It was only after the summer program ended that Eduardo and I really got to know each other. During the MSLI, Eduardo was notorious for finding humor in any situation. His jokes were invaluable when material became so serious that students and instructors felt like shutting down. About one month after the program ended, Eduardo and I began e-mailing and instant-messaging each other to see what was going on in our lives. We built a unique trust over the Internet. Eduardo shared some very personal information with me that moved our relationship to a different level. We shared confidence and trust in each other. By the time the study formally commenced, I felt like Eduardo and I knew each other more intimately than most of the other students. My visits with Eduardo doubled as opportunities for us to build our virtual relationship in the material world.

Antonio, the Political Scientist

Antonio left a life of relative affluence in Mexico City to live with uncles in a large California Central Valley city. Mexico City had become a dangerous place for him and his sister, having narrowly escaped one attempted kidnapping at the age of thirteen. The decision to move Antonio to the Central Valley meant that he would go through high school while living apart from his mother. Reconnecting his family has been a goal for Antonio since beginning his U.S. education. At times, Antonio struggled with a transition from living as an upper-class pre-adolescent in Mexico's largest city to living as a working-class adolescent in California. He pushed himself to figure out what school was about in California's public education system—very different than in his elite *secondaria-preparatoria* (middle-high school) in Mexico. Antonio became one of the most involved students at his school, participating in every academic and service club or activity the school offered.

Antonio balanced his involvement in school with his dedication, commitment, and responsibilities to his newly formed family. His uncles operated a carpet cleaning business, and by his senior year, Antonio was functioning as the company's *de facto* chief financial officer. He took care of all the finances and supplies.

As Antonio put it, "I do everything except the actual cleaning and the appointments."

In addition to his family responsibilities and his school involvement, Antonio worked a series of part-time jobs throughout high school, and shared his earned income with his family. With both him and his sister living in the house, the household's expenditures had increased at a faster rate than its income.

As an undocumented student with aspirations for law school, Antonio has involved himself in political movements since he first became a member of the school's debate team. When the immigrant rights movement gained momentum in the spring of 2006, Antonio put his experiences in political analysis from the debate club into practice. He helped organize marches and rallies throughout his home city. His leadership in the movement was mentioned when Antonio was recognized as student of the year in his metropolitan area.

When I first met Antonio, I wanted to ask him to back off. It was the second day of the MSLI, and I was frustrated that Antonio seemed to respond to every rhetorical question with a response that suggested he already knew the journey we expected students to take that summer. He had an opinion about everything. He made me feel stupid. Luckily, I shared these thoughts with my instructional teammates, and we talked about remediating Antonio's participation to allow more divergent voices to be heard. I was afraid he was shutting other students out. Antonio approached us at the end of the first week. He let us know that we were not nearly as motivating as his experience in a migrant program he participated in the previous summer. I was floored. We all chatted together, and I became Antonio's biggest fan. His confidence in critiquing us was inspiring, and when he did, he approached it in terms of learning and teaching together, which had been our framework from the beginning. We worked with Antonio to reorganize some key elements of the classroom. He worked with me to reorganize the foundations of our relationship. I have been learning and teaching with him ever since.

Carlitos, the Fighter

Carlitos spent five years apart from his parents when he was a young child. At the age of 11, he and his grandmother moved from their village in Southeastern Mexico to work in the agricultural industry in Northern Mexico, along the Mexico-U.S. Border. They lived with Carlitos' uncle, who put Carlitos to work in the fields and regularly beat him when he came home. When he and his grandmother first moved to Northern Mexico, neither of them spoke even a single word of Spanish. Their native language is an Indigenous tongue spoken only in their village. It has three dialects, each building on the other. Carlitos' family spoke the third dialect, which meant they could also speak and understand the first two. Carlitos spent two years living in his uncle's abusive household, learning Spanish as he worked alongside grown men in the fields. His parents had long since migrated north into California. After one failed attempt to send for him, his father finally sent word that he had arranged for Carlitos and his grandmother to cross the border with the help of a *coyote*.[4] It took four days to get through the desert of the border. Carlitos, at the age of 12, was responsible for himself and his grandmother. They had one gallon of water to share between them for the entire journey. Once in California, Carlitos and his grandmother found their way to the Central Valley, where his parents had been raising his younger sister and brother, whom Carlitos had never met.

Carlitos immediately enrolled in school for the first time since he was nine years old. Gifted in math, he took calculus in his sophomore year, sadly, the last math class available at his high school. Although he demonstrated mastery of the English language in reading, writing, and speaking while at the 2005 MSLI, Carlitos' school still mandated that he enroll in English Language Development support classes. Carlitos loves to play basketball and soccer, but does not participate in any school-based activities. His extra time on the weekends and during school break periods (e.g., spring break) is spent in the fields with his parents, earning extra income for the family. The only school-based activities that he has participated in have been related to the immigrant rights movement. Upon returning home from the 2005 MSLI, Carlitos tried to start an organization at his school to assist and support fellow undocumented students prepare for college. In the spring of 2006, amidst the national debate on immigration reform, he also helped organize student participation in a protest march from his high school in his small, mostly migrant-occupied town, to the city hall of the nearest large city—at least a ten-mile march. They were on the front page of the metropolitan area's newspaper the next day. Carlitos aspires to attend the University of California and become an astronomer or mathematician.

I was in awe of Carlitos after the first time I read his writing in class. He wrote with the sophistication of a graduate student, except with more technical and grammatical errors. He was quiet, reserved, respectful, and attentive in class during the summer program. At first, I mistook this to mean he was shy. I was wrong. One night, I was tutoring in the residence hall where the students stayed, and I sat with Carlitos to look over his essay. He kept talking and talking about the reading we were focusing on that week. I could hardly get him to breathe or slow down. I asked him what he wanted me to work on most with his essay, and he replied, "Everything. I came here to learn. Teach me!" It was like something out of an after-school special. Always kind and considerate, Carlitos has a gentleness to his presence that makes me feel at ease, and safe and secure. When I visited him, we spent most of our time in conversation in his bedroom. We would remember things from the summer. We would share new things going on in our lives. We would laugh. We would smile. And then whenever I asked Carlitos to re-tell a story from his life, he would go there with me with a kind of trust that I felt deeply honored to share with him. In those moments, Carlitos became the teacher, and it seemed at times, that he would change his tone, or choose his words carefully, based on how he was studying me and my responses to his stories from his life.

Yaneth, the Believer

Yaneth is the third child in her family to go to college. Her older sister and brother were admitted to CSU and UC campuses, respectively. Her parents migrated to California from Mexico before her older sister, the oldest child, was born. Both parents worked in the fields for more than 20 years. Yaneth won the prestigious Gates Millennium Scholarship, which covers all expenses for her post-secondary and post-graduate education. She had also won upwards of $14,000 in additional scholarships, of which she could keep approximately $9,000. She was named Migrant Student of the Year for her region in her senior year of high school. She volunteered at various social organizations throughout her high school years, most notably the city parks and recreation department, where she landed a summer job in her junior year.

Yaneth believed that all of her hard work would pay off. She said that it had to pay off, because there were times when she felt that it might all be for nothing, but that she could feel a greater purpose to everything her family encouraged her to do, including her volunteering and studying. Beyond her work in the community, Yaneth was involved in academically oriented school activities, and maintained an active social life. Indeed, it was Yaneth's social skills that I noticed first when we met at MSLI.

Yaneth was part of a small group that met with me in the afternoons for tutoring during the program. Our group connected so well together in the first week, that students made an effort to organize themselves so that our group could remain intact throughout the institute. From day one, Yaneth put herself out there by asking questions about key terms she did not understand from the complex graduate level texts we were reading (e.g., Eduardo Galeano's *Open Veins of Latin America*). Her belief in the work of the Institute was made apparent when she encouraged other students to do the same. She was never shy about discussing her parents' histories as fieldworkers and situating the group's learning within their shared sociocultural experiences. It was no surprise to me when she shared that she would be attending one of the flagship UC campuses in the fall of 2006.

Greater Los Angeles Area

The Los Angeles metropolitan area (LA) is littered with community colleges, small private four-year colleges, seven California State Universities, and four research universities (three UC, one private). It is the largest, most populated metropolitan area in the U.S., and the city of LA itself is the second largest city, behind New York. LA was the most diverse environment in which I conducted fieldwork. Still,

LA was one of the most segregated places, and the two participants living in LA were far from integrated into a pluralistic community. One participant lived in East LA, one of the most notorious neighborhoods in the city with longstanding social narratives of poverty, violence, and drug use that have been represented in countless popular culture media such as film and music. Another participant lived in one of LA's older suburban cities, which has become more urban as decades have passed. Public schools throughout LA are generally portrayed as pitiful in the national discourse on public education.

Alex, the Caretaker

Alex is one of the most caring individuals I have ever met. His life has trained him to take care of people. Alex and his mother left his abusive father in Alex's first year of middle school. The transition to relying on each other has influenced all of Alex's decisions thereafter. Alex is the oldest child in his immediate family. He tries to emulate the responsibility and integrity that his uncle has shown throughout Alex's life. Indeed, Alex once told me that he felt like he was raised by his uncle. He considered his uncle to be his new dad, and he wanted to make sure he honored the sacrifices and struggle that his uncle and mother had made for him and his younger brother.

Alex's caretaking flowed over into his schooling. He matriculated into high school with a close group of friends from middle school. Based on Alex's suggestion, they made a pact with each other. They agreed that they would make sure all of them went to college. None of their parents had attended a four-year institution. They recognized early on that they needed support beyond what the school would provide, and they saw each other as a valuable network to supplement the support provided by their parents.

I met Alex through other students I was working more closely with in MSLI. We quickly connected, and Alex joined the tutoring group I worked with in the afternoons. Alex and I began to seek each other out in the cafeteria on the occasions that I ate with students by the residence halls. We chatted about relationships, mostly. At the time, Alex was consumed by his romance with his girlfriend. He sought my advice, which I gave with a huge qualification that I was no expert. Our conversations were fun and filled with jokes. Living in Los Angeles, Alex and I were in close proximity after the Institute ended. He was the first participant to volunteer for the study, and I was honored when his family included me in his high school graduation celebration. Alex is the first person in his family to enter a four-year university directly after high school. He went to a nearby California State University, commuting from home while continuing to provide care and financial support to his family.

Cristina, the Singer

In response to the perceived pitiful schooling conditions in her neighborhood, Cristina's parents sacrificed a good portion of the family income to send her to a private Catholic school twenty minutes away from home. Neither of Cristina's parents attended college, but her mother had been part of a mentoring program for newly arrived Latina's. Her mother's employer paid for job training and helped her get sustained employment as an administrative assistant.

Cristina was a solid student in school, but struggled to get along with her teachers and peers. During and after the 2005 MSLI, Cristina began to develop an identity as *Chicana*. She made no excuses for her practices of identifying racialized processes in schools, including highlighting the ways in which inequality was being perpetuated in their curriculum. Becoming *Chicana* for Cristina was integrally tied to her college-going. "It's the whole point. Who cares if I can sing if I can't see the inequality that's keeping me from getting ahead?" she once asked me.

Cristina's singing voice rocked the halls of the 2005 MSLI. She sang for the talent show and the commencement ceremony. For her, singing was another outlet for social analysis. In the classroom, Cristina was eager to investigate systems of oppression and to find applications for her learning in her real life outside of MSLI. Over the course of the study, Cristina and I investigated colleges together. Our goal was to find schools that would foster her commitment to the *Chicana* movement she so desperately wanted to take part in, yet struggled to realize in her restrictive high school.

North San Diego County

Bordering the Pacific Ocean on the west with beachfront homes below Interstate 5 and cliff-balancing mansions just above, North San Diego County is known for its affluence and its privacy. A string of small cities populates the political map of the area. The greater San Diego area stands as one bastion of California's most conservative residents. Just a quick 30 minutes from the busiest political border in the world (Tijuana-San Diego), the ever-present military and border patrol makes clear who the desired residents are. Schools are heavily segregated in these north county beach cities. The underperforming schools serve predominantly Latino and low-income students, while the high-achieving schools are predominantly white and wealthy. The Latino community of the area seems to exist under the radar of the dominant image that the north county puts forth in its tourism brochures and its lists of fine dining beachfront establishments.

Butterfly, the People Changer

Once every few years, one of the national newsmagazines in the U.S., such as *Time* or *Newsweek,* feature profiles of what might be considered *underprivileged* or *disadvantaged* students who *against all odds* manage to *overcome barriers* and make good of their lives. Butterfly could easily grace the cover of such an issue. Butterfly grew up in a mobile home park just off the interstate in a city dominated by million-dollar homes overlooking the ocean. She and her older sister lived there with her single-mother and at different times her older brother and/or an uncle as well. Butterfly's parents divorced while she was in elementary school. She had another brother who passed away while she was in middle school. Their home could be featured in the magazine as a fragile yet steadfast touchstone for recuperating from the racialized, class-based prejudices they endured outside. Butterfly could be heralded for her high GPA, her 30-hour work week outside of school, and her countless volunteerism. As well she should be.

The newsmagazine might leave out the ways in which Butterfly lives her life, not as underprivileged or disadvantaged but rather, as a young Latina struggling to sustain her family's commitments to each other and honor her mother's sacrifices for her education. The newsmagazine might not analyze Butterfly's academic accomplishments in context of being the only Latina in her honors and advanced placement classes, while her neighborhood friends were tracked into a vocational or remedial curriculum. The newsmagazine might portray Butterfly in the same way that she felt her peers in the college-preparatory track did, "Like, I'm not a Mexican, but that I'm one of them." After the excitement of appearing on the cover of a national magazine wore off, I suspect that Butterfly might have the same reaction to *Time* or *Newsweek* as she did to her classmates, "They don't even know me. They can't see past themselves."

When I first met Butterfly, she was a quiet, attentive, and congenial young woman in class. After visiting the residence halls one night for tutoring, I found out she had been playing me in class. Butterfly was loud. She was silly. She eagerly made friends and organized study sessions. Back in the classroom, the instructional team decided that we did not want students to bifurcate their experiences in MSLI. We wanted them to bring the fun from the residence halls into the classroom. Butterfly was reluctant at first, but in the end, she changed more people's concept of learning than most other students. She thrived on the changing nature of the classroom. Change seemed to be part of the fabric of who Butterfly was. She did not take on traditional leadership practices in the classroom, but was subtle, almost stealth about her influence within the classroom. My relationship with Butterfly over the course of this study developed into a shared confidence, trust, and respect that I count on from some of my closest colleagues. I did not hang out with Butterfly extensively in her community. Most of our encounters were in her family's house. Occasionally her sister or mother would be around. I was always made to feel like a welcome and well-respected visitor, which was an honor I took to heart.

Imperial Valley

When I surveyed online physical maps or satellite images of the Imperial Valley, I could not tell the difference between lands claimed and governed by Mexico and the United States. If I did not speak English or Spanish, and I were driving or walking around any of the towns and cities that populate the Imperial Valley, I also might not know the difference of my locale. The area, on both sides of the 32nd parallel,[5] has commercially dense streets nearby agriculturally expansive fields. People might speak in English, Spanish, or both languages. People have longstanding roots in their communities, and people have recently relocated themselves and their families for different opportunities in the area. The one definite thing that sets the northern side of the 32nd parallel at the 115th perpendicular apart from the southern side, as I drove across the highways to my destinations, was the persistent presence of the U.S. Border Patrol. Despite, or perhaps in spite of, the fluidity of crossings from each side to the other, this was by far the most militarized and policed region that I visited.

The public schools serve predominantly Latino students. The smaller of the two cities has twice as many private secondary schools as it does public, many of which are attended by students from the southern side of the 32nd parallel. In other words, elite families in Baja, Mexico, send their children to private schools in California, United States. Agricultural work is one of the major employment opportunities, as the area not only has expansive fields within the Imperial County of California, but also is commuting distance to fields in Arizona to the east and California's Coachella Valley to the north. The participants living in this area came from two neighboring cities, one of which had its own school district, while the other was part of a valley-wide unification district. The closest U.S. metropolitan area is 125 miles west in San Diego, which hosts both California State University and University of California campuses. There is a satellite campus for San Diego State University within Imperial County, and there is one community college.

Lorena, the Helper

As the youngest child and only girl in her family, Lorena is the last chance for her parents to see their dreams fulfilled of having more educational opportunity for their children. Her parents crossed the political border between Mexico and the U.S. before Lorena was born. They reside in the U.S. with legal documentation, and they also retain and practice their rights as voting citizens of Mexico. Trips to Mexico were a common and cherished experience for Lorena while growing up. She benefited from the wisdom and comparative experiences of her cousins, older brothers, and grandparents on both sides of the political border.

As a student, Lorena worked hard to make things happen. She was involved in endless school activities, including the two she was most recognized for: cross-country and student government. Lorena valued these experiences, in part, because they extended her social network. She worked tirelessly to sustain study groups, which she used invaluably to help make sense of her difficult advanced placement courses. In turn, Lorena was always the first to offer assistance to other students.

I only knew Lorena through tutoring during the MSLI. She was not in the same regular classroom as me or most of the other participants. Still, everyone knew Lorena. She was known to me as "one of the coolest kids, ever." Lorena could carry on a conversation with anybody, and she was genuinely interested. Lorena sought out the connections to bring people together in order to help each other in our mutual struggles. Lorena aspired to attend an elite campus of the University of California.

Jesus, the Scholar-Athlete

Jesus makes mean tackles. He holds an aggressive line on the football field. He also carries the field portion of the school's track and field team to success. Most importantly, Jesus gets good grades in the college-preparatory track at his high school. Staying involved in school and getting good grades has been ingrained in Jesus since he began schooling. Both of his parents went to a California State University campus in southern California. He is the only participant in this study who has parents with bachelor's degrees.

Despite their level of educational achievement, Jesus' parents have struggled throughout their lives to sustain the lifestyle they desire for their family. They both worked in the agricultural industry of the Imperial Valley for long periods of time. At the time of this study, Jesus' dad still worked in agriculture, but as an import inspector at the border between Baja and California. Their experiences with the California public higher education systems have proven useful for Jesus and his younger sister. He and his sister have known about college, what it can be like, what it can be used for, and how its systems and processes can be quite confusing their entire lives. Jesus is on target to graduate from high school as UC eligible. He hopes to attend one of the flagship UC campuses.

I was somewhat surprised when Jesus volunteered to participate in the study. I liked him a lot during the 2005 MSLI. He was eager to learn and apply critical skills that might help him achieve his goal of getting into a UC campus. He was very proud to be participating in a program at UCLA. Still, I walked away from the program feeling that Jesus was one of the students I never really got to know. I wanted to know him better. My encounters with Jesus throughout this study showed me that the more I got to know Jesus, the more time I wanted with him, and the more I wanted him to know me.

Renaldo, the Cheerleader

Similarly to his neighboring colleagues in the Imperial Valley, Renaldo was a superstar at his high school. He was involved in almost every club that was available. He was also captain of the cheerleading squad, which at times seemed to be his most valued achievement. Indeed, cheering people on was, in many ways, Renaldo's *modus operandi*. Renaldo's entire family worked in the fields. He was often left in charge of his younger sister, for whom he strove to set a good example. Renaldo was the supportive hub in his family. He made sure that everyone knew how much their efforts for the family were appreciated.

Renaldo has vivid memories of his life in Mexico. On one visit, Renaldo recounted a story to me about the time when he broke his leg, and the doctors did not know if he'd be able to walk normally again. He and his best friend were playing around each other's houses, and Renaldo fell out of a tree. When Renaldo told me this story, it was filled with hope and energy, because he worked through the struggles of rehabilitating his leg and becoming the active and athletic teenager he is today. At the same time, while telling this story, Renaldo expresses a certain melancholy associated with his memories of Mexico. When his family entered California, he left behind a whole set of friends and family relations. Returning to Mexico is risky for Renaldo, because he does not have legal documentation to reenter the

U.S. The artifact of Renaldo's migration north of the 32nd parallel complicated his college-going trajectory in many ways, which are explored further in chapter five. Still, Renaldo graduated from high school in 2006 as a UC eligible college candidate. He has since begun his post-secondary studies at the local community college.

I grew quite fond of Renaldo very early on during the 2005 MSLI. His personality was magnetic to me. He was high energy. He was eager to participate. He wanted to get along with everyone. He reminded me a lot of myself at his age. There was also a vulnerability that I sensed in Renaldo. I had a hunch that Renaldo had a lot more to say than the mood-elevating cheers and chants that he bellowed throughout the Institute. I made an effort to include Renaldo in the tutoring group that I worked with regularly. He made an effort to make sure he got assigned to my group. Since then, Renaldo and I have shared hundreds of stories together, and I made special efforts to visit him when I would drive to my family's home in Arizona during holiday breaks. Renaldo and I share many similar interests in pop culture, fashion, dance, and music. Working with him on this project was like working with a good pal on something that we both felt very strongly committed.

Migrant Students as Subjects Learning College Access

Human subjects are constituted by both external and internal forces. Sociocultural understandings of identity hold that the individual does not manifest absolute autonomy over one's self (Bettie, 2003; Vadeboncoeur & Stevens, 2005; Holland, Lachicotte, Skinner, & Cain, 1998). Rather, a confluence of social, cultural, and individual influences mediate the construction and performance of the person. Further, identities are fluid and change across the different spheres and moments in life. In thinking about how migrant students are constituted in college-going—the learning of college access—it is useful to draw from sociocultural understandings of the relationship between learning and identity. Socioculturalists Lave (1996) and Gee (2001) each argue for conceptualizing learning as identity shifts. As Moje and Lewis (2007) summarized, "one learns to take on new identities along with new forms of knowledge and participation" (p. 19). At stake in seeking college access then, is students' appropriation of college-going identities wherein they not only understand the seemingly objective facts about college admissions (e.g., college knowledge), but also think and act like people who are going to go to college. However, these identity shifts become hazardous when external and internal forces intertwine and potentially conflict. Historically marginalized communities have been systematically excluded from certain identities of opportunity. Thus, the making and remaking of identities from Mexican migrant students seeking higher education opportunity becomes a struggle. In resolving that struggle, even if only temporarily, migrant students disrupt the master narrative of college-going.

The rest of this chapter builds on the descriptive portraits of students and analyzes the external and internal forces to which migrant students are subject in their college-going activity. Insights can be drawn from interpreting the constitution of the migrant student subject in college-going that can help inform future inquiry. These interpretations also suggest how future educational designs might incorporate social justice perspectives into work that might seem only tangentially related to promoting higher education opportunity, yet could contribute to a more powerful extension of students' repertoires of practices toward the goal of developing college-going literacies.

I present an analysis of forces that were in conflict with one another in their construction of the migrant student subject, and discuss external forces of racialization and social class as they intersected with internal forces of analytic feelings and liberatory ideals. There are a multitude of other forces and other points of conflict to which migrant students are subject, but I have chosen to focus discussion on these because students expressed them most often and as having the most at stake for their lives. The chapter concludes with an example of a migrant family's mitigation of the conflict between these external and internal forces—ultimately positioning the student as a family project. This reframed construction enabled students to more comfortably shift into college-going identities, thus contributing to their development of college-going literacies.

External Forces

All of the students' racially identified themselves as Latino. They also named themselves Mexican, *Chicano, Chicana,* or at times, Mexican American. Students rarely made a direct statement such as, "I'm poor," or "I'm working class." Rather, students more often signified their social class identification by sharing how they did not identify.

"We're not really middle class."

"My family can't afford that kind of stuff."

"I don't know how, but my parents always seem to find the money we need."

"I know they're not like, making as much as people who work in offices and stuff."

This inquiry did not seek to deconstruct students' race-based or class-based identities, but rather to investigate how external and internal forces constituted them as college-going subjects. As such, I sought to understand how students were racialized and what potential consequences accompanied those racializations. This approach follows in sociocultural commitments to understanding identity as interactive process among individual performances of self and materials that make these performances meaningful (Lewis, Enciso, & Moje, 2007). Race and social class operate in tandem with any college-going activity system. Students who lived in predominantly Latino areas and attended predominantly Latino schools seemed to privilege the workings of social class more so than the ways in which others racialized them. Students who attended schools that were predominantly white, or where Latinos and Asian/Asian American students shared a majority of the population, definitely related their racialization in a more privileged position. Moreover, the labor contexts of migrant farm-working ubiquitously circulated in students' sense of self and their performance of possible selves overall. Migrant farm-working as a labor context carried with it both racializing and class-generating discourses.

Racializing students as poor Latinos in students' college-going took shape largely in schooling activities and interactions with higher education institutions. Schools, colleges, and universities were sites where students recognized differences in their college-going across racialized and class-based demarcations. Racialized and class-based external forces took shape in how institutions treated students, whether by tracking them into specific educational trajectories, or by ignoring their educational needs. Forces of racialization and social class also took shape in how individuals within schools and higher education institutions treated migrant students in talk and physical body language.

To illustrate how these external forces constituted students in college-going, I draw from Butterfly's portrait as previously described in this chapter. Butterfly worked between 20 and 30 hours a week outside of school. Her income supplemented her life with some of the things that other students at her school took for granted, such as a cell phone or a new shirt for the first day of school. She also contributed to the household income when necessary. Butterfly recognized that class influenced how she thought about college as she shared with me,

> I would have liked to do more extracurriculars, but, like, I can't. I have to work. Some kids at school don't get that. They're like, 'just don't work as much.' But, they don't even have to work. If they do, it's just to like, pay for gas in their brand new car or something. But, like, yeah. If I could do more in school, I would like to, but I have to work. I have to work a lot. Kids are like, 'You're such a worker.' It's kinda lame.

Butterfly's interactions with her peers constructed her as a worker, someone whose family needed more income than they had. Her class status kept her from participating in college-going in some of the ways that other students participated. This process of othering was further made evident by Butterfly's reflections on her position as the only Latina in her advanced placement courses. Butterfly said:

> Yeah. Like, I'm the only one. The only Latina or Mexican or Hispanic, whatever. In my AP classes, there's no one else. A few Asian kids and then a lot of white kids. It's not like that at my friends' school. They mostly go to this other school, but my mom and I wanted me to go here because it's supposed to be better. Anyway, there aren't that many Mexicans here, and I'm the only one in my class in honors or AP. … And like, that shouldn't matter, maybe, and usually, like, it's no big deal. But sometimes, especially when we talk about immigration, I just can't believe what some people say. One kid, said, 'Who cares, they don't do anything. They don't even like, go to classes.' And I told him, I asked him, 'Who? Who are you talking about?'

> And he told me, like,'The immigrants.' I was like, 'Don't I look like I could be an immigrant?' ... like I am *not* in their group. ... And they look at me, and even tell me, like, 'Well, we don't think of you like them [Mexicans].' I was so upset, and they couldn't even understand why. I'm not really friends with anyone in my classes. There's one kid that I might ask for help from sometimes, but usually, I just have to work on my own.

Butterfly explains how her racialized relationship to other students cast's her as an individual entirely responsible for her own circumstances. Her narrative also captures the ways that being alone can be experienced as being excluded, and it hints at how her very body was politicized in her college-going. Critical race scholars might interpret this moment as a racial microaggression (Solórzano, Ceja, & Yosso, 2000). Racial microaggressions are behaviors that implicitly perpetuate racism, dehumanize members of non-dominant racialized groups, and yet might appear as innocent opinions of a dominant group member. In Butterfly's example, her peers' comments, which sound like they might be meant as a compliment, indeed stand as an insult to her, her family, her heritage, and her lived experience. In these ways, the external forces of social class and racialization situated migrant students as intellectually inferior and individually responsible for any inequities in their lives.

These forces of racialization and class shaped migrant students as subjects in college-going in three consequential ways. These external forces painted migrant students as incapable of college-preparatory work. They positioned migrant students as needing to compete for college in solitude, rather than as members of a broader community of college-goers. Finally, these external forces of racialization and class politicized the migrant student subject in college-going as bodies whose futures can be determined by public opinion, specifically through immigration reform.

Internal Forces

Internally, students expressed being subject to a knowing of their world that pushed them into social circles and politically motivated them to combat the oppressive external forces they encountered in schools and institutions of higher education. Students often spoke of a nexus between feelings and thoughts that created new knowledge in determining or constructing them in their college-going identities.

"I know it's not fair. I just know it."

"I can feel that something's wrong. I just can't always name it until after."

"I just know that we need to stick together if we're going to make it."

"The marches are about more … who we are. Like, the education inside us."

The internal knowing expressed by students indicated that they were acutely aware of the inequities they faced in their lives, and they were engaged in on-going, sophisticated mental and emotional analysis about the world around them.

During one of my visits with Alex in the greater L.A. area, we were having coffee at a local coffee house when a few men within our earshot began to use language that was derogatory toward queer people. Alex looked at me with his eyes wide-open. It was as if he wanted to do something, but didn't know what it would be. I just kept talking. Alex interrupted:

> Ryan. It's everywhere. There is really uncool stuff everywhere. Do you think white people see this? Like, other than you? Like, I can feel it. Our schools aren't as good. I mean, I like my school, but we don't have the things that other schools have. And I live in a good neighborhood. But then I hear stuff like that. And it's no different than hearing stuff about Mexicans. I mean, it's different, but it's still oppressive, you know? And there are so many barriers it seems. … That's why we [his group of friends] have to go to college. To make more of a difference in kids lives like me. Like, kids that have had troubled backgrounds or whatever. And that's why my family is so important.

Alex, like other migrant students participating in this study, was constantly identifying inequities and oppressive practices in the world around him. He knew that he was preparing for college in circumstances and conditions unequal to other students. He knew and recognized that these inequitable conditions extended beyond education. Facing inequity was political, and he sought a social network in which he could activate his political investment in education. Alex's last statement hints at how the conflict between oppressive external and liberatory internal forces was addressed in migrant students' college-going.

A Family Project

These internal and external forces were mutually engaged by the ways that students participated in college-going; their college-going became a family project. The conflict between the external and internal forces was addressed by the private acts of migrant families. They worked to mitigate the intersection of the oppressive external forces and the liberatory internal forces. Throughout this project, when students spoke of support and the significance that higher education opportunity played in their lives, they mentioned their families first. When students spoke of assistance with college-going tasks, they mentioned their families first, even when their families could not provide the assistance they needed. It became clear to me that college-going is a family project for the migrant student participants in this study.

The family, then, is a site of identity possibilities. It simultaneously nourishes the desire to try on new identities by protecting available identities from the dehumanizing external influences that subject migrant students to racialized discourses of failure. This is not to say that family is a cure-all, or indeed strong enough to fully combat the external forces that sought to support the master narrative of Mexican migrant college-going, but rather that family needs to be incorporated into understanding the identity shifts made available to Mexican migrant students as they engage in college-going. Families are both internal and external in the constitution of the migrant student subject.

As will be discussed throughout the next four chapters, migrant students in migrant families is a multidimensional theme that spreads across migrant students' college-going literacy development. In chapter five, the family project theme will emerge in discussion about (im)migration as a mediating artifact in migrant students' college-going. This discussion will be embedded within a larger discussion of the potentially transformative opportunities that present themselves in understanding the tools and rules that mediate college-going for migrant students. The family project theme emerges again in chapter seven as I map the division of labor in migrant students' literacy development. These students were constituted in college-going in the conflict between oppressive external forces and liberatory internal forces, emerging as projects of migrant families seeking social opportunity. Constituted from these nexes of activity (external, internal and family), migrant students draw from a wide array of social texts in reading their educational opportunity. As re-presented in the following chapters, these social texts are the ubiquitous contexts within which students simultaneously write, and rewrite, their imagined educational futures, harnessing the mediating power of cultural tools from their repertoires of practice to achieve college access. Students come to know college access from contested identities as projects of their family's struggle for social opportunity.

Notes

[1] Migrant education programs in California are politically organized by region. There are 14 regions in total, which generally follow county lines.

[2] These portraits were coauthored by the individual participants and me. Whenever possible, I shared my analysis and writing as it was in progress with the participants. For these portraits, I presented them with bulleted lists of the salient characteristics I identified from my analysis of our encounters. I then asked them if they would like to construct a couple of paragraphs that captured those bullet points and one paragraph that described our relationship to each other. I pitched it to them as introducing themselves as a character in a story.

[3] HR4437 was federal legislation approved in the U.S. House of Representatives in 2006. Immigrant rights groups, civil rights groups, and other progressives have critiqued the bill for being anti-immigrant, too narrow in scope, and punitive in its proposed enforcement.

[4] A *coyoté* is the vernacular term for people who are paid to help individuals cross the political border between Mexico and the U.S. without government documentation. Popular presses have documented violent, dangerous, and Machiavellian business practices of some *coyotés* working throughout the borderlands area.

[5] The geographic location of Mexicali, Baja, Mexico, is approximately 32° 40' north latitude and 115° 28' west longitude (Wikipedia, 2007). I use these scientific, yet European/European-American-centric signifiers of the political border between the areas of southeastern California and northeastern Baja in order to deemphasize the hegemonic notion of political control over the relationship between lands and humans, while at the same time highlighting the vacuity in my own rhetoric, which refuses to name it the U.S.–Mexico border, while retaining the real consequences experienced by those who have, will, or cannot cross this site of the globe.

Chapter Four
Mapping Tools and Rules: Mediating and Regulating College-going

According to sociocultural theory, knowing an object of activity is always a mediated process (Chaiklin, 2003; Cole, 1996; Engeström, 1999; Gutiérrez, 2004; Vygotsky, 1978). In a simple illustration, writing is mediated by the pen that implements the mind's ideas onto paper; reading is mediated by the text that appears on the page. Communication is mediated by the language used to express oneself. The pen, text, and language are cultural artifacts that have been made and remade over time in order to mediate learning and development. These mediating artifacts are the tools that humans use in coming to know any object of activity.

There are countless tools in migrant students' college-going, each mediating the object of college access in diverse ways, and always contingent on the cultural-historical position/ing(s) of the subject. An exhaustive list of tools used in mediating migrant students' knowledge of college access would require an extensive and invasive ethnography of students' lives. Even then, the list would remain incomplete, as the historicity of tools is dynamic, and many functional definitions of some tools could become obsolete without notice. For example, just five years ago, the internet was only beginning to serve as a major information source about colleges and universities. Today, all California public four-year institutions require students to submit online applications. The changing technology used to mediate students' profiles from high schools to colleges can affect how students participate in the activity of college-going. At the same time, online applications sustain the practice of students' submitting credentials to institutions for review in order to gain admission. The example of online applications illustrates how tools are dynamic, yet also retain sustainable elements over time.

As this study was not designed to uncover an exhaustive account of the tools used in the mediation of college access for migrant students, analyses to this effect cannot be presented. However, this study did aim to understand how students came to know college access as a recursive process between and across understanding the object (college access) and participating in college choice processes. As such, the design sought to capture the cultural practices of students' everyday lives that worked toward learning college access. In analyzing students' practices, I looked for mediating artifacts that contributed to transformative learning opportunities—tools that assisted students in extending their repertoires of practice. I discuss two of these tools in depth in subsequent chapters.

Socioculturalists also contend that all human activity is governed by rules (Cole, 1996; Engeström, 1999; Gutiérrez, 2004; Vygotsky, 1978). These rules might emerge organically, such as when children play a made-up game on a playground. Or, rules might be imposed from broader social structures, such as when English language learners are restricted to using their home language for "x" number of minutes in the school day. Rules regulate the normative practices of an activity.

There are always explicit and implicit rules in any activity. These rules are legitimized to students through participation in them. Rules generate from beliefs or folk knowledge about college-going that grow out of a history of participating or not participating in a set of official practices. Over time, these beliefs are instantiated and mediate students' participation in college-going as rules.

Explicit rules are those widely available and sanctioned in the public domain. They can be verified from official sources (e.g., admission officers). Explicit rules carry consequences that are generally made known and can be easily anticipated. For example, in California, the A–G course requirements for admission to public universities are a set of explicit rules. If a student fulfills them, she can rest assured that she will be admitted to the public university system. If she does not, she can anticipate denial of admission.

Implicit rules are those understated, colloquial, or assumed regulations by which things get done. They carry consequences that may not be widely agreed upon or easily anticipated. Some implicit rules might be accompanied by unanticipated consequences. Continuing with the example of the California A–G course requirements, it is explicitly stated that a student must satisfy them. However, the implicit rule-of-thumb is that in order to be admitted to the campus of your choice (e.g., top-tier UCLA or UC Berkeley), you must not only satisfy the A–G course requirements, but you must do so "better" than most other students. "Better" in terms of the A–G requirements often translates into a curriculum that includes as many advanced placement courses as possible, strategizing students' course-taking to optimize their grade point averages (GPA) during the sophomore and junior years, and perhaps taking courses that are not available as advanced placement at a local community college. It is the subjective, prejudicial, and negotiable "better" that makes a host of other rules implicit in learning about and getting into college.

Dichotomizing rules of learning activity as explicit/implicit is not neutral. It is simply one way to think about how the rules of the activity are organized, which in turn help to understand the social organization of the activity itself. Both of these qualities of rules (i.e., explicit/implicit) can share qualities such as official/unofficial, or expert/novice.

An extensive and intrusive ethnography would perchance uncover all of the rules of college-going. However, this study was designed to understand the disruptions in the normative experiences of college-going that uniquely shaped migrant students' development of a college-going literacy. As such, the normative, primarily explicit, rules were accounted for in data collection and analysis, but they did not lend themselves to transformative opportunities that extended students' strategic actions toward college-going. Rather, the implicit rules, which were instantiated in the practices of the broader college access community and had historical ties to migrant students' participation in college-going, provided much deeper insight into moments of rupture when transformation became plausible.

To illustrate how tools and rules operated in these Mexican migrant students' college-going literacy development, I provide a traditional qualitative representation of their engagement with what I term, the *mechanics* of college-going. The mechanics of college-going, put simply, are the required tasks that are bound by explicit rules, such as assisting students in completing appropriate coursework. Mechanical college-going practices contrast with *organic* dimensions of college-going. The organics of college-going, put simply, are the tasks equally integral to students' college-going, but tied up in a web of implicit rules. Organic labor moves the imagining of educational opportunity from an abstract to a concrete idea.

I return to the notion of mechanical and organic dimensions of college-going in chapter seven, further theorizing how the work (or labor) of college access must be understood from these mutually re-enforcing dimensions. After summarizing the mechanics of college-going for migrant students, I present a genetic analysis of three implicit rules that govern Mexican migrant college-going. These rules affect students' engagement with both mechanical and organic college-going labor.

Illustrating Tools and Rules: The Mechanics of College-going

There are sets of clearly defined, *explicit* rules in college-going. These include college entrance requirements (i.e., coursework, grade point average, and standardized testing requirements for admission), the ability to pay tuition and fees, and the regulations for state and federal financial aid. In California, college entrance requirements are prescribed for students in the extreme and include course-taking and academic performance. Known as the A–G requirements, this set of expectations for students' academic preparation has been established by the governing bodies of the California public higher education institutions.

In addition to the explicit rules around college access, there are additional rules directed toward the regulation of students in their daily lives as they work toward the object of college access. All but one of the students in the study were enrolled in California public high schools (Cristina, from East Los Angeles, attended a parochial high school.), which subjected them to a litany of enforceable behavioral and cognitive expectations. These explicit rules, which are sanctioned and enforced from either, or both, the higher education

Mapping Tools and Rules 93

institutions and the K–12 schooling institutions mediate students' understanding of college access by regulating, to some extent, their use of tools in the mechanics of college-going. The mechanics of college-going are the material expectations that students must perform via cultural artifacts that have been designed or appropriated as college-going practices. One such artifact is standardized testing.

It is an explicit rule that students must take a college entrance examination (e.g., the SAT) in order to gain admission to a four-year institution. It is also an explicit rule that students must pass the California Assessment of State Standards Exam (commonly referred to as the California exit exam), in order to receive a high school diploma. A high school diploma is required to enroll at a four-year institution. These rules dictate the specific use of the SAT and the California exit exam in students' college-going. These rules and tools are part of the mechanics of going to college in California.

Students' use of these tools mediates their learning of college access. As voiced by Lorena and Jesus, standardized tests shaped their understanding of what college access meant in discouraging ways.

Regarding the SAT, Lorena said:

> Oh, they are stressful. The SAT because they are like, 'Well, it is a very hard test, you are just not worth it.' Like, 'if you want to go to UC Berkeley, you will have to get like something, something, [indicating a specific high score], and then if you want to go to UCLA, you will have to get something, something, or you will have to go for others.' And they will just start saying like where you can get like the lowest scores …

As an artifact, the SAT stood as a challenge to Lorena's aspirations. It was used by other members in her college-going activity (teachers and counselors in this specific case) to temper her aspirations. Lorena's own use of the tool was required by the explicit rule that colleges require the SAT for admission. This requirement was problematic for many students, including Jesus.

Jesus said:

> I think they should tell us, like, that the SAT doesn't, it doesn't have to like depend on us getting into college, because, in most colleges, like, the information they give us, like, you have to score this to get into and that discourages you because most people don't do well on the test. I didn't do well.

Jesus suggests that the SAT be made less influential in college-going decisions. His experience with the exam shaped college access as a process that was unfair and negligible to students' experiences. The California exit exam mediated college access in similar ways. When asked what some obstacles to educational goals might be, Lorena responded:

> The exit exam because ... Well, I took it last year, and last year in my PE class I met Ariana, but she barely moved; she is from Mexicali, it was her first year here and right now she is a senior, and I was like ... Why are you so worried about the exit exam, like they told me that it was so easy, and I took it and I passed it like nothing, and then she said, 'Like, you know English, and I don't.' So, oh. ... That is when it hit me, and wow, I am going to help her, and I did. We got together some weekends, and we just study out, words and worksheets, and she passed it, she passed the exit exam, so she is graduating.

The fear of failure on the exit exam, which is an explicit rule in college-going, mediates college access as a threatened practice—access to college could be denied, no matter how meritorious a student might be, no matter how well someone might learn, if they do not learn how to take the exit exam. In California, that means learning how to pass a standardized exam in English.

Standardized testing is just one example of how the basic mechanics of college-going, the explicit rules and their correlating tools, help mediate college access for students. As noted before, there were too few instances across the data to substantively suggest transformative opportunities of learning—moments of literacy development in relation to these tools. However, two tools that were not tied to the mechanics of college-going emerged from the data that clearly contributed to transformational possibilities in students' learning. These were tools of (im)migration and *confianza*; each mediated college access in ways that ruptured normative understandings and fostered new opportunities for students' literacy development. I discuss these tools in depth in the subsequent two chapters. I turn now to a more in-depth discussion of how migrant college-going is mediated by implicit rules instantiated over time in migrant communities' histories of participation in higher education.

Regulating Students' College-going Literacy Development

Three implicit rules emerged in students' college-going literacy development as especially salient to student experiences. These rules regulated how tools could be used and how various members of students' college-going community could participate. The three implicit rules uncovered in my analysis are:

1. Migrant students should temper their post-secondary aspirations.
2. Migrant students need to seek out financial aid.
3. Migrant students have to work harder to get into college.

These rules are based on beliefs about college-going that have grown out of a history of participating or not participating in a set of official practices that over time have evolved into rules, which then mediate students' participation in the activity of college-going and coming to know college access. These rules function as hegemonic official practices. They work in conflict with goals of coming to know college access for migrant students. In order to illustrate how these rules manifest in migrant students' college-going, I present a genetic analysis (Vygotsky, 1978) based on students' experiences as they were shared with me during time spent with participants. A genetic analysis looks at the constituent parts of the rules themselves. In the case of implicit rules, I sought to identify the beliefs or folk knowledge from which students' cultural practices were based. I then investigated the history of those practices from which the rule emerged.

Migrant Students Should Temper Their Post-secondary Aspirations

As will be discussed in more detail in the next chapter, migrant students' aspirations for post-secondary education were generally developed early and set high.[1] Students' families placed high values on education and reinforced these values through positive affirmation when students demonstrated dedication to education or succeeded in school. All of the students in this study had aspirations to attend a four-year college. Most of these aspirations developed by the time students entered high school. The notable exceptions to this were four undocumented students who migrated northward in middle school.

Still, by the end of their first year of high school, undocumented students also aspired to a four-year college education. Indeed, education seemed to be important across all families, and the undocumented students' delayed aspirations appeared to be an artifact of their unfamiliarity with the U.S. educational system. It by no means represented a weaker emotional or intellectual investment in education by the family.

Despite students' relatively early and high aspirations, they reported conflict between their personal goals and the institutional expectations that seemed systemic in the social practice of college-going. The dominant beliefs suggested that community college was the place to start higher education for migrant students.

Lorena put it plainly when she said, "It just seems that they want you to stay at CC [a local community college] (she let out an exasperated gasp). ... [It makes me feel] bad, because they have so many students that want to stay here, but there is hardly any help for the students that want to go out [of the area for college]."

"Out of the area" for college for Lorena, as with most other students in this study, meant a UC campus. Leaving home, although associated with a number of emotional and financial considerations, was generally believed by participants to be a necessary future action in order to get the higher education they wanted. Lorena's case was complicated by the fact that there were no four-year institutions in her immediate region. Lorena's thoughts also point to the history of participation in college-going and in higher education institutions.

Higher education has been a privilege reserved for the elite since its inception (Cohen, 1998). Although non-dominant groups have made significant gains in the sheer numbers of individuals participating in higher education over time, large disparities persist. These disparities continue across higher education institutional types. The historical trend is that when Latino students have participated in higher education, it has been at community colleges, not at four-year institutions (Horn, Flores, & Orfield, 2006).

Over time, the practices in which students engage, whether rhetorical or physical, enforce a rule that tempers students' aspirations. Conversations with teachers, teachers' pedagogical practices, school administrations' structuring of college-preparatory curriculums, and higher education institutions' involvement (or lack thereof) in migrant students' college-going all seemed to reinforce this rule.

As Butterfly put it, "I think people are just so used to seeing Mexicans fail that, like, if anything, they think we might go to community college."

Over the course of this study, four students graduated from high school, all of whom were UC or CSU eligible. Two of those students chose to attend a local community college. A constellation of influences mediated their decisions, but community college was a readily available alternative for them. It was, as Renaldo put it, "the easiest thing to do."

Renaldo contrasted the ease of the community college by explaining that the UC to which he was admitted:

> Seems like a world away, and I have no idea how to afford it. ... Plus, like, what if I go there and don't do well. Then I've wasted my time, my family's time, and all that money. ... At CC [local community college], like, I'll be a rock star. I know that. It's like, what people do here. Not just undocumented, but like, a lot of people.

Embedded in Renaldo's reflection was that he had been well prepared for entering community college, whereas, even though he qualified for the University of California, he did not feel as well prepared to attend the more prestigious institution. There had been no institutionalized pathway for him to follow, in part, related to his status as an undocumented resident, but also because the community college was viewed as the normative pathway for people like him.

Migrant Students Need to Seek Out Financial Aid

The students participating in this study were surviving conditions of poverty. The artifact of students' family economic backgrounds supported folk knowledge that migrant students could not afford to go to college. This relationship was confounded by the belief that college is for people with money. Migrant students' families lived month-to-month, often relying on any savings to carry them through months when work was scarcer.

As Carlitos said, "We don't spend money on things, because we don't know when there won't be money. My mom and dad and I are really careful. That's why I work [in the fields] on vacations."

Eduardo added, "I know they [his parents] want me to go to college. But, like, it just seems so much like something for other people. Like, how are we going to pay? It's not seeming like something for me. Maybe State [local CSU campus]."

Alex said directly, "College is supposed to be for rich people. But me and my friends are changing that. We're finding ways to do our thing, you know?"

These class-based analyses from students' real-life experiences are based in the financing of higher education, historically. As scholars have documented, college costs and financial aid ideology have moved from viewing higher education as a public benefit to a private one, with the onus of affordability put on the individual student (Price, 2005; Heller, 2002; Swail, 2004; Perna, 2005b). The public has decreasingly invested financial support for sending students to college since the early 1980s (Heller, 2002). The 1990s saw an exponential increase in predominantly loan-based aid packages (Price, 2005). Higher education tuition and related college costs have risen at rates beyond inflation (St. John, 2003), while migrant farmworkers' wages have proportionally declined (Rothenberg, 1998; Thompson & Wiggins, 2002; Foner, Rumbaut, & Gold, 2000). The state-subsidized tuition at public institutions is prohibitive to most migrant students and their families. Plainly put, migrant students and their families cannot afford higher education. Without financial aid, they do not have the ability to pay for college.

Over time, the historical practices of raising tuition, and lowering the public's investment in making higher education affordable to all students, reinforces the belief that migrant students cannot afford to go to college, which is seen as something for people with available money anyway. In historical context, these beliefs get instantiated as the rule that migrant students need to seek out financial aid. This rule mediates how they participate in college-going. Yaneth's experience with financing higher education speaks to the ways in which this implicit rule affected her college-going practices.

Yaneth said:

> I went after everything. I spent all of Christmas break applying to scholarships. I had to talk to teachers for recommendations. Even if I didn't like them very much. It was a sacrifice, like, not playing some sports, not spending time with friends, not doing things that a lot of teenagers do. But it was worth it. I'm going to UCLA. How many migrant students get to say that? ... Too few. I'm lucky. My family can support me so that I can do that stuff. It was okay for me to spend all that time. So many just don't even see the worth, like, there's no guarantee, you know. Or they never even get to learn about scholarships. It's not easy. It's confusing. I had my brother and sister to help me.

Yaneth, and the other students in this study, worked against the grain to alleviate the ways that this rule about financial aid seemed to prohibit their participation in college-going. The implicit rule that migrant students need to seek out financial aid suggests that exclusionary social assumptions might further mitigate students' development of college-going literacy. They must negotiate complex economic terrain without assistance from institutional actors.

As Armando said, "They [schooling and higher education personnel] don't get it. They don't understand me. And I don't know how to help them."

Armando's frustration underscores how this rule puts the onus of responsibility for financing higher education on the individual student. *He* tried to help *them*. For students whose economic and social circumstances are exploited by public education already, this rule reinforces the dominant, oppressive discourse that works against migrant students' college-going.

Migrant Students Have to Work Harder to Get into College.

Feeling under appreciated for their achievements was ever present among students. Whether a student was recognized as traditionally high achieving (i.e., high GPA) or as a special needs student (i.e., English Language Learner), they each reported critical moments in their schooling careers in which they felt like their efforts were unrecognized or rendered unimportant. For example, Jesus responded to students in a school assembly who, from Jesus' perspective, accused him of not being as good a student as they.

Jesus shared:

> There is a lot of people in school that are not involved, and I think it is easier for them to maintain like high grades. But for people who are involved, like sports, we don't have that much time as them, because we are doing more stuff. But I think that we deserved better recognition than them… because it shows that you are a well-rounded person. That you are not only smart, but that you could do other things. You are involved in the school and sports. You're a hard worker. Like, that's what my parents taught me.

Renaldo's active participation in his schooling community illustrated another dimension of the experiences of under recognized achievement.
Renaldo explained:

> It's really hard when they tell you to get involved and that it will help, and it's really the best part of high school, but then the kids who took half the classes you did and did half the activities you did get the awards. Plus, like, their families are not like mine [migrant farmworkers].

Renaldo and Jesus show how family values of working hard translated into their schooling practices, and how these values-based practices, which at times were encouraged by schooling personnel, indeed went seemingly unrewarded. Yet, the belief that hard work begets rewards, persisted.

To make better sense of how working hard became a component of the college-going rule, I turn to Carlitos' analysis of the political economy of college-going. According to Carlitos, he will have to work harder to get to college, because:

> Capitalism makes the rules. You have to do better than someone else. I have to beat someone. Even if I'm as smart as someone else, capitalism makes it like, whoever can somehow get better gets to go. It's like, the bad side of sports. Like, when the competition makes people ugly, because they take it [sports] too seriously. … But really, it's just the people with more money that keep getting better things. We [migrant students] have to work harder to get less.

Carlitos' analysis speaks to the connection between a capitalist society's adherence to market competition and academe's historic meritocratic ideals. These beliefs have a more recent history that

Mapping Tools and Rules 101

presses in on students' experiences. State-based percentage plans, like the California Education in Local Context plan that guarantees UC admission to the top 4% of all students in any graduating class, perpetuate the competitive nature of college-going. Within the historic condition of discriminating schooling practices toward migrant students (previously discussed), the myth of the meritocracy becomes the rule that migrant students must work harder to get into college.

The following excerpt from field notes covering time I spent with Antonio provides another example of how this rule was ever present in migrant students' lives:

> While grabbing lunch during one of my visits to the California central valley, Antonio told me a story of when he figured out that he needed to work harder than others in order to get to college. He told me of a time in high school when teachers were deliberating who would receive an award that carried a cash prize. They decided to give the award to two young women who had a GPA that was .01 higher than Antonio, and that GPA was the only criterion they would consider. Antonio thought that was unfair, because the only reason the other students' GPAs were higher was because they took fewer courses than he had the previous semester. Antonio took six courses, four of which were computed with extra points in the GPA computation because they were honors or advanced placement courses. The two students awarded the cash prize each only took four courses. They happened to be the same four that Antonio was taking in the honors or advanced placement programs. As an artifact of the mathematics of averages, the other two students' had a slightly higher cumulative GPA, even though Antonio had taken more courses and received more As than either of them.
>
> For Antonio, this was devastating. Anger filled his voice and eyes when he relayed the story to me. I asked him how he handled the situation. I was curious to hear if he challenged the schools' practices. He let me know that this was just the final version of ways in which he needed to work harder in order to reap fewer rewards than other students. It was noth-

ing new for Antonio. He had become used to lowered rewards for higher labor.

As a rule, understanding that migrant students had to work harder in order to get to college mediated college-going as an intense activity of labor. It reinforced dominant, hegemonic notions of who deserved to go to college and who would be excluded from higher education. This rule had direct implications for students' college-going practices. Participants in this study took this rule to heart. They were some of the most active and hardworking students in their homes and schools.

Between Tools and Rules

Tools and rules share reciprocal relationships. Many tools accompany specific rules. For example, the SAT, as an artifact (potential tool), accompanies the explicit rule that students must take college entrance exams and pass the California high school exit exam in order to go to college. The reciprocity between tools and rules is not always as clear. They might correlate directly, as in the case of the SAT, but they might also contradict each other. These contradictions offer potential sites of rupture, where future transformative learning opportunities might be fostered. Furthermore, the congruence between tools and rules, such as the SAT, might contradict elsewhere on students' college-going map. For example, the rule about standardized testing, which correlates directly to the SAT and high school exit exam as artifacts, clearly contradicted Jesus' and Lorena's participation in other college-going tasks, such as developing and sustaining aspirations for higher education. In this chapter, I focused on a generalized understanding of tools and rules, with more specific, in-depth discussion of three implicit rules that regulated students' college-going literacy development.

Finally, I suggest that talk is a tool that my data collection and analysis could only uncover as being present, but which holds promise for greater understanding into how students make sense of college access. Indeed, regardless of other tools students shared with me, and in what dimensions of activity the tool(s) were used, researchers are compelled to explore the ways talk functions as both an artifact and an object that mediates and organizes students' understanding of college access. Discourse in general, and talk in particular, as related to college-going, is an important line of future research to more fully understand migrant students' college access.[2]

Notes

[1] Literature on college choice indicates that students who develop college aspirations before entering high school are more likely to attend four-year institutions immediately after high school, whereas students who develop aspirations for post-secondary education after entering high school are more likely to attend a community college or no college at all (Hossler & Stage, 1992; Hamrick & Stage, 1998).

[2] For more information on talk as a unit of analysis in educational opportunity research, see Hunter, J. D. (2006, April). *Like you're worthy of playing against me: Hybrid language practices that organize chess instruction.* Paper presented at the meeting of the American Educational Research Association, San Francisco, CA.

Chapter Five
(im)Migration as Tools for College-going

The most salient experience in students' lives was by far their families' histories with (im)migration.[1] Whether students had migrated northward from Mexico to California themselves or they had been born to parents who had made the journey years earlier, (im)migration was an artifact that permeated all aspects of their lives. In this section, I analyze how (im)migration mediated students' literacy development. Previously, college access literature has understood immigration as a static influence on students' education that signified a lack of information about college-going (Conchas, 2006; Louie, 2005; Súarez-Orozco, 2001). From a literacy development perspective, my qualitative analyses uncovered that (im)migration mediated students' understanding of college access by framing college-going as a politicized process tied to their family's everyday efforts toward family sustainability. Politicizing college-going in this way influenced students' negotiation of their under resourced lives and oftentimes oppressive schooling circumstances.

My analysis treated (im)migration as a tool that mediated students' coming to know college access. This tool was both enabling and constraining in students' college-going goals. Furthermore, the tool of (im)migration was not used synonymously across all students' practices. Rather, there were similarities and differences across the cross-section of students participating in this study. The differences fell along lines of legal residential status in the United States. Undocumented students used (im)migration differently than students with legal residency papers. The tool of (im)migration mediated college access differently for students whose parents had been undocumented at some point, as compared to students whose parents had established legal residency before becoming parents. Still, (im)migration was a powerful tool in mediating college access for the migrant students in this study. It was a tool that had potential to transform students' learning college-going and higher education opportunities.

I present three narratives that I constructed from multiple data sources in order to illustrate, exemplify, and serve as the basis for discussion on how (im)migration mediated college access. These narratives are constructed composites from formal interviews that I conducted with students, informal conversations I had with students, and my own field notes from the time and activities in which I participated with students since meeting them in the 2005 MSLI. The narratives I use to re-present my analyses of the ways that (im)migration served as a tool in students' college-going draw from diverse writing genres. One of these genres, the ethnographic vignette, has a longstanding tradition in critical qualitative scholarship. However, in choosing how to represent some of the dimensions of (im)migration's mediating influence, I found the traditional vignette limiting and inadequate for the compelling affect students' experiences carried with and for them. To achieve the affective dimension of (im)migration in students' lives, I have co-constructed new narrative forms in qualitative research. These forms respond to calls for more creativity in qualitative research reporting (Ellis & Bocher, 1996; Lincoln & Denzin, 2005; Piirto, 2002; Tierney, 2002; Tierney & Lincoln, 1997) and follow in the footsteps of other critical access scholars who have sought to craft more compelling representations of evidence and analysis (see for example, Solórzano & Yosso, 2001; Tierney, 2009; Tierney & Colyar, 2006; Yosso, 2006). As such, I briefly introduce each new form before deploying it, qualifying in some ways the methodological choices I have made.

Each narrative form serves to represent one of three coalitions of students, demarcated by their family's experiences with (im)migration. These three coalitions are most clearly delineated as: 1) undocumented students, 2) students whose parents were undocumented at some point in the students' education, and 3) students whose parents held legal residency before the student was born.

Although there are three different coalitions of students, it is important to remember that all of the students who participated in this study share the saliency of (im)migration as part of their everyday lives. Even students who were born as citizens of the U.S. to parents who were considered legal residents, were also children of immigrants, as are the students who migrated from Mexico to California themselves.

Undocumented Students

Carlitos' journey toward knowing college access traversed five significant moments before taking action explicitly directed at his educational trajectory in a sixth moment.

First Moment

Born in a small agricultural village in the state of Oaxaca, Mexico, Carlitos' first language was the third dialect of an indigenous language spoken by only a handful of villagers.

Second Moment

By the time Carlitos was six, both of his parents had migrated into California, leaving Carlitos as the charge of his grandmother. In order to make ends meet, Carlitos had stopped attending school and instead helped his grandmother earn more income by assisting her arts and crafts work.

Third Moment

When their life in the village became unsustainable, Carlitos and his grandmother migrated to the northern provinces of Mexico in search of his uncle. They found him in the sprawling agricultural economy of the area nearest the political border established between Mexico and the U.S. Carlitos immediately went to work with his uncle in the fields. He learned Spanish quickly while working alongside other fieldworkers. Over the next three years, Carlitos was enrolled in school for less than nine cumulative months. He suffered verbal, emotional, and physical abuse from his uncle.

Carlitos and his grandmother grew increasingly frustrated by their circumstances. Carlitos' father was made aware of their still unstable economic conditions, as well as the abusive relations between Carlitos and his uncle. He arranged to bring Carlitos and his grandmother into California, but at the last minute, plans were cancelled. Carlitos' parents had two more children that had been born in the U.S. Their own economic condition was at a subsistence level. The *coyoté* they had planned to use to get Carlitos and his grandmother across the border became too expensive. The climate with the U.S. Border Patrol was deemed to be too dangerous. The entire trip seemed too risky at the time.

Fourth Moment

Months later, however, new arrangements were made, and Carlitos and his grandmother were to meet a man on a specific day at a specific time in a specific place. They were going to cross.

Carlitos and his grandmother were allowed to bring a small backpack of essential belongings and food. They were provided one gallon of water to share. They set off on a six-day hike through the desert borderlands. When they met their *coyoté*, they were almost denied, despite the fact that their passage had already been paid for. They were told that they needed more money, and that Carlitos could not cross because he was wearing a red shirt. The red would be too easy for the U.S. Border Patrol to spot, and it would endanger the entire trip. Carlitos had long since taken responsibility as the primary decision-maker for him and his grandmother, as she had not learned Spanish and was physically less able to contribute to the household economy. Carlitos, at the age of 11, stood up to the *coyoté* and informed him that Carlitos and his grandmother would be crossing on this trip. Their payment had been received in full, and Carlitos was willing to risk the entire group's safety because he was wearing the only shirt he owned.

Two weeks later, Carlitos and his grandmother were reunited with Carlitos' parents, and they met his younger siblings for the first time.

Fifth Moment

After working in the fields with his parents that summer, Carlitos, at the age of 12, entered compulsory education for the first time. Carlitos' primary language has never been part of his U.S. schooling. Rather, with a Spanish surname, and a corporeal presentation similar to other Spanish-speaking students in California public schools, Carlitos was immediately placed in Spanish-to-English language development classes. He was subjected to racially discriminative practices that often plague public schools.[2]

Schooling was a nightmare.

Schooling was a dream.

For the first time in his life, he was afforded the opportunity to safely indulge in the development of his mind. He excelled in math. Carlitos' performance on the school's placement test placed him in a higher level than the school offered. By the time he reached his sophomore year, Carlitos was taking college-level calculus, the highest level offered in his high school. He voraciously read every book and textbook he could get his hands on, whether it was written in his developing Spanish or developing English languages. He was relieved from working in the fields for weeks at a time. He only worked with his parents during school vacations and in the summer time. He made friends on the basketball courts in his neighborhood.

Education was recognized as a necessary achievement to further his family's goal of sustainability. Without an education, Carlitos' future looked like the darkest parts of his past. In the ninth grade, Carlitos' math achievements placed him in a class with college-bound students in the advanced placement track at his high school. Carlitos had become adept at negotiating his environments and figuring out what he needed to do in order to survive. He learned that in the U.S., a college education was necessary for the stability his family so desperately longed for. Yet, neither he nor any of his family members, knew what a college education was.

Carlitos asked some of his friends on the basketball courts what college was. Their response was not as optimistic as his inquiry. His friends were mostly older boys in the neighborhood who had either departed school or no longer aspired to post-secondary education. When Carlitos questioned their disinterest in what Carlitos believed to be the surest way to achieve his family's dreams of living a more sustainable life in California, his friend reminded him that neither of them had papers.

As Carlitos told me, "Suddenly, we were illegal."

It was as if he had found the golden key to opportunity only to find out it was actually made of brass.

A fear of government authority had plagued Carlitos his entire life. In Oaxaca, he and his grandmother feared the ongoing militarization surrounding their village community. Near the Mexico-U.S. border, he and his uncle witnessed the lack of effectiveness and disinterest of officials in regulating and enforcing fair labor practices. As he crossed into California, the threat of the U.S. Border Patrol was palpable. In the San Joaquin Valley, his family had already mastered a litany of strategies for avoiding *La Migra*. Believing in the state's commitment to make life better and safer was not part of the family's constitution. Believing in the dreams of opportunity was.

Sixth Moment

Despite the ever-present dangers of state authority, Carlitos yearned to find a way to make his family's sacrifices matter in their quest for stability. After participating in the MSLI, Carlitos turned his (im)migration into a powerful tool that he used to interrogate the injustices he had already known and continued to face in his daily life. As political interest in immigration continued to fester during the fall and spring of 2005–2006, Carlitos increasingly used his family's history with (im)migration as the lens through which to make sense and take action in the world. Carlitos started a school-based initiative to educate teachers, staff, and fellow students about California's AB540.³ When mass protests around HR4437 emerged across the nation, Carlitos helped organize a school wide walkout and march in protest of the racist, anti education, anti opportunity, and dehumanizing discourse of the bill. Carlitos was coming to know his educational opportunity as a politicized process with dire consequences.

Carlitos appropriated language from the MSLI as he told me, "Immigration is why I have to go to college. ... without immigration, I wouldn't be here. I might not be alive. ... If I don't go to college, it will be like I am back in Mexico. It will be more of the bad that I have fought so hard to leave behind. ... I can't let the oppressors take away any more of my family's humanization."

These six moments in Carlitos' story help to explain the history of (im)migration as a tool in Carlitos' college-going literacy development. (im)Migration's historicity comes to a head in the current political debate in the U.S. around issues of immigration reform, and Carlitos links his family's (im)migration story to his educational trajectory, explaining college access in his world as a political battle for the imagined future his family has sought since he was six years old. The first moment in the vignette established the genesis of the story—Carlitos was born into a specific set of social circumstances, as are all human subjects. The second moment signifies his family's direct entry into the practices of (im)migration in the Mexican United States corridor of human mobility, while also highlighting the dire economic circumstances from which such entries emerge. The third moment shows the complexity of negotiating (im)migration in the local lives of individuals, and it highlights how nonlinear the processes and consequences of (im)migration can be for families.

The fourth and fifth moments illustrate how (im)migration can afford new possibilities for students, while also constraining individuals in paradoxical ways. Carlitos and his family were reunited. The agricultural economy of the San Joaquin Valley provided opportunities (however limited) for the family to sustain hope of economic stability. The schooling that Carlitos entered provided him an education that had been long denied. At the same time, there were now more mouths to feed and only one additional part-time laborer to bring in income. The working conditions for migrant farmworkers have been well documented as some of the poorest in the United States (Rothenberg, 1998; Thompson & Wiggins, 2002; Foner, Rumbaut, & Gold, 2000). Carlitos suddenly found himself with a newly ascribed identity that was accompanied by enhanced threat and diminished hope. (im)Migration is never neutral.

The sixth moment explains how Carlitos appropriates the family's complex history with (im)migration toward knowing college access. The politicization of the self, the family, the education and aspirations they hoped to benefit from by migrating—all mediated Carlitos' future post-secondary participation via his recursive practices of standing up for what he believed in and organizing to learn more about how college access (a political and economic goal) can be realized.

Children of Undocumented (at some point) Parents

As noted earlier, data collection for this study occurred over a timeframe that coincided with an increase in political debate and popular democratic protest across the United States. I shared a commitment to the immigrant rights movement in which all of the other participants were becoming involved. We exchanged e-mails, MySpace messages, and phone calls about upcoming actions, protests, and marches, usually around HR4437, but also about efforts to link the movement to an anti-war struggle. The political climate emblazoned my conversations with students. For a time, it seemed that every topic we discussed related to (im)migration. In fact, through my conversations with students, we came to the conclusion that every topic did relate to (im)migration. (im)Migration permeated their lives in every way imaginable.

Some of the most active measures to directly support and participate in *el movimiento* came from students with the security of being native or naturalized citizens of the U.S. Students who themselves were free from the threat of *La Migra*, but clearly recognized the dehumanizing practices of immigration enforcement and reform in the U.S. were also the students whose parents more recently acquired their own papers. Some of these students had vivid memories of days when their parents or an older sibling did not qualify for healthcare or job protections, yet they themselves could provide a social security number on demand.

For these children of immigrants, the processes of (im)migration had not stopped when their parents obtained legal documents of residency or citizenship. (im)Migration was still in process, as they navigated and negotiated the California terrain in hopes of reaching the goals their parents had set out for when they initiated their moment of entry into the global phenomenon of (im)migration. When I visited with them for this project, or when I participated with them in political-social action, students' reflections on higher education were contextualized in these processes of (im)migration. College access became a family project, regardless of who in the family had the capacity to help with any specific college-going tasks. College access was political action in itself; it was picking up the baton of the family's (im)migration relay for opportunity.

These children of undocumented parents were some of the most outgoing in their schools and communities. They took initiative to organize school events within *el movimiento*. Their teachers knew them as "good students." Oftentimes, our conversations that explicitly sought to understand the intersections of (im)migration and education in their lives seemed to take the form of political speech-making. I have constructed this narrative as such a speech. Using almost entirely students' own words, as documented in interview transcripts or field notes, I have co edited a political speech to illustrate how (im)migration mediated college access in these students' lives. This speech was shared with the students whose words constitute it. They provided insightful revisions and assisted in its final editing.

"My immigration is now!"

A political call-to-action by *Los Estudiantes Migrantes y* RyanEG

Being a Mexican-heritage kid, I know my parents. They are immigrants and they were illegal at one point in time. I don't know how they did it, but they managed to become residents. A few years ago, in one of the proudest days of my family's life, my mom became a citizen. There is still discrimination. There is still danger. Someone needs to do something about it.

We need to do something about it. So many are still what they are calling, 'illegal,' and if that were me, I wouldn't have the opportunities that I have now. I probably would be living in Mexico, getting raised over there. Right now, my sister's husband is 'illegal.' I don't have to go that far back. I am going to some of these marches, and I am organizing this forum, because we are fighting for people's rights, you know. My immigration is now!

My education is my immigration. My parents sacrificed a lot for me to be here today. My parents had the option of saving up the money and going back to Mexico. We choose not to do that. My parents would rather spend the little money they make on *us*. School supplies. Anything and everything at school. Since I was young, my parents always enforced education. Without education, you can't be anything here. I know what I have to do. And it is not just because they told me. Now, it is something I want, too.

My parents came here for opportunity. My mom worked in canneries. My dad did a lot of farm work in the fields. His opportunity was working artichokes, lettuces, strawberries. And my mom was passed up for raises, promotions, and better hours. My mom would come home around the time I would wake up. I would find her sleeping on the couch and nudge her awake. "Mom, it's time to wake up." She had just worked nine hours straight, but she did it. She woke up to get her *mi hijo* ready for school.

I don't know if my parents know that we do appreciate it, and that I do respect that. When I think back on it, and now that I'm talking to you about it today, I carry an imagined image of my mom in her hair net and my dad picking produce. One of them always telling me the other will be back later. It makes me proud. She is strong. He is strong. That is why education is important to me. That is why immigration rights are important to me. Showing my parents that I am someone. Like them, showing them I am like them. My opportunity is my education. My education is my immigration. My immigration is now!

Although (im)migration is primarily used as a tool for the relocation of bodies across new terrains of land, the politicized use of (im)migration by these students shows how it can be used secondarily as a tool for mediating college-going. In this case, college-going, and by extension, college access is mediated as a family project in their (im)migration process—a family project of opportunity.

Children of Legal Residents of the U.S.

A significant difference in how (im)migration mediated college access for students in families that had either established legal residency long before having children, or initially entered California with papers, was their (im)migration status. These students reflected, as if in a mirror, the tool use of (im)migration. These students used (im)migration as a tool via their analysis of others' experiences, noting how they themselves were implicated in struggles for educational opportunity. As a lens through which to view the social world, (im)migration displayed the contradictions in individual experiences and the hypocrisy that permeated the dominant discourse around educational opportunity.

The vignette I've constructed to illustrate how migrant students from more established homes where there were fewest threats from legal residency status comes from a series of conversations I had with Cristina while hanging out at her *Abuela*'s house in East L.A. Cristina's articulated her relationship to (im)migration and education with a sophisticated analysis that made my job quite simple. Other participants whose families share similar characteristics reported practices that followed similar principles to Cristina. As will be illustrated, all of the participants in this coalition of students recognized racism toward (im)migrants, implicated themselves in that specific subjective position, despite others' assertions that they were not like the people at whom the oppressive comments or actions were directed, and they connected these experiences to their college-going practices.

Cristina's family of four had struggled for years to sustain residence in the same neighborhood. For a short period of time, Cristina moved in with a friend's family while her own was in a housing transition. Her experiences at that house were an example of how (im)migration mediated educational opportunity through a looking-glass effect. As heard in Cristina's words:

> I'm in her house and you see all these elephants and they're all just like republican or whatever, so she wanted to talk to me and I wanted to talk to her. I wanted to sit down and see what she was about and everything ... like, I thought I was going into a conversation, but she acted like, she already knew my responses. She already knew how to completely, like, almost try to convince me. I was like, 'whoa, I can't ...' about marriage, about schooling. And she herself, like, immigrating here as a teen, had to go to community college because she couldn't go to college. She didn't go to college till she stayed there for like, four years, and then she moved on to a university. And, like, she argued, and she told me that, 'No, we don't need programs. We don't need outreach. It's the individual and their motivation. They need to work hard to get to the top.' And like, I couldn't believe that her, even though she had to struggle, she, coming to this country. She didn't get equal opportunity. I know she didn't. She went to CD High. She was telling me that kids are there because that's how their parents raised them, basically they're getting themselves into these problems and people like that, ... it's really scary. She isn't helping anyone here.

Cristina related her challenges in understanding people who did not recognize the sociocultural dimensions of (im)migration experiences to her own goals for higher education. She indicated that experiences like the one illustrated above informed her future thoughts about political activism in school. She said:

"I don't know if I want to be the minority, like, *the* minority or have a group of us, because, how do things get started in colleges? I wouldn't mind initiating something like a Chicana movement in the school, but if it's already there, that's even more helpful."

When I asked Cristina if there were other experiences that informed her identity construction as a Chicana, she informed me:

> When I was living with my friends, her husband was Mexican American but like, generations have been here, so they don't know Spanish. They hate Mexico, like it's dirty, or something, but while I was living there, even before this, the oldest daughter, she had a boyfriend and then in college she got pregnant. She had the child. The guy left her. He was a Mexican. So that ... made her hate almost the fact that he was Mexican and she was like, and then the fact that her daughter was impregnated by a Mexican man who left

her and now she has to do it on her own and like that animosity became like, him now making it a broader racial issue.

Cristina's struggles to make sense of how people could be so far away from understanding the place she occupied as a Chicana continued to be tested. She finally came to an analysis that strengthened her convictions after further reflection.

> Me living there, like, family would come over and they'd have discussions about politics, discussions about immigration, and I had to listen and kind of like, take it. People, they would laugh, and I was, I would not laugh, but I was called like 'the Mexican houseguest in their home, and I don't know, like, I'm treated like one of them in a sense, but I kind of have to do, I kind of had to take that and every time I'd be like, 'Please, can you call me something else? Like, Cristina?' But it's like, 'Oh, well, get over it. We're not racist. We're not like …' I would never ever say that to someone, but like so many things that I've had to just, like just take it. … They put me down like that, but then they pick me up by saying, 'Well, you're different.' It gets me more upset, because I'm like, I'm the exception to this culture? I'm the one that defines our heritage and becoming something better? Something more American? Something? It's like all this crap, and even though, this family—I love them so much, but I still, I can't love them in a certain way.
>
> And so, like, I know I'm getting my education. And everyone deserves that. Like, if I have such a hard time, and I'm like, not really even an immigrant. My parents are. But, like, as much as I'm different, I'm like, the same. I have to fight for immigration, because immigration is fighting for me.

Cristina's narratives illustrate that (im)migration mediated college-going in more ways than just direct experiences. Her family had never been threatened directly on the basis of their legal residency status. Her parents entered California with papers. Yet, (im)migration persisted to shape and reshape her knowing of college access, its purpose and its imperativeness to her political convictions. Reflecting on personal experiences with others around issues related to (im)migration and the oppressive racialized practices stemming from (im)migration troubled students like Cristina. Although it frustrated them, it also provided a meaningful lens through which to view and manifest the commitment they felt they needed to make college a reality.

A key dimension to students' uses of (im)migration as tools for coming to know college access is having the opportunity to reflect on and put into action their use of (im)migration in their lives. This process underscores the recursive nature of literacy development, especially in the social practice of college access. The take-home message from understanding how (im)migration might serve as a tool in coming to know college access is to recognize how (im)migration mediated college access as an object of learning. (Im)migration moved the ideology of college access into learning, not a rite of passage or a ritual or a logical next step, or a recognition of merit. Rather, (im)migration eschewed the concept of college access as recognition of merit and fostered a rethinking of access as a process of reaching, a journey, and a fulfillment of the family's (im)migration trail.

Next, I discuss a second tool that emerged as significant to the participants of this study and enabled transformative learning opportunities in which students could renegotiate their practices and/or re imagine college access. This second tool focuses on a specific type of relationship that proved useful for students as they developed college-going literacy.

Notes

[1] I strategically put the prefix "im" in parentheses in order to discursively form the process of human movement across lands as one that can be contested politically, yet retaining the significance of the migratory experience.

[2] See, for example, Oakes (2004); Moll & Ruiz (2002).

[3] AB540 is the California legislation that extended in-state tuition benefits at public higher education institutions to all residents of California, regardless of their (un)documented (im)migration status.

Chapter Six
¡*Confianza!*

From field notes after a visit to the East San Francisco Bay and greater Monterey Bay areas:

> I was so honored to be invited over for breakfast. Just the day before I had driven six hours from L.A. to the bay, just in time to participate in Armando's cousin's birthday party. Armando's *madre* prepared some of the best *pozole* I had tried—not too salty, but still spicy enough to know it was from her kitchen, not some bulk warehouse recipe. After visiting with Armando and laughing with his family about the funny things that his one-year old cousin got into when crawling around, I traveled another two hours over and down the coast to kick it with Nené for the night. By the time I lay down in the (dis)comfort of my local cheap motel room, I was exhausted. Nené and I had hit the town, as much as there was a town to hit for a 17-year-old boy, in Watsonville. We visited with friends of his at the bowling alley, the local Starbucks, and we grabbed some food at a fast food joint where he used to hang out with those other kids during high school. Finally, Nené helped me build my MySpace page online until about 1:00 in the morning. As I dropped him off, he said, "Hey! *Mi mamá's* making *menudo* in the morning. I asked her to make *enchiladas* for you last night, but she didn't have the stuff for it. So, she's making *menudo* instead. What time are you coming over?"
>
> On my drive back to the motel, something hit me. *I am just as much a part of his life as he is mine.* I had felt this before, especially when Nené would call me on occasion to share big news, like getting crowned homecoming king, but sometimes I need to be reminded of the ways in which my relations manifest and play out across contexts. Here, in front of his

family's home, I was invited to breakfast, not as a visitor, but as someone who was part of Nené's life.

Typically, I was late. I had stopped to pick up flowers for *Señora* (*Sra*, Nené's mother) and deodorant for myself. I only found the deodorant. I felt like a jerk, but at least I would be a jerk that smelled nice. Speeding onto their street, I quickly parked my car in front of their house and eagerly knocked on the door. What I did not realize was that hardly anyone else was going to be around at what, to me, was a typical weekend breakfast time. Nené's father had already left for work hours before me. He would be managing a fruit stand near the highway for most of the day. Nené's brothers were either still asleep, having come home from a late night of work, or already gone to another job. I would join only Nené and his mother over homemade *menudo* that morning.

For me, conversations over special meals, and breakfasts in particular, have always played an important and subtly distinctive role in my life. These are the confessional meals. The meals where problems get exposed, worked through, and perhaps, if lucky, set on a process toward resolution. Thoughts and feelings get aired that must remain bottled during other daily interactions. They are rebuked or legitimized by the way others at the table take them up, shoot them down, or appropriate them for their own experiential sense-making. This meal proved to be both similar and different from my own breakfasts.

Sitting down at the table, Nené and I began to eat. *Sra* joined us at the table, but did not eat. Within ten minutes, the confessions began. *Sra* began asking me questions about Nené's plans to start community college in the fall. Nené, serving as translator between his mother and me at first did not really try to elaborate on either *Sra's* questions or my responses. After another few minutes of *Sra* asking me about other parts of Nené's life, like his relationship with his girlfriend, it was established that *Sra* and I both agreed that Nené spent a lot of time, late at night, talking to his girlfriend, and perhaps that was why he became so easily tired during the day. Nené kind of chuckled and asked if we had planned ahead of time to get together in order to pick on him.

"What is this, pick on Nené hour?"

We all gave out a relaxed laugh. *Sra's* questions kept coming. Nené, as translator, had the opportunity to qualify or editorialize them. Finally, Nené relented. He let it all out.

He turned to me and said, "We had a fight this morning, and she thinks that what you're saying is proving her point. You see what I mean? It's like I said last night. They think they know better than me, but they don't. They think I'm just hanging around here to be lazy or something. I don't want to be here for that. I'm trying to do something better."

Nené's decision to attend the local community college was not devoid of other options. He had been admitted to two California State University campuses, but opted to begin at community college in order to achieve his goal of graduating from UCLA. Nené had adjusted his goals shortly after I met him in MSLI. Unfortunately, his fate as a freshman-admit to UCLA had already faltered by that point. Nené did not have the grade point average necessary for "competitive admission" to the UC system, nor did he have the opportunity to take the advanced placement courses necessary to raise it. For Nené, community college was a critical decision to go beyond what he once thought the pinnacle of success.

This decision was contrary to his parents' understanding of community college. Having participated in numerous parent involvement programs with the migrant education programs of their region, *Sra* had been informed that community college was a last resort, and indeed a dangerous option for students to take if they were serious about obtaining a bachelor's degree. There was friction hovering over the *menudo* that morning—friction I did not feel until suddenly *Sra* started to cry as she explained to me in her developing English that,

"I am so proud of my son and he doesn't think so. He thinks because I cannot buy him a car that I am ashamed of him. Because when his brother went to college, we bought him a car. I am a little ashamed because I cannot do what I want to do for him. I want for him the things that will make his education, and his life easier. I do not want for him what his father has to do, what I have to do."

Through tears of his own, Nené responded with condolences and statements of his own pride for his parents. He tried to explain how he did not care at all about a car, but how he was actually trying to do something better. He told *Sra* about his conversations with me, and about how we had talked about how important their struggle was for him and his goals of graduating from college.

After a few minutes of silence, with Nené having retreated to the sofa and *Sra* in the kitchen, I remained seated at the dining table. *Sra* turned to me and said,

"I share these things with you because I see that my son has, um, how to say, *confianza*, with you. Like you, I do not know how to say, but you are important to him, and you are from the migrant program, and we see how that has changed him. And we want him to be that way."

I was floored with responsibility. I was floating with acceptance. I was beginning to understand how "relational learning" could really mean something much more powerful than content knowledge or effective execution of specific social tasks. *Confianza* afforded the possibility for transformation through our relationship.

Confianza,[1] although commonly translated into English as "mutual trust," indeed, means something more complex. At its most basic level, *confianza* is a cultural expression of trust. However, within the circumstances in which I use the term, it means a great deal more. In this chapter, I describe how *confianza* can become an invaluable tool used to foster college-going literacy by analyzing the specific relationships that students reported having transformed their ways of knowing and their ideological assumptions about college-going. I describe the ways in which these relationships of *confianza* mediated students' development of college-going literacy. The individuals in students' lives that most clearly gave rise to relationships of *confianza* were most often found outside of traditional schooling environments. This chapter summarizes and suggests ecologies that might help foster *confianza* for the intention of developing students' college-going literacy.

Others on *Confianza*

Many scholars have used the concept of *confianza* to describe or analyze relationships that influenced students' performance and participation in schooling. *Confianza* has been adopted into models of students' resiliency in schooling when faced with adverse circumstances (Franquiz & Salazar, 2004; Velez-Ibanez, 1996; Aspiazu, Bauer, & Spillet, 1998; Stanton-Salazar, 2001). It has been used to describe the relationships between students and adult figures involved in shared activism related to students' schooling (McLaughlin & Bryan, 2003). I am extending these uses of *confianza* into students' college-going activity, arguing that *confianza* can be a transformative component to the ways in which students learn college-going. I seek to highlight relationships within students' college-going communities that might transform college-going into college-going literacy. *Confianza* is a site of trust, respect, mentorship, teaching and learning, legitimacy, reliance, and commitment. The *confianza* shared by students and another adult is where the transformation from college as a potential to college as a real opportunity can happen.

Missing is the relation between the navigation of school for "school success" and students' educational aspirations, preparation, planning, and commitment to post-secondary education. Salinas and Reyes (2004) detail the efforts made to help migrant students persist through high school by "advocate educators,"—another relationship of *confianza*. They were geared toward retention in high school and high school graduation. They are not geared toward a definition of success contingent upon being prepared for higher education opportunities.

Confianza in College-going Literacy

Used here, the concept of *confianza* signifies more than "sharing confidence" or "mutual trust." Its manifestation is not contingent upon an extension of students' social capital, as in Stanton-Salazar's (2001) conceptualization, although, that might be one of the consequences associated with a student's constellation of *confianza*. *Confianza*, in my analysis, indicates a mutual relationship of exchange, beyond *quid pro quo*. It can mean being treated like family, but without losing the distinction of being someone outside of the family. Indeed, that distinction is important, because sharing *confianza* often means being able to share some things that one does not want to share with family.

As a quality, *confianza* transforms an existing relationship into something in which there are new potentialities. For example, my relationship with *Nené* began as a teaching assistant in a summer outreach program. The *confianza* we developed allowed us to become friends after the program ended. It also provided us with the potential to engage in this research process together. In a crude sense, Nené played the role of research subject, and I played the role of researcher. Yet, our mutual involvement in each other's projects—*Nené* transitioning from high school to college student, and I working through my research project—extended the potential ways in which we could relate to each other, even within the roles of subject and researcher. Nené quite often pointed out to me things or ways in which I could better understand how he has learned college-going. Reciprocally, I often listened to Nené work through issues with his girlfriend related to his moving on from high school and her finishing out her last two years.

The new potentialities afforded by the *confianza* that I speak of allow participants in students' college-going literacy development to break and reinvent the rules assigned to their specific division of labor within the student's college-going activity. Nené and I get to establish new rules for our relationship—that might not be followed in the expected relationship between a researcher and a participant, and rules that might actually break existing rules in the dominant discourse of relations across TA and student. In this sense, the development of *confianza*, and the development of the relationship itself might indeed work from a separate activity system that intersects with the activity of college-going for an individual or collection of student(s). Furthermore, in order to develop *confianza* of the quality that I speak, it requires a thread of honesty and shared vulnerability. There is a buy-in between the subjects of *confianza*.

A relationship of *confianza* was identified in each participant in this study. Students unanimously recounted at least one relationship with a "more expert other" (Vygotsky, 1978), through which their college-going literacy was transformed. The specific transformation took different shapes and affected different dimensions of their college-going activity, but the influence of these particular relationships was explained to be tremendous.

How Relationships of *Confianza* Mediate College-going Literacy

Below, are two specific examples of *confianza* within migrant students' college-going. I present these examples in the context of college-going, highlighting the new potentialities *confianza* afforded students. These new potentialities manifest from the transformative service that *confianza* provided in students' college-going literacy. These examples also serve as context for discussion on some of the components/elements of the social ecologies that can promote and foster such *confianza*.

These relationships did not mediate students' literacy in identical ways. Rather, what is significant about relationships of *confianza*, is that each contributed to transformative learning in very specific ways for each student. As explained in greater detail below, the *confianza* I shared with Nené, for example, helped reaffirm his decision to follow his goal toward UCLA, whereas the *confianza* that Lorena shared with Juan helped her align her appreciation for her family and the different ways that they could and could not serve as a resource for her. These are but two examples of how the ways that *confianza* can serve as a mediating tool in students' literacy development.

Nené and Me: The Relationship

When Nené and I first met, neither of us expected that we would become very tight with the other. I initially viewed Nené as one of those cool kids that would probably be respectful in the classroom, but harbor ill feelings toward me, and anticipated that, most likely one of his judgments against me would come out in class sometime during the summer program. I remember being extremely deliberate in challenging myself on this assumption during the second day of class. We were using an ice-breaker that related to social literacy—

reading and writing in the social world—which required us to pair up and share some personal information. I strategically asked Nené to be my partner, and I could feel his slight disappointment at having to do the exercise with one of the so-called teachers. Keeping in mind that the social organization of learning in MSLI was radically different than traditional high school or college classrooms, I allowed my choice of Nené as a partner to occur under the guise of subverting the dominant ideas of teacher-student/expert-novice, rather than revealing my truer motivations, which were to force myself to get to know him beyond his initial presentation and vice-versa.

"I think you might be a person who presents himself as one way—wanting to get along with everyone and help things have a good time—but actually has a lot more insecurity in figuring out what you really want to be about," I said at the beginning of our exercise about what we were reading from our one-day interactions with each other.

"Well, you're probably right. But I think that you're trying to figure out what you want to present yourself like, even if you do know what you want to really be about." Nené replied.

I acceded, "Okay. You're pretty astute."

Nené asked, "What do you mean?"

I said, "I mean you're pretty perceptive there, and at the same time, you're reflecting on who you are. It's pretty cool."

Nené replied, "Yeah, Ryan. I try to be a pretty cool guy. See, you're not so different."

I smiled and jokingly said, "Yeah, well, don't tell nobody yet. Let's keep 'em guessing for a while."

Smiling, Nené responded, "No way, man!"

Thus, Nené and I began to involve each other in our teaching and learning processes. Throughout the Institute, I provided feedback to Nené, who emerged as a leader in our classroom, volunteering regularly to share both assigned writing and personal poems that he was working through. I joined the students for dinner in the residence halls, and during a few of these, Nené eagerly invited me to sit with him and his friends. He even referred me to one friend who wanted advice on his relationship with his uncle, whom he suspected might be gay. The three of us had a long conversation, and at the end, I remember being really proud because Nené's friend asked each of us why I was willing to listen to him.

Nené said that he asked me because, "I told you [Nené's friend], Ryan's a pretty damn cool guy."

I said, "Because if Nené's got a friend who wants to talk, I want to talk to that friend. Nené's a pretty important person to me."

We all said *"¡Salud!"* and clinked our glasses of milk together.

Nené and I remained in contact after the Institute. Our conversations were usually over the phone, and generally fairly evenly distributed as far as who initiated contact with whom. Nené would call me at times to share major things that happened in his life. For example, he once called me to let me know that he'd organized a major event in his community about the immigrant rights protests that were erupting across the nation in the early part of 2006. I called him to share my involvement in the movement. We talked about different strategies that groups were taking, and how we each felt we could best serve the cause.

I also called Nené to ask him explicitly about school, and how his college plans were evolving. He would update me with his applications, his concerns about financing, and his ultimate plans to attend the local community college before transferring to UCLA. We met up once in Santa Monica when his local Migrant Education Program counselor had organized a trip to visit Southern California colleges. Nené invited me to join his group for dinner, and we talked a lot about his solidifying plans for after high school.

It was during another meal during one of my visits over the course of this study that Nené explicitly shared what my friendship meant to him. We were eating dinner together at some restaurant in his hometown. He was relaying a story to me about his girlfriend and how that relationship was going in light of his graduating from high school soon. Somehow the conversation turned to discuss who he shared what sort of things with.

Nené informed me:

> And Ryan, man, like, you're one of my best friends. I mean, other than my brothers, like, dude. I can tell you just about anything. Even some stuff that I can't talk about with my brothers, well, like, not in the same way at least. Yeah, man, like, I don't really think I have any other friendships like you.

Like, we're so different, you know, but like, it doesn't really feel like that difference gets in the way, like, it kinda helps.

About eight months before, Nené had said something similar in front of our entire MSLI classroom, when he mentioned, "Look at me and Ryan. Like, if you just thought about us, like, you would probably only say that we're totally different, but really, like, there's a lot more that's the same between us than the stupid differences." That comment inspired me to immediately begin working through and honoring the relationships that had begun in MSLI. It also represents the initial *confianza* that changed and grew in strength by the choices that Nené and I made to stay in touch and rely on each other after MSLI ended.

The Transformative Service / New Potentialities

The relationship fostered between Nené and I afforded him the possibility of working through his vision of college studies. He could explore different imaginations of what studying in college was about, and simultaneously figure out some of the challenges of negotiating his college-going practices with his family values and expectations. During one of my visits with Nené, we were eating Chinese food at one of "Nené's Bests" (favorite spots in town). He brought up his interest in pursuing Chicano studies in college, under the context of reaffirming his decision to hold off on a four-year school until he could transfer to UCLA.

Nené: "Like, I used to be thinking about business, because, like, it would be cool to make a lot of money and stuff."

RyanEG: "Yeah. Is that what you're about? Money?"

Nené: "Well, money's pretty nice, don't you think?"

RyanEG: "No doubt. But, like, hey! I don't make a lot of money. I'm pretty happy."

Nené: "You make a lot of money."

RyanEG: "Oh really!"

Nené: "For just you. Heck yeah. I mean, you can come up here and visit me and stuff."

RyanEG: "Well, that's true. I live a very lovely life. But trust me, I don't make a lot of money. I'm cool though. I make plenty for what a person like me needs. You're right."

Nené: "Anyway, so, like, I was thinking business, right? But, like, I don't know, I really like, like, Chicano Studies and stuff."

RyanEG: "Seriously, way cool."

Nené: "Yeah, but like, what does that really mean?"

RyanEG: "Well, like, I have some friends who did Chicano Studies. They didn't have it at my school. We only had, like, American Studies or maybe Latino Studies, I think. Maybe just American. That was a pretty cool major, though. Sometimes I think I should have studied that."

Nené: "But, like, your school was private, right? Occi ..."

RyanEG: "Yeah. Occidental. It's a small private liberal arts college. So, there's not a whole lot of really specific or specialized stuff to major in."

Nené: "I heard that, like, UCLA has a good Chicano Studies."

RyanEG: "Yeah. They do. They just became a department kind of recently, like, before they were just a program, which is like, not as good, I guess."

Nené: "Like, didn't people have to fight, like, fasting and stuff?"

RyanEG: "You know about that?"

Nené shook his head and kind of smiled as he chewed his food.

RyanEG: "Yeah, there were like huge campaigns and stuff. But officially, they are like a full department now. Which is really cool. It means they have the same status as like, all the old white man departments."

We both chuckled.

Nené: "You're gonna be an old white man someday, Ryan."

RyanEG: "Nah!"

Nené: "Nah! You could never be an old white man, dude. You're too cool, rock star. You're Ryan."

RyanEG: "Ri-eee-ight!"

We both laughed.

RyanEG: "So, what's up with Chicano studies? You know, UCSB has a good department too. Yeah. They just started offering the PhD degree, too. The first PhD in Chicano studies anywhere."

Nené: "That's what you're doing, right?"
RyanEG: "Uh-huh."
Nené: "You're going to be Dr. Ryan. Or Professor Ryan?"
RyanEG: "Something like that."
Nené: "That's so cool, dude. I want that."
RyanEG: "Dr. Nené. Or you want to be Dr. Ryan?"
Nené: "Huh, huh."
He let me know my joke was lame.
RyanEG: "Well, Dr. Nené, so what's up? Chicano studies."
Nené: "I dunno, like, it sounds cool. It's like, all about my life, you know, but like, my life that I don't get. Like, the ways that we'd like to be but can't, kinda."
RyanEG: "What do you mean?"
Nené: "Like, it's all about Mexicans, right?"
RyanEG: "In a sense, yeah, I guess."
Nené: "But like, I'm Mexican, but I don't really get to live like a Mexican. Like, we do Mexican things. We *are* Mexican, like anyone will tell you. But, like, we'd like to live like Mexicans without all the crap that happens because we're Mexican."
RyanEG: "You mean from the whities."
Nené: "From anyone, but yeah, from the whities."
RyanEG: "Sounds cool. Yeah, like, Chicano studies, like, what I really liked about the classes I took, and like, I think the programs are sorta set up like this too, like, it's really interdisciplinary. So, like, there's like a lot of social science stuff, like sociology and anthropology and stuff, but there's also a ton of like, humanities, like theater and poetry and literature and history, and you can really work with all of them all together or like, just a part. And they're all considered like, cool."
Nené: "Yeah, man. Like, that's what I want. Like, that sounds really cool. But, like, what I do with it. Like, what do I tell my parents I'm doing?"
RyanEG: "You can actually move into a ton of stuff with Chicano studies. You'd be totally set up to go to graduate school. You could go into education. You could work for stuff like the Migrant programs. You could start a non-profit. You could go into politics."
Apparently, I'd become a bit excited.

Nené: "Ryan, calm down, dude. I get it."
RyanEG: "You could totally kill with your poetry, too, man."
Nené: "You think so, man?"
RyanEG: "Umm, yeah. But, like, tell your counselor or whoever's supposed to help you at registration, because you want to make sure you set yourself up for UCLA from the beginning."
Nené: "I know. I know. You said that before."
RyanEG: "Yeah, but I really mean it. Like, if you there isn't someone to help, then find someone. Ask questions. Call me. We'll figure it out together."
Nené: "Alright man. So how's your thing going? ...."

Two months later, Nené registered for community college. He told his transfer coordinator that he wanted to major in Chicano studies, but was still maybe considering business. He enrolled in his first Chicano studies course, Chicano Art History.

The preceding conversation is both a micro example of *confianza* at work, and a representative example of on-going conversations that I shared with Nené.

Nené's affirmation of his decision to pursue a UCLA education via the community college is significant in this conversation. Nené and I explored what it meant to major in Chicano Studies. We explored what it meant to begin post-secondary education at the community college. Each of these explorations were contextually specific to Nené's life. I could not have participated in this conversation with Nené without sharing the relationship. Part of understanding *confianza* as a tool implicates Nené in a recursive process whereby our relationship mediates his understanding of college access as an object to be known—and informs his actions toward college access as a social practice.

Lorena and Juan: The Relationship

"Juan is my hero. He's got a huge place on my MySpace page."

Lorena and Juan developed a unique relationship during MSLI. He worked as one of the resident assistants that summer. Juan had just finished his first year as an undergraduate at UC Berkeley, and he had participated in MSLI two summers before. Lorena explained having an instant connection to Juan:

> He was the first person I met at UCLA. He helped me move in to my dorm room and just made me feel right away like, okay, I can be here. I can do this. I didn't know he was from Berkeley or anything then. All he said was that he was an RA and that he'd done the program a couple summers ago. He was just really nice and supportive from the beginning. ... He also said that he was there to learn from us as much as we were there to learn from him. He said that he came back to the program because he needed strength from it. I really liked that, like, his honesty about needing people.

Over the next couple of weeks, having spent almost all of their non-class time together, Lorena began to confide more in Juan, and look to him for support. A turning point happened one night when Lorena's group in the program had a conflict with their parent liaison. Lorena recounted:

> I remember we were having problems with our mother RA, because she wouldn't let us speak up and do the things we wanted to do. We always had to like what she wanted to do. And then like one day, like, Juan went up to me because I said something about that teacher (a controversy from her own high school), and then Ana (the parent RA) made it seem like we never did anything to get her (the controversial teacher) out of the school, when, well, we did.
>
> We did do a lot of things to try to get her out but we couldn't and she made it seem like ... No, it is because you didn't know what to do, and well ... She was really mean about it, and I was like, 'Okay,' I didn't want to argue or ... But then Juan came up to me and he said, 'You know, like, don't be afraid. Don't be afraid if you know, like, you are right. Don't be afraid. Don't do it in a rude way, but you know, if you know you did something, and if you don't know what to do, like, talk to people, and find out what you can do because having a teacher like that it is not fair. That she shouldn't be teaching.'
>
> And yes, I always listen to Juan. Just like everything he says it's, like he is not going to tell you always it is easy—you are going to get the scholarship, you are going to get it like nothing—No. He is going to tell you, you know, that it is tough. It is going to be tough, and you are going to have to face it, but there are people that are going to help you.

Lorena and Juan remained in touch after the program ended. Juan happens to be a Gates Millennium Scholar,[2] and has continued to encourage Lorena, as well as other students from the 2005 MSLI, to apply for top-tier schools and scholarships. Lorena reported calling or e-mailing or sending MySpace messages to Juan whenever she needed help "figuring out what to do."

Lorena said she goes to Juan, specifically. "I choose Juan. I kind of think he really likes it. Not like he doesn't have anything else going on, but like, he said once … it's about strength through each other. When Juan calls, I always call him back."

Lorena and Juan relied on each other. They supported one another during and after the summer program, extending their relationship into friendship. They were invested in each other. Lorena continued, "Like, I can call him when I don't know how to deal with a teacher, or what exams to take, or when I think that something's unfair that I need to get into college."

Lorena planned a visit to Juan so that she could see Berkeley's campus and test out the environment. It was cancelled due to a family vacation, but the significance of her parents' letting her visit him remained.

"I think it's a big deal for me to go away, especially for my dad, especially where there will be boys. Because, like, I'm the youngest one, and I'm the only girl. My mom is all about it, especially after she saw me at UCLA. But my dad, I think it's kind of hard on him."

Lorena's respect for Juan transferred to her parents. According to Lorena, they, too valued him as her friend and confidant. Visiting her at UCLA and seeing her on that campus, with Juan as her RA opened up new possibilities for the dimensions of Lorena's relationship to him. Lorena further explained how she felt Juan was like family, in part because of the similarities between their parents. Lorena said:

> And also like his parents are a little like mine. Like, I got the chance to talk to him about like how my parents are, and it is not that, I know it is not that they don't care about me, 'cause they do care a whole lot. But it is just that they are working so much that sometimes they don't have the time, and his parents are just like that, and my parents didn't even know that I was going to go to college… And his parents, he kept it a secret until graduation day because he wanted to give them like the big surprise, they didn't have to worry about anything.

Lorena's relationship with Juan transformed the roles that Lorena saw her parents playing in her college-going. Although Lorena did not go to the extremes of withholding successes such as the Gates

Millennium Scholarship from her parents as Juan did, she adjusted her reliance on her parents, but without feeling bad or thinking poorly of her parents.

Lorena informed me, "My parents are a wealth of support, and they're really helpful when I think of places to go, especially because of my health problems, but I don't really go to them for help with a lot of the 'you have to do this, you have to do that' kinda stuff."

The assistance with negotiating the cultural practices of family with the cultural practices of the dominant institution (education), was a transformative influence. Lorena often spoke of how Juan served as a model for her when it came to honoring her parents, yet acknowledging that there were limits to what their involvement might be in her college-going. This was tremendously important for Lorena who valued her family's integrity above everything, but also felt conflicted about how to negotiate her individual goals with her familial goals. The parallelism shared between Lorena and Juan was both part of what fed their developing *confianza* as well as part of what their *confianza* afforded them to understand in each other.

The Transformative Service / New Potentialities

The *confianza* shared between Lorena and Juan allowed Juan to encourage Lorena to think about college differently. Namely, Juan had the opportunity to serve as a corporeal representation of college as a reality. As a student at an elite university, his encouragement for Lorena to consider goals beyond those she had considered before carried a weight of legitimacy. As a migrant student himself, Juan represented someone who was similar to Lorena. Indeed, Juan and Lorena shared a *confianza* that was also connected to a specific sociocultural geography, or a cultural ecology—MSLI. In discussing Juan's influence on her thinking about college, Lorena reported:

> Because I thought it was extremely, extremely hard to get into UCLA. Like you have to be like some bookworm or something. That is really what I thought, and even though, like I liked it, I am not going to even apply like, that is just a waste of $35, and I'll just go to like some other school that it is easier to get in. I guess I didn't have, like, a definite goal like I do now. That I didn't know. I didn't even know they [broader goals] existed like ... And then there were examples of people like Juan. Well, Juan is at Berkeley ...

You know I was like, 'Why can't I make those courses, and things? I will try, and I am going to work hard for it.'

Lorena's prior idea of college was limited to community colleges or a non competitive state university. Sharing the trust and deeper belief in one another with Juan allowed her to conceive of college as an elite institution, requiring different preparation than her prior concepts. Simply put, the possibility of a UC campus as the next step in Lorena's education moved UC from being an exclusive institution to becoming the goal of Lorena's college-going activity. In the space of the *confianza* shared between Lorena and Juan, Lorena was able to re-imagine the relationship between her and higher education. As with Nené's re-imagination, Lorena's reconstruction of the object entailed more than thinking that a UC was a reality. It was accompanied by a task-oriented pragmatism, represented by the new strategies in course-taking.

Ecologies That Fostered *Confianza*

There are six notable ecological traits that cut across each relationship of *confianza* reported by the participants in this study. These ecological traits afforded both subjects of each relationship to mutually buy into each other's efforts and struggles toward humanization. These traits are presented here in order to describe ecologies that have the potential to foster *confianza* for students' college-going. These ecological traits are not intended to serve as a prescription for *confianza*, as ultimately, it is an interpersonal process that requires individual commitments. However, when designing learning environments with the intent of working toward students' college-going, these ecological traits might prove extremely useful.

First, even though most of the relationships of *confianza* included one subject who was vested with more institutional or positional authority in the contexts in which the two subjects met and operated, that authority was not accompanied with consequential assessment responsibilities. In other words, there was no grading. Students were free to explore and experiment in their work and in their imaginations without the fear of failing, and without the competition of doing better than peers. The other person, whether teacher, mentor, or friend, was not bound by an obligation to make an assessment of the student that might have consequences for their future educational or social endeavors.

Second, students' home language(s) were validated in all communication between, across, and amidst the individuals in *confianza*. Language was a tool of communication, not an index of competence. Students, and the "more experienced other" were permitted, and in most cases, encouraged to express themselves in the ways they found most effective for the task at hand. If this meant speaking or writing in Spanish, additional tools would be used to include non-Spanish speakers or readers. Validating the home language of students also mediated the risk of using languages that were less familiar for either person.

Third, all parties mutually engaged in shared as well as different familial cultural practices. Relations between individuals were encouraged and expected to connect learning activities to their own lives. Drawing on their own experiences, and sharing those experiences in both narrative and physically experiential ways added to the repertoires of practices that participants (students and adults) could draw from in making sense of the figured worlds in which they lived and learned.

Fourth, there were opportunities for relationships with students' parents to develop. Although this ecological trait was used less often in the relationships of *confianza* reported by students participating in this study, the opportunity for parents to engage and participate in students' relationships was notable. This trait seemed to carry symbolic power, suggesting that just the structural ability for parents to meet and get to know the individuals in students' relationships was meaningful.

Fifth, each individual who shared *confianza* was structurally able to go beyond their explicit job expectations. If an instructor in a supplemental educational program was asked to go to lunch with a student, the time was available and culturally accepted. Any cultural taboo around spending time with students over periods of time was removed.

Sixth, the learning environments that gave rise to *confianza* were socially organized to assume greatness in students, rather than to identify and address something in them that needed to be fixed.

There was an operating assumption that all students and other participants in *confianza* had ability to learn. This was most often achieved by structuring the "teacher" and "student" relationships as mutually interdependent and dynamic, wherein all teachers were active learners and all learners were actively teaching simultaneously.

MSLI as an Ecological Example

The 2005 MSLI is the ecological context that I am most familiar with from the collection of *confianza* spaces that students reported. In part, that is why I focused the previous discussion and illustration of *confianza* on two relationships within the 2005 MSLI. The college-level work that students engage in during MSLI includes reading graduate level texts, such as Eduardo Galeano's *Open Veins of Latin America*, Paolo Freire's *Pedagogy of the Oppressed*, and Gloria Anzaldúa's *Borderlands/La Frontera*. Students also write every day. There are four assignments that anchor the curriculum around specific writing genres and social lenses (e.g., history and labor, schooling vs. education). In-class writing assignments might include poetry writing, journaling, quick-write responses to questions raised in class, and draft after draft of the anchoring assignments. The emphasis of instructional feedback is on the process of writing, using writing as a process of sense-making to take action toward addressing social and individual problems related to oppression and opportunity. Grades are never marked on students' work, yet meaningful feedback is provided by instructors' participation in students' writing processes and practices.

The MSLI uses what Gutiérrez, Baquedano-Lopez, & Tejeda (1999) called, "hybrid language practices" (p. 287), where multiple languages are used in the classroom and across all activities in the Institute. Attention is paid to translation needs of all participants (students, instructors, residential staff), and most conversations include both Spanish and English phrases, sentences, exclamations, questions, and other utterances. Some participants were monolingual in English. Others were monolingual in Spanish. Many participants had various degrees of written, spoken, and auditory comprehension of English, Spanish and other languages.

Grounding learning in participants' lived experiences achieved a mutual engagement in shared and different cultural practices. Abstract understandings of material were constantly questioned with their practical, material, or cultural implications for real life. Making learning tangible assumed that knowledge about migrant leadership came from migrant lives. Extending participants repertoires of practice to work toward specific learning goals (e.g., recognizing oppression in schooling, even when school might be students' favorite place to spend time), drew upon the diverse sets of meaning-making experiences across all participants. In this way, the strength of the Institute came from both the shared histories and the divergent practices of all persons in the MSLI. Traditional indicators of academic achievement (e.g., GPA) spanned a broad range. Instructors' life experiences prior to becoming well-educated instructors from UCLA were equally diverse. This cultural diversity was used to expand the possibilities and potentialities for meaning-making across contexts.

Each year, the MSLI hosts a parent institute for one week following the students' month-long program. This is a formal way for parents to participate in something similar to their children, providing opportunities for parents and some staff to become familiar with each other. Additionally, parents are invited to spend the final day of the Institute with their children and witness the recognition of all MSLI participants' achievements. Beyond these formal ways in which parents are included in the MSLI ecological context, instructors and students are able to spend time together outside of the (in)formal classroom. Ethical involvement in student's lives after they leave UCLA is a normative practice. These extensions of the relationship provide opportunities for students and instructors (or residential staff) to develop relationships over time and for instructors to meet students' parents, on their terms. The emphasis of these practices, as an ecological trait, is on the ethical participation among all subjects.

Finally, the MSLI worked diligently to fight deficit orientations of student learning. Participants' cultural backgrounds were used as valuable sources of meaning-making and knowledge construction. Following pedagogies informed by cultural wealth models (Villalpando & Solórzano, 2005), Vygotskian (1978) and Freireian (1970;

2004) derived theories of learning, and privileging the historically oppressed experiences of migrants in California (Tejeda, Espinoza, & Gutiérrez, 2003), the MSLI organized learning as a dynamic process in which all participants were expected to learn and to teach. Effective assistance strategies were constantly remediated in order to sustain a dynamic learning environment in which all participants contributed.

A Note on the *Confianza* Fostered in MSLI

Special relationships develop in any intensive residential educational program. MSLI is no exception. However, MSLI is exceptional in a number of ways that differentiate the relationships fostered in it from other residential education programs. One of the most salient ways in which MSLI relationships are different is the commitment to a mutual cause of liberation and humanization by all participants (students, instructors, parents, and administrators). Historically, some groups have referred to this as participating and committing to *el movimiento*, broadly understood as the struggle to end the oppression of Latinos in the U.S. In MSLI, *el movimiento* is extended to include all oppression, and specifically to address the social problems associated with oppressive practices. Participants work hard to develop a shared sense of responsibility for this cause. What sets this apart from some other political agendas that educational outreach programs might espouse, is that this cause of liberation and humanization centers on and privileges the experiences and expertise of the migrant community in California. This action casts light and focus on an otherwise largely ignored community. Indeed, some scholars have gone so far as to suggest that mainstream dominant discourse renders migrants "invisible" (Harrison, 2004).

In order to sustain this mutual commitment to liberation and humanization, and in order to afford participants with transformative learning experiences, MSLI organizes learning and its larger social organization within a decolonizing pedagogy (Tejeda, Espinoza, & Gutiérrez, 2003). Decolonizing pedagogy takes into account the histories of people, institutional structures, and power relations among and between dominant and marginalized bodies, and focuses on social change. This framework affords instructional staff, residential staff, parents, and students to access a vulnerability, built upon trust that can weight the object of learning with greater social, personal, and political purpose than traditionally understood in schools. It also affords participants the freedom to live and work within new rules and to deploy a greater sense of self-determination in regulating activity. Borders, boundaries, expectations, and responsibilities are reimagined and made more capable of sustaining respect and support for each other's racialized, classed, sexualized, gendered, and abled bodies.

There is a special collective *confianza* that develops through MSLI that is necessary for the Institute to achieve its goals. This preexisting *confianza* most definitely contributed to the *confianza* experienced between Nené and me, as well as that expressed between Lorena and Juan. However, the *confianza* described in this study is also new and original. It is more than a regeneration of a previously developed *confianza*. I presented these specific relationships as examples of relationships of *confianza* within migrant students' college-going. They also serve to highlight some of the components/elements of the social ecologies that can promote and foster such *confianza*.

Confianza in Context of College-going

The transformative learning opportunities of *confianza* mediated the organics of college access for students. Two major psychosocial barriers to higher education opportunity faced by under-represented students are the perceptions of feasibility and the perceptions of what getting to college means in terms of one's place in life. According to sociocultural scholars focusing on the decolonization of students of Mexican descent (Tejeda, Espinoza, & Gutiérrez, 2003; Nunez & Jaramillo, 2005), a sense of entitlement to a better life, as commonly felt by middle-class whites, is a key transformation for students' success. This assertion is rooted in Freire's (1970; 2004) notions of humanization and dehumanization and the requisite literacy needed to interrogate one's own human condition. In this context, feasibility entails the sense-making work of recognizing one's unequal status and ways to take action toward alleviating that inequality. Making higher education opportunity feasible means that attending college is itself feasible, as well as the actions available for students to take in working toward that goal. This newly manifest entitlement to basic human rights (e.g., education), makes feasible the goals of higher education opportunity. In short, making higher education opportunity a feasible endeavor is complex work, and the *confianza* shared between these students and their adult counterparts contributes to sustaining that feasibility.

Furthermore, it has long been established that parents wield the most influence in students' college-going decisions (Cabrera & La Nasa, 2000; Hossler, Schmit, & Vesper, 1999). This well-established understanding of parental influence has, in some ways, held captive the methods for investigating students' college access and choice. Surveys generally do not seek to question students about relationships like those represented as *confianza*. My findings do not conflict with the longstanding assertion that parents are the most influential relationship in students' lives related to college choice and access. My findings do point to newer ways of understanding how students use different relationships in learning about college-going, and how the roles that various individuals play in different students' college-going activities are dynamic across subjects in the same population. Parental influence is paramount. Some parental influence is delimited to the aspiration and expectation of attending college and the realities of affordability. For all but one of the students in my study, a relationship of *confianza* was integral to students' navigating and negotiating their environment toward college-going.

As demonstrated by the examples of *confianza* presented in this chapter, reducing *confianza* simply to mean trust does not capture the complex relationship-building and procedural dynamism intended by this new conceptual tool in students' college-going. *Confianza* outlines the development of a new system of belief shared between students and a more experienced adult and/or peer. It was not that Lorena trusted Juan or that Nené trusted me, and therefore they believed us and followed our advice. Rather, Lorena and Nené believed in Juan and me and in the larger social project in which we engaged each other. Therefore, they invited us to participate in their college-going project with them, and we invited them to practice their college-going with us. College-going, in this sense, indicates the larger social practice of college access, as mediated recursively by these relationships of *confianza*, as well as the tool(s) of (im)migration and the rules that were discussed in earlier chapters. *Confianza* and (im)migration mediated students' college-going literacy development as tools. As mentioned previously, these, and other tools, were used within an activity that was regulated by explicit and implicit rules. *Confianza* and (im)migration were two tools that assisted the emergence of transformative learning opportunities.

Notes

[1] I specifically use the Spanish word, *confianza*, to express the concept under analysis in this chapter for two reasons. First, it was the word that came up empirically in the data to describe most of the specific relationships I report on in this chapter. Second, my analysis of the specific *confianza* at work in the college-going literacy development of these students is beyond any simple Spanish-English translation. That is to say, there is no word for the concept of *confianza* in the English language.

[2] The Bill and Melinda Gates Foundation "Gates Millennium Scholars" is a scholarship program that provides full tuition, room, board, fees, and additional living expenses for minority students to attend any university to which they get accepted. It also includes funding for graduate school. It is an extremely competitive scholarship program.

Chapter Seven
Mapping the Community's Division of Labor: Who Does What in Migrant Students' College-going?

The literature on college access points to many individuals who contribute to students' college-going. Findings from this study confirm much of the previous research; however, they also point to new insights about how these individuals participate in migrant students' college-going. They form a community that works toward students' coming to know educational opportunity. I broadly organize these members of the community into four ecocultural groups: family, schooling, higher education, and outreach. Some members of the community in each of these four ecocultural groups have been observed and documented previously in the literature. Interestingly, however, my study also uncovered novel members in the community and new insights into their ways of participating in migrant students' higher education learning activity. For example, older siblings with college education provided critical assistance to students, which transformed their sense-making practices around college access.

Each member of the four groups within the community contributed to students' learning in both similar and different ways. Within an activity theory framework, community members' assistance in the college-going literacy development of the students is understood as labor and discussed in terms of the division of labor among the community. I organize the labor, or work done in students' college-going activity, into two categories: mechanical and organic. *Mechanical* work includes the specific tasks that students must complete themselves as well as the concrete task-specific information that students need to actualize higher education opportunity. Juxtaposed to task-oriented work, *organic* work is based on developing students' understanding of college-going as a social practice.

I present a conceptual model of how migrant students' college-going is a social practice embedded within a community division of labor. I came to this model from my analysis of the ethnographic and ecocultural data gathered for this study. Members of the community were established by coding each person (e.g., mom) or position (e.g., high school principal) whom students referenced in our interactions around their college-going practices. I then sought to make sense of this list of individuals and groups by their ecocultural role in students' lives. Thus, I organized these individuals into groups based on the ecocultural contexts in which they assisted students toward college-going. I achieved this by coding each of the tasks that students named in their practices toward coming to know higher education opportunity in the data. After reviewing these coded data, I came to an understanding that there were both mechanical and organic work in the activity. This moment in analysis came about early in the analytical process, as Cristina, during one of our formal interviews commented,

"There are those things that you have to do, like the things that are required, and then there are the things that like, really help, like making college more real, like, my parents letting me come to UCLA."

I followed Cristina's intuitive analysis and found that it was productive to think about the work of college-going in mechanical and organic tasks. Mechanical labor are the required tasks that are bound by explicit rules, such as assisting students in completing appropriate coursework. Organic labor are the tasks equally integral to students' college-going, but tied up in a web of implicit rules. Organic labor moves the imagining of educational opportunity from an abstract to a concrete idea.

Tables 1–8 are visual representations of how the four ecocultural groups in the community related to the mechanical and organic labor involved in students' college-going literacy development. The four ecocultural groups in the community are each comprised of individual or group members. The two types of labor are constituted by 12 tasks that students must complete in working toward college-going.

This study was designed—and data were collected and analyzed from a person-centered framework (Hollan, 2001)—to focus on how students experience college-going.. The labor presented in this study examines how various members in the community of college-going activity support the tasks that students perform. Therefore, my analysis does not capture system- or institution-centered labor, for example, establishing and evaluating admission standards. Indeed, these tasks are taken up in ways "hidden" from students in their learning process. This is not to say that the actors involved in this hidden labor are not part of students' literacy development, but rather these actors themselves are often invisible.

Explanation of Labor Terms

Below, I present a bulleted list of simple definitions of the labor terms in tables 1–8. Each of these tasks will be elaborated on later as I work across the tables, describing how each ecocultural group assists both mechanically and organically in students' college-going.

Mechanical Labor Tasks

- *Coursework* entails both choosing and completing a college-preparatory curriculum.
- *Testing* refers to all standardized testing to which students are subject throughout their college-going preparation. Testing includes state-enforced standards-based testing, which all California public high school students must pass in order to graduate, as well as traditional college entrance exams such as the SAT. The work of testing includes becoming familiar with what tests to take, when to take them, how to prepare for them, and how to finance them.
- *Application* to colleges includes filling out the actual applications but also includes the preparatory work that students must complete in order to understand what an application requires of them. Many scholars have documented micro-pieces of this labor task as students' college choice process (McDonough, 1997; Hossler, Schmit, & Vesper, 1999; Cabrera & La Nasa, 2000). Application, in

my model, includes the deliberation over where to apply, including what kind of college, and is closely tied to the "financial aid" task and most of the organic labor tasks.
- *Financial aid* includes understanding what types of aid are available and how to apply and/or garner that aid.
- *Resource allocation* indicates dedicating the time in students' lives to pursue college-going tasks or practices, such as studying or becoming involved in school. Time allocation becomes a key concern when students have an increased expectation of responsibility to the family, such as childcare or generating income. Money for college-going activity is also included in this task, for example, paying for tutoring that might enable students to complete coursework with higher achievement markers (i.e., grades).

Organic Labor Tasks
- *Ideologies* refers to the guiding ideas that frame how college access is understood. One prevailing college access ideology in dominant discourse today is that of the meritocracy, wherein individuals who work hard (e.g., earn good grades) can achieve (e.g., get honors and graduate from high school) and will be rewarded accordingly (e.g., gain acceptance to an elite college).
- *Aspiration development* is a longstanding task that is well documented in college access literature (Hossler & Gallagher, 1986; Stage & Hossler, 1989; Freeman, 1997; McDonough, 1997; Smith & Fleming, 2006). It refers to the student's desire to accumulate education and pursue post-secondary schooling.
- *Politics* as a task includes contextualizing college-going in sociopolitical terms. For example, some educators worked to assist students in understanding California Proposition 209 and its impact on the admission of students of color to the University of California.
- *Making college real* means that college, as an idea, becomes something more concrete than a rhetorical goal that students keep in the back of their minds. It relies heavily on the imagination of student futures, and student skills at re-imagining that future.
- *The hidden curriculum* of college access is very similar to Margolis' (2001) concept of the hidden curriculum in higher education. The

task at hand for students in the hidden curriculum is dispelling rumors about how higher education opportunities happen and constructing new truths, based on insider information, such as building relationships with teachers so that they can write powerful letters of recommendation to scholarship and college admissions offices.

This conceptual model functions in malleable categories, although empirically derived. Much of the mechanical work has organic consequences, and vice-versa, but in general, the mechanics of college-going can be understood as being different from the organic work of imagining college, and then moving that imagined idea from an abstract to a concrete state of understanding. Furthermore, members of the community might be engaged in work that is both mechanical and organic at the same time. Rarely are members responsible for solely mechanical or solely organic labor.

The following sections present descriptive analyses of each interactive piece of the model, organized by the ecocultural groups in the community.

Family

Within the ecocultural group of families, students reported assistance from parents, siblings, extended family members, and people who had known them for a long period of time and were close to them; these people were treated "like family." By far the most popular members of family that students related their college-going to were their parents, followed closely by their siblings. This is congruent with existing literature that has well documented parents as the primary influence in a student's college choice (Hossler, Schmit, & Vesper, 1999), and emerging literature that explains how some first-generation college students use siblings in lieu of parental experience with the college choice process (Freeman, 2005). This was confirmed early on in my visits with students.

Lorena captured the influence of family in her college-going activity quite eloquently. She said:

> My family is so important to me. I rely on them, a lot. And they help me out a lot. I know they do everything they can, and if I really needed them to do

something, I know that we'd find a way to do it. But there are some things that they just can't do, you know. Like, we just don't have a lot of money, and stuff. So, I try really hard not to ask for too much. But I would say that everything I do, it's not just for me. It's also for my family.

In thinking about how the family's influence assists the student toward college-going, I connected parents to the tasks in which they assisted students. My response to Lorena, and other students who reported similar feelings about their family's influence would regularly ask what, specifically, their parents, brothers or sisters might do that helps them with their educational goals or makes college more understandable for them. Most often, students relied on what Lorena began to share in the last half of the quote above. These families were working-poor and working-class families. Parents' time was largely devoted to working long hours, hard days, and maintaining a safe, clean place for students to live. Parental experiences with college were limited, based mostly on their participation in migrant education programs that talked about college and how important it was for their children's future success. As such, students actively chose not to rely on parents for too many specific tasks.

As denoted in Table 2 below, the only mechanical task where parents provided assistance was in resource allocation and development. In order to work on other tasks, be they mechanical or organic, students must garner the resources necessary, most prominently, time and money. *Only* parents took responsibility for assisting their children. Often times, resources such as time and money, were allocated from parents to students with the explicit goal of college-going in mind. As Jesus explained:

> My parents don't let me work, because they want me to focus on school, and being like, more than just a student. Like, to get into a good college and get scholarships. Like, activities and stuff. Yeah, like, if I need something, they just give it to me, because if I had to work, then, like, I wouldn't be able to do sports, like, as good as I do, or like, I probably wouldn't be making the grades that I do. Right? School is my work. That's what my parents say.

Jesus benefited from parents who had graduated from a California State University and managed to secure jobs that allowed them to supplement their family income by purchasing a rental property in the neighboring town. Jesus' mother explained that the investment's primary role was to provide for her children's college from the earnings. Although Jesus' family might have been more economically stable than most in the group of students that worked with me in this study, their sentiments were nearly universal among the other families in the study. Whenever possible, students were encouraged by their families to focus on school and preparing for their next step (i.e., college).

Despite parental desires to provide the time and money needed for their children to pursue their education, half of the students in this study held full- or part-time jobs at some point during the academic year, even if only during vacation periods. All of these students used the money earned for either educational expenses (e.g., exam fees), to support their own personal expenses (e.g., cell phone, lunch money, or clothes), or to contribute to the general family income. When committing money to educational expenses or in support of their own personal expenses, the usual sentiment among the students was that they "did not want to burden my parents with that stuff." Thus, even when students' income was not directly dedicated to the family income, it was always an important piece to the family's economic practices. This background information on the context of students' work and parents' resource allocation more fully clarifies how crucial this task can be for students. The allocation of time or money to students' college-going can come at great cost to the family. It can mean more than just an additional expenditure, but a loss of potential income as well.

The four students with older siblings who had matriculated into a public university, found their assistance invaluable. Older siblings were able to decode much of the mechanical labor into tasks that seemed less daunting or formidable to students. From the students' perspectives, older siblings' first-hand experiences had the legitimacy and trust afforded to a family member, and an older sibling's investment in the students' lives was similar to that of their parents. These siblings had the content knowledge to help students with coursework requirements. They were familiar with the college application and financial aid processes and had even sifted through various options themselves. Having the first-hand experience of already applying for college acceptance and financial aid and having met other students at the university who had taken similar or different pathways to campus, older siblings were able to help students discern among the multitude of choices that students must make in the mechanics of college-going. A segment from Butterfly's college-going activity exemplifies this nicely.

Butterfly's older sister was commuting to a nearby California State University. Over a series of conversations, Butterfly explained how her sister was helpful in the development of goals and decision-making about how to complete mechanical tasks such as seeking financial aid. Butterfly said:

> Well, mostly I talk to my sister because my mom doesn't, she doesn't really know much about it, but she's always telling me, she's always just telling me, 'Don't worry about it.' Because she knows that there's money. She just doesn't know how I'm going to get it, but my sister—she's [Butterfly's mother] always telling my sister to talk to me about it, because my sister's been through all the process and stuff. And so my sister's the one that's pretty much telling me, 'Don't worry about it,' and then she's telling me 'There's this scholarship or this and that,' or, 'I got this. Maybe you should apply for this' or something. She's the one that tells me all this stuff.

Butterfly's older sister clearly steps in for what their mother cannot provide—assistance with understanding the financial aid process. In this case, Butterfly's mother is proactive in recommending that Butterfly seek out her older sister's expertise based on her recent experience of entering a California State University. However, as much help and assistance as older siblings might provide to their younger fellow first-generation siblings, there are limits to the resonance and the confidence of older siblings' expertise. When I asked Butterfly how she figured out what questions to ask or what kinds of information she needed, Butterfly responded:

> Well, I pretty much ask everything, because I'm not sure. So, I pretty much ask as many questions as I have, or that I need to cover what I need to know, because … I mean, my sister's gone to college, but she didn't really have that much … I don't know. She had other people helping her too, because she was the first one, so she's not like … and she barely did it like last year, so she's not like an expert on that. She just tells me to go and ask my teachers or stuff because … yeah.

Seeking out information about various college-going tasks can be extremely daunting to first-generation students. Relying on older siblings helps, clearly, but it is not a panacea, as Butterfly's older sister exemplifies by redirecting Butterfly to the institutional actors that have yet to take responsibility for assisting Butterfly in these tasks. Still, the assistance of older siblings who are attending or have attended college contributes with transformative potential in the college-going practices of students. Butterfly recognized how important her sister's assistance was. When asked what could make her college-going easier, Butterfly replied:

> If I could have had, like, more influences and stuff, because I know my sister, she's a really good influence because she's already in college and everything. But, I see my brother, and my brother sometimes ... well, he didn't graduate from high school. Because he didn't want to. And so, if I could have had him, like he could have helped her [Butterfly's sister] even more, and then she could have helped me even more.

Butterfly expertly recognizes that the ecocultural group of the family has tremendous potential to provide assistance in the tasks of college-going. She can look backward and forward in time, acknowledging how her older siblings experienced different assistance that contributed to a different outcome than is planned for her.

When neither parents nor older siblings were available for assistance in the tasks at hand for students' college-going, occasionally an extended family member, or a close family friend who was treated "like family" might take responsibility for assisting students in figuring out what it takes to apply to college. These interventions were rare for the participants in this study. When they did occur, they were always contingent on the availability, accessibility, and interest of the extended or outside family member, and the responsibility taken on by the member was figured as primarily supportive assistance, that is, reinforcing work that students had already done. As Renaldo put it, "yeah, like everyone wants me to go to college. They're like, supportive and helping, like, asking me things like, 'Did you remember to do that application?' or like, 'Did you get to visit these colleges when you went on this [outreach] program?' and it's cool."

An exception to this was Alex, whose uncle figured prominently in his life. As mentioned in the section introducing *estudiantes migrantes*, Alex considers his uncle to have raised him. As such, I have treated his uncle as a parent in my analysis.

Table 1, below, represents the various members of the community in the family ecocultural group and the mechanical labor for which they might take responsibility.

Table 1: Family Division of *Mechanical* Labor

	Coursework	Testing	Applications	Financial Aid	Resources
Parent(s)					X
Older Sibling(s)	X		X	X	
Younger Sibling(s)	X				
Extended Family			X		
Like Family			X		

Siblings figure most prominently in the family division of mechanical labor. Similarly, where and when parental experiences restrict them from assisting students in some of the organic work of college-going, siblings take responsibility for both initiating and reinforcing assistance. This can be seen in Table 2, which represents the organic labor assistance offered by members of the family ecocultural group. When older siblings had experience in college, they could significantly assist students move college from an abstract to a real, concrete idea, often in conjunction with dispelling the hidden curriculum of college access. By this, I mean that older siblings informed students about things they could do to give themselves an edge in the admission process, for example, developing relationships with teachers who might then write letters of recommendation for scholarships. Students often spoke of how visiting an older brother or sister at college helped them "really see what college is like." They also benefited from older siblings' mis-steps. Stories from an older brother or sister about things *not* to do equally contributed to how students made sense of their own college-going.

As Yaneth explained:

> Well, first of all, I learned about college from my older brothers and sisters, since I'm the third child. ... how to get into college, the things you need to do, all the testing you take, and they kind of taught me what it was all about. You know, 'It's not going to be easy.' They prepared me for that, and they prepared me so I can get into college, into the university, what you had to get done. ... Since I was a freshman, they've been telling me about it. They've been telling me you have to get good grades, and you have to study now and just start getting involved in school and stuff, extracurricular activities always count for a university. ... My older sister, she didn't have nobody to tell her. You know, we're first generation to go to college, and my parents never went, they never went to college, so it was kind of hard for her. So after her going through that, she thought it would be helpful for her to help me. ... Our family is very close, and it's a good relationship. We're very open and we trust each other, and we help each other out whenever we can.

While hanging out together, Yaneth pointed out to me that it was in similar situations that her older siblings would pass on valuable information to her. Just by spending time together, they casually, but effectively shared their expertise in taking advanced placement courses, taking advanced placement exams for college credit, and participating in extracurricular activities that were meaningful for gaining competitive college admission. For Yaneth, once her sister was in college, talking about going to college became a natural thing. Her ideas about how to get there were transformed into actionable plans, co-mapped out with her older sister and brother. Keenly aware that their parents' assistance was delimited by their own experiences, Yaneth's family divided the labor differently than some dominant cultural communities might, drawing on the strength of their already-present practices, i.e., sustaining a close-knit and interreliant family.

Yaneth represents the current crown jewel of the family's project of educating all their children. Her older sister attended a nearby California State University. Her brother currently attends a University of California campus. Over the course of this study, Yaneth herself was named a Gates Millennium Scholar and began attending one of the most competitive of the University of California campuses. Yaneth shared the news of her award with me during a telephone conversation when we were planning our next visit together. Yaneth humbly said something to the effect that her sister, her brother, and she won the Gates Millennium Scholarship; she just happened to be the recipient.

Butterfly's experiences add to an understanding of how older siblings supplemented the aspiration development assistance provided by parents and contributed to a transformation of college-going. Butterfly shared:

> With my sister, it's always about what I have to do ... she's always stressing the fact that I have to go to college and this and that. It's not pressure, but it's like important kind of. She's going to Cal State right now, but she told me that she wants me to go to like a more prestigious school or whatever. Because she told that she didn't have the chance because she had to start working ever since she was little to help around because my parents are divorced, and she told me, 'I want you to ... just don't worry about anything right now, and I want you to go to a better college.'

The transformation came from the new standard of what the object of college-going should be. For Butterfly, aiming for "a better college" translated into figuring out what "a better college" might be, attending more closely to her preparation.

Finally, Nené's brother, living away from home at a nearby California State University campus, helped bridge the idea of college into a palpable reality and a refurbished goal toward learning. Nené related many stories to me of visiting his older brother. For example:

> Nené and I were searching for something to do. The Starbucks? The bowling alley? The hotel's Internet? We'd each eaten just a couple of hours before, so food was not really on the top of our "to do" lists. We just kept driving around until suddenly we realized, Nené was giving me a tour of his hometown.
>
> "Yeah, man. This is my town, I guess." Nené said with a casual pride that allowed for either a disappointed or a cool interpretation.

"Well, show me your spots, man," I replied with a cool enthusiasm.

We continued to drive around. I learned about the best Chinese food restaurant. We found the best burger in town. We passed by the best place for chillin' on the sidewalk. We discovered the best place to meet up with anybody who was out that night—Jack in the Box.

"But I don't hang out there anymore, man." Nené informed me, foreshadowing a story I wanted to follow up on.

"Who's there?" I entered the story.

"It's like, that's where I used to go all the time, you know. And like, it was cool when my brother was around, because, like, we'd look out for each other and stuff. But, now he's gone, and like, it's just kind of lame."

"What makes it lame, just 'cause he ain't there anymore?"

Nené explained. "Nah, it's not just that, but like, I gotta work hard to keep myself in line, you know. Nobody else is gonna do it. And those guys there, like, that's all they do. 'Let's hang out at Jack in the Box, yo!' And then they talk about being drunk or trying to be drunk. I just can't be like that anymore."

I was impressed with his self-awareness. When I was in high school, taking classes seriously was important, but if I had been welcomed where the cool kids hung out, I would have been there in a second. Homework could've waited.

"The homework always waits with them. It waits so long it never happens." Nené seemed to have read my mind.

"Well, like, when did this all happen, dude? Like, when did you grow up so cool?" I asked, trying to figure out how a 17-year old boy fights off the pressures of being down with his peers while remaining cool with his friends.

"Like, when my brother left, like, he had me visit him. Like, I love going up there, man. He like, parties all the time, but it's like, they also take shit seriously. Like, they all get their work done. Then they party. And it's a whole lot more fun than hiding out in the parking lot at Jack in the Box. It's like, in order to celebrate something, rather than making something to celebrate. Like, sometimes they even talk about school like's it an okay thing to be proud of, you know?"

"So, you're ignoring the kids who get in trouble here so that you can party there?" I asked with a bit of incredulity.

"No, man!" Nené let out a bit of a laugh. "It's like, that's a real place, you know? And like, when I get there—to UCLA—like, I'll be doing something important, and then I can party because I'll be taking care of stuff. Like, the partying's not the point. The point was that I've seen it now, like, kinda like when we were at UCLA [for MSLI 2005] but even more real. That's why I don't just sit around doing nothing with those other kids now."

The context provided by this vignette, excerpted from one of my field notes written while visiting Nené, importantly illustrates the relationship that siblings can play in first-generation, migrant students' lives. By accounting for the development of their relationship to each other and to other peers in their hometown, Nené's brother contributed his assistance to the task of making college more real, as shown by Nené's changed behavior toward his immediate environment, including "those other kids."

As demonstrated by Yaneth, Butterfly, and Nené, older siblings with college experience can take responsibility for assisting in both mechanical and organic tasks. Siblings who had not attended college also assumed responsibility for some organic work. Like other siblings who had attended college, those who had not attended drew on their own life experiences to foster students' aspirations toward college-going. The family investment in individual students' college-going included this dimension of mutually fostering student ambitions to go to college. Lorena explained this well. She said, "My brothers, they like tell me stuff, like, 'Don't act like we did. Don't be like we were in high school. You have a chance.' It means a lot, but it's a lot of pressure, too."

Generally, younger siblings were partly responsible for reinforcing students' aspirations, but younger siblings occasionally played a role in supporting students' coursework. For example, Nené informed me that his younger brother was "wicked smart" and often helped him with his essays for English classes. Younger siblings often served as part of the students' family obligations. It became an obligation to set a good example, and make the pathway easier for those who came after them. This parallels the roles of older siblings in families where older siblings had already attended college.

Aspiration development, as noted in Table 2, is the most popular task that members of the community took responsibility for assisting students to perform. In fact, all members of the family ecocultural group were involved in fostering students' aspiration development. Table 2 represents the various members of the community in the family ecocultural group and the organic labor for which they might take responsibility.

Table 2: Family Division of *Organic* Labor

	Ideologies	Aspiration Development	Politics	"Real"	Hidden Curriculum
Parent(s)		X			
Older Sibling(s)		X		X	X
Younger Sibling(s)		X			
Extended Family		X		X	
Like Family		X		X	X

As shown in Table 2, the family ecocultural group ignores students' work at understanding the ideologies and politics of college access. Indeed, not a single student related the various ways of thinking about college access or the potential political dimensions to college-going to practices they engaged in with family members. Also noteworthy is that only older siblings, extended family, and close family friends who were "like family" who had also gone to college took responsibility for assisting students' in making college more real and disclosing the hidden curriculum. This finding underscores the power of prior college experience in assisting students during college-going literacy development. However, this power should not be overestimated, as students spoke of the extended family and people who were "like family" in a fairly passing manner, indicating a passivity in their assistance.

Antonio once explained how his cousin's assistance was "nice, but not totally helpful." He expanded:

> Yeah, like, my cousin, she went to State a couple of years ago, but we're not like, close or anything, but she shared some stuff with me about how some majors are easier to get into than others. But then I found out from a counselor that that's not true everywhere, so I was like, well, big deal.

In this example, Antonio's cousin shares some of the insider information (i.e., the hidden curriculum) she had discovered through her own college choice process, but it turned out that Antonio had other resources with more accurate information. Still, Antonio maintained that his cousin's efforts were supportive in his coming to understand that there was more than perhaps met his eye in college admissions.

Schooling

The existing literature discusses school personnel and pupils separately. I have categorized them together because they both represent and function from the same ecocultural context—high school. This context is significantly different in its constitution, and plays a significantly different functional role in students' lives than the ecocultural context of family. When thinking of school as an ecocultural context, it is helpful to think of it in terms of schooling, that is, within the social institution of compulsory education in the United States. Conceptually organizing the community in this way also allows for the possibility of creating and fostering pedagogy to work toward the object of higher education in and across each of these contexts. Therefore, since students reported the assistance provided by peers and school personnel primarily in the same context, I choose to discuss peers and friends within the schooling ecocultural group. This group also includes teachers, administrators, and counselors. Schooling was largely inactive in students' college-going activity, yet ever-present. School personnel and pupils often took primary responsibility for the mechanical work of completing coursework and secondary or supporting roles in organic work such as developing aspirations.

Table 3 represents the members of the schooling ecocultural group that took responsibility for assisting students in mechanical tasks.

Table 3: Schooling Division of *Mechanical* Labor

	Course-work	Testing	Applications	Financial Aid	Resources
Teacher(s)	X	X			
Admin.		X			
Counselor(s)			X		
Pupils/Peers	X	X	X		

Coursework and testing were both supported by teachers and peers, with high school administrators playing a minor role in the support of standardized testing. Structurally, both teachers and administrators are expected to assist students in these tasks. It is in their job descriptions to do so. Much of the task of "coursework" is the learning that takes place in the classroom. That is, students must master the content of their coursework and perform well in order to be college eligible. Interestingly though, students did not speak of their teachers as mediators toward college-going. Rather, it was the assistance they sought, provided, or mutually enabled with their peers that had a college-going emphasis to it.

As Lorena said, "There just aren't that many teachers that really help me. My friends, or like, just other people in classes are like, more like who I go to for help." This was a common response to describe how teachers help students in their coursework.

The assistance provided through peer support for coursework was directed toward college-going. Coursework was given purpose in college-going through its mediation in peer study groups. All but two students in this study talked about forming groups with their peers in order to master the material in their courses and figure out which courses to take.[1]

Butterfly informed me, "Like, when I can, I study with other kids in class. Not with the teachers. ... And yeah, like, us Mexicans try to tell each other which classes to take, especially if we know that they want to go to college. Then it's like, really important."

Alex emphasized how significant the assistance he received from his friends was to his college-going, "There's this group of us, and we all said we were going to go to college. This was like, freshman year or something. And all of us are going. Like, without their help, I don't know ... I'd still be going, but probably just to Mt. CC [a local community college], you know?" It was in these peer groups that students found, and at times provided for others, the assistance they needed to complete coursework toward the goal of college access.

As powerful as peer assistance could be for students, the inverse was also true. Peers had equal opportunity to work against college-going, especially when the assistance they took responsibility for led students to do worse in school. As Nené explained to me about a group he would come to call "those other kids," it was as if they were helping him "not be anybody, not get into college."

Returning to the vignette presented about Nené's brother's assistance in making college more real, "those other kids" Nené often referred to were the group of friends who hung out at Jack in the Box, "getting drunk so that they could talk about getting drunk." To Nené, breaking out of that group was transformational, because while a part of them, he was made to feel "like we were brothers, or some crap like that. But I have a real brother, and like, when I was almost failing, like scared of flunking out even, like, they weren't there for me." Indeed, Nené had faltered from his goal during his junior year, which he largely attributed to how "those other kids" represented the way high school was supposed to be. It is important to acknowledge that assistance in college-going tasks does not always lead toward college-going literacy. Nené's friendships with "those other kids" were based on assumptions that they each had each other's best interests in mind. At the time of their hanging out together, it made perfect sense that "kicking it at Jack" was meaningful work for teenage boys.

When teachers, administrators, or counselors did take responsibility for mechanical tasks, students received such assistance in generally banal ways. Schooling seemed to matter less in the effort of getting to understand and achieve higher education opportunities. If a teacher or counselor had walked through college applications with students, the general response was similar to what Eduardo said,

"Like, big deal. That doesn't teach me anything more than like, filling in my name and stuff. And they still didn't help me figure out if I took the right classes or not."

However, when exceptions happened, they illustrated how much potential the schooling ecocultural group has in transforming students' literacy development. As illustrated by Antonio's story of becoming a college-bound student, narrated below, when teachers took responsibility for assisting students in college-going tasks, transformation became a possibility.

Antonio and I grabbed a quick bite at the cafeteria on City College's campus. He was taking a political science course to get a greater head start on his general education requirements at his future institution, Fresno State University. Antonio began to reminisce about his high school experience. He was one of the most active students in his high school, participating in every academic activity available from academic decathlon to student government and mock trial. I, myself had participated in similar activities in high school, and I remembered that for me, they were safe havens from the overtly favored athletic activities at my middle-class, suburban high school. I inquired if he had always been so involved in school.

When Antonio began high school, he had only been in California for a few months. He had migrated north from a major city in Mexico in an effort to escape some of the treacheries he had experienced as one of the elite members of society there. Antonio learned English quickly, immersing himself in what he called "the American culture," which, he said was only different in two ways: people spoke English, and school really mattered. While Antonio lived in Mexico, he rarely focused on schooling. He told me stories of being dropped off at the front of his elite private school only to walk around the main building, meet his friends, and spend the day fooling around throughout the city. Antonio said that in the U.S., fitting in was not really hard for him.

"As long as you go around trying to buy things and pretending to behave, you make friends pretty easily." Antonio said. For him, it seemed a natural transition to appropriate middle-class teenage behaviors, despite the fact that he now lived with his working-class uncles and their families in their shared single-family home.

"But the difference was when it came to school. Like, it didn't really matter in Mexico, because everyone had money, and it didn't really matter what you did in school, because they would just pass you on anyway."

Antonio's older sister had migrated with him, and the Migrant Education Program counselor for their region had recruited her into some of the MEP services provided at their school. Antonio followed. As Antonio's English language skills accelerated, he was identified to take a test for a special academic program by one of his older sister's teachers. His sister had been a high achiever in the English Language Development courses, and this particular teacher had also volunteered to work with the MEP. She took it upon herself to encourage Antonio and his sister to apply for this special academic program.

Antonio said:

> When she found out that I was her brother, she asked me, 'So, are you as bright as your sister is?' And I said, 'I dunno.' 'Cause I always thought that my sister was really smart. She did good in school in Mexico. But then the test came back, and I scored higher than her, so like, then I was like, 'Hey, I can be a smart kid, too.'

Following the testing, his sister's teacher took it upon herself to move him out of the ELD program and into the advanced placement track.

Antonio said, "Like, suddenly, school was important, and I started to hear about colleges, and it was like, everyone was trying to go to someplace." To keep fitting in, Antonio figured out that getting involved in activities like academic decathlon not only helped him sustain friendships, but worked toward greater goals in his broader life. "Believe it or not, I was kinda shy at first."

I gawked at this comment, as Antonio was one of the most outspoken participants in MSLI as well as in this study. He and I shared long conversations about politics and school policies. He was never short on something to say, and he was always willing to volunteer for activities.

Mapping the Community's Division of Labor

Antonio replied to my facial gesturing, "Seriously, that's why I joined decathlon. I wanted to get better at English and more comfortable debating things. And then I learned that it was good for getting into colleges, and I just kept trying to do more."

Had Antonio not been identified early in his high school career as one of the students the school could prepare for college, his eagerness to contribute might never have emerged. His sister's teacher, who had volunteered with the MEP, took the responsibility of assisting Antonio in completing his coursework. She remained interested in Antonio throughout high school, and Antonio continued to participate in academic programs that she organized (e.g., mock trial).

However, similar to the ways in which peers did not always work to extend students' literacy practices, teachers' participation could be potentially damaging.

From field notes from a visit to the Imperial Valley:

> Lorena, Jullian and I were hanging out in the front room by the fan, trying to stay somewhat cool in the intense heat of the Imperial Valley's onset of summer. They were telling me how their junior years were ending up, and then Jesus seemed to raise the temperature a bit.
>
> "Oh! And this one teacher, Mrs. Sanchez!" Jesus exclaimed. "You know her." He said to Lorena.
>
> "Oh, yeah. Ooh. She is not a good teacher." Lorena foreshadowed the gist of the pending story.
>
> "No. Like, she's just not nice, and then, like, if things aren't exactly perfect, exactly as she wants it, she marks you way down. She tells you, like, 'What's wrong with you? I told you what to do, and you still couldn't do it right.'" Jesus explained.
>
> I learned that even when explicitly asked about college applications or planning, this particular teacher seemed to try and steer students in another direction.
>
> Jesus said, "It's not like she says that we shouldn't go or nothin'. She just like, makes you feel like you can't do the work, so why should you even try."
>
> I was appalled, but not shocked to hear this. It reminded me of conversations with other participants. As I was asking

for more details, Jesus' mom came home. She had bought pizza for all of us to share as we hung out.

"Mom. Tell Ryan about Mrs. Sanchez." Jesus said.

"Oh. That woman should not be teaching. She won't teach my kids again." Jesus' mom began. "She wasn't going to let him pass the class because he put numbers on his flashcards. Silly numbers just to keep them in order. And that's an A-G class. A college class. I had to march down there and tell them that he will be getting the grade he deserved in that class, and it will be whatever he would get based on those flashcards, despite the silly numbers. I mean, it's like she had no idea what her stupid rule would do to kids."

"Yeah, and then she was all weird to me, mom." Jesus reminded her.

With a bit of a laugh, Jesus' mom said, "Yeah. She was, wasn't she. She made you, like, student of the month the next month too, didn't she."

Lorena laughed, "You probably scared her."

"I hope so. That was just the beginning of it, too." Jesus' mom said.

Later on, I learned that Jesus' parents were extremely vocal in the local schools. They attended almost every open district meeting and requested meetings with their children's teachers. Sadly, the family's plans to avoid Mrs. Sanchez as a repeat teacher seemed to be up for a battle. She was the only teacher available for an advanced placement course that Jesus planned to take his senior year.

"Maybe I could take it at community college." Jesus suggested.

Lorena summed up the potential negative assistance that teachers like Mrs. Sanchez could put forth when she said, "The sad thing is, like, not everyone has a mom like yours, Jesus. Like, my mom wouldn't do that, because, like she speaks Spanish. She'd be mad, but then I'd have to go and fight. And like, I might, but how many of the kids at school probably just deal with it and then don't go anywhere."

"A lot" was the consensus around the pizza.

Unfortunately, stories like Jesus' were not isolated to him. Many of the participants talked about teachers who seemed to take an interest in subverting their plans for college. Most of them also commented on being lucky that they had sources to defend them against the negative assistance. Sometimes these defenses were more transformative assistance providers, like Antonio's teacher. Other times, students reported that their experiences in MSLI had taught them what they were entitled to as Chicanos, and they refused to accept anything less. Whatever the defense was, it was usually accompanied by a sentiment similar to Lorena's—that they knew some students were falling prey to the subversion of school personnel like Mrs. Sanchez.

Both Antonio's teacher and Mrs. Sanchez in the Imperial Valley were exceptions. By and large, teachers, and school personnel in general were not popularly discussed by students. As members of the community, their assistance was not salient to students' college-going practices. However, the illustrations provided by Antonio, Jesus, his mom, and Lorena show that there is great potential for teachers to contribute to transformative learning around college-going.

The assistance provided in the schooling ecocultural group, whether potentially transformative or potentially damaging, contributed to students organic as well as their mechanical tasks. Table 4 represents the organic labor for which schooling personnel and pupils took responsibility.

Table 4: Schooling Division of *Organic* Labor

	Ideologies	Aspiration Development	Politics	"Real"	Hidden Curriculum
Teacher(s)	X	X			
Admin.		X			
Counselor(s)	X	X			
Pupils/Peers	X	X			

Again, aspiration development was the task that was most prevalent in the ecocultural group's assistance. However, with the notable exceptions of teachers such as those Antonio and Jesus experienced, the assistance that schooling personnel took responsibility for was generally banal. At most, it served to support the development of aspirations that families had previously and continuously fostered. Distinct from the family's ecocultural group, schooling members contributed to students' understanding of ideologies that guided their conceptions of college-going. They did this by supporting the propaganda of specific ideological assumptions. As the ideological work that schooling members took responsibility for was more passive in nature, and the data collected does not substantively afford description for interpretation, I return to a more detailed discussion of ideological work in the section on the outreach ecocultural group, noting how/when data suggested schooling members' participation.

Higher Education

Although far less prevalent in students' lives than family and schooling ecocultural group members, the personnel from higher education institutions can play pivotal roles in students' college-going activity. The most obvious personnel associated directly with students' college-going literacy development include admission officers, financial aid officers, and college or university faculty. Interestingly, these members of the community were far less often present in students' lives, yet if they were, the work done by them was oftentimes transformative in students' learning, especially faculty.

Table 5 depicts the mechanical assistance in which higher education personnel provided assistance.

Table 5: Higher Education Division of *Mechanical* Labor

	Course-work	Testing	Applications	Financial Aid	Resources
Faculty			X		
Admissions Officer(s)			X	X	
Financial Aid Admin.				X	

When higher education personnel—whether faculty, admission officers, or financial aid administrators—took responsibility for assisting students with mechanical tasks, students did not necessarily complete the tasks more fully or responsively. Usually, students commented similarly to Yaneth, that their interactions with admission officers and financial aid administrators were "Nice for practicing, but not really important."

Students like Jesus and Lorena noted when certain colleges and universities were not present at events that elicited participation from higher education institutions. They each reported, as did other students, "Even at college fairs, it's like, the big schools don't really come. We didn't see anybody from Berkeley or Stanford." Part of the flagship UC campuses' lack of presence might be an artifact of physical geography, as the UC campuses are, in part, designed to serve specific regions of the state. Nonetheless, their absence was noted. Even when schools were present, the effect of visits and college fairs seemed to be inconsequential for students.

As Eduardo noted:

> Yeah, they came and talked about the requirements and stuff, and we even filled out a practice application, but like, it's all online now, and it's still confusing. Plus, like, they all sort of said the same thing, so I don't really know what the difference is besides UC being better than Cal State, you know?

Embedded within Eduardo's insight is a potential misnomer. Although the UC system is at the top of the California public higher education system's hierarchy, the assistance provided to students in figuring out what schools to apply to, how, and how to finance their education seemed to neglect that students had a choice and the opportunity to figure out their own personal fit with different institutions. Perhaps a California State University campus might better serve the needs of some students than UCLA or Berkeley. These types of deliberations were left out of the assistance that higher education personnel provided students in their college choice processes.

As indicated by Jesus and Lorena's comment about Stanford's absence, the other participants in this study had been neglected by assistance from private colleges and universities in the mechanics of college-going. As Alex put it, "I don't know much about private schools, except that they're expensive. Which ones are good? And I've heard that some of them will actually cost less, 'cause they have more money to give away? But, like, how do I know?" Without the culturally reproduced knowledge that college-educated families can instill in their children, the lesser-known schools in the public domain, such as elite private liberal arts colleges, remain elusive and confusing to first-generation college students.

As an alumnus from Occidental College, a top-tier national liberal arts college located in northeast Los Angeles, I often took it upon myself to explain what a liberal arts college education can be like. I emphasized the potential funding possibilities that some private institutions could provide. My long-winded exhortations on the benefits of an Occidental (or other comparable institutions) education were almost always met with uncertainty.

"Really? But is it a good school?" was a common reply. To me, this response suggested a distrust of the unfamiliar. I found myself qualifying the qualifications of my alma mater. Students seemed unimpressed with the number of Rhodes Scholars that emerged from Occidental College in the past ten years, or the 90% rate of top-choice graduate school acceptance the alumni reported. These hallmarks of liberal arts educations held little caché in students' lives. Furthermore, my descriptions of the close-knit community and intimacy with faculty seemed to echo some of their least favorite aspects of high school, especially for those students seeking to move to more metropolitan areas during college.

There was a fair amount of variation in the schools that made assistance available to students. This generally followed a geographic pattern, where students closest to UC campuses were most familiar with UC personnel, and students in areas predominantly served by California State Universities were most familiar with that system. The two sophomore-year participants, both of whom happened to be undocumented, had experienced the least assistance from higher education personnel. In general, the institutionalized practices of college fairs and high school visits from admission officers or financial aid administrators provided nearly inconsequential assistance to the students.

Mapping the Community's Division of Labor 169

As Renaldo put it, "They all seem to be the same after a while. But I still go, because it's fun to go on the trips when they [school or outreach programs] take us places."

The exception in higher education assistance came in the organic labor tasks that brought students closer to knowing college access. Table 6 presents the division of organic labor within the higher education ecocultural group.

Table 6: Higher Education Division of *Organic* Labor

	Ideologies	Aspiration Development	Politics	"Real"	Hidden Curriculum
Faculty	X	X	X	X	X
Admissions Officer(s)		X			
Financial Aid Admin.					

Although there were not many faculty members who participated in the students' college-going tasks, when faculty did take responsibility for assisting students, it was tremendously powerful. As seen in Table 6 above, faculty had the capacity to assist students with all of the organic tasks that helped constitute their college-going literacy development. The participants in this study all had exposure to faculty in the 2005 MSLI. These were the primary faculty identified by students as playing a part in their college-going. Cristina spoke eloquently about how one faculty member, *Profé*, formerly affiliated with MSLI, assisted in transforming her literacy development. Over the course of our conversations, Cristina recounted:

> Like, Profé made us feel like we're a part of something. Like something larger than ourselves, part of a movement. ... And people told him, 'Your GPA is not that good. Don't go to college,' and he applied, and he's been to Harvard, he's been to SC and so it's just—that makes it [college] tangible to me. Like, he's like a walking example of where I can go and he's talked to me about UCSB, that it has some Chicano Studies. ... And that's what I think I'm gonna do. Like, he taught us that it's not just about if you get good grades, you get to go to college. There's like, capitalism. ... We [her family]

used to drive by here, by UCLA, like, I don't know, on the way to a swap meet or something, and I used to just think, that's so rich. It's like just for the rich. But, like, not anymore. Like, we can help each other. We can help ourselves. ... Just the idea that you don't just come here to learn, to get, to make money. You come here to learn things that aren't exposed to you, aren't exposed to you in school: why we are how we are, why we are the way we are, who we're meant to be. I know this isn't necessarily what college is about, but I would much rather learn about that than get my degree in like, business, to keep the cycle going of winning, losing, and all that stuff. So I think these courses and people like him prevent new minds like myself from falling into that capitalistic, just, mess. ... Yes. I'm going to be Dr. Cristina Lopez. Profesora Lopez.

Cristina connected higher education opportunity to high school inequities and greater inequities across society and across social contexts. Profé's influence over her understanding of competing ideologies around college access—such as the meritocratic ideal of getting good grades followed by college acceptance versus something more socially complex tied to economic practices embedded in capitalism—also served to make college more real for Cristina. As an example of someone who shares her struggle in "a movement," Profé re-presented college as a possibility for Cristina in her life. Indulging in "learning" with Profé's assistance assisted her in re-imagining what UCLA was, and at the same time, exposed part of the hidden curriculum of college access—namely, how certain degrees might actually help inscribe "that capitalistic mess," whereas other goals might nourish her desire to be a part of "something larger than ourselves."

Cristina returned to her school and began making demands for her coursework to be college-prep, her voice to be heard, and her goals to be taken seriously. She was met with some strong resistance. Cristina said, "I'm like, the trouble student, now at my school. But I don't even care. Like, they can tell me that I'm 'acting Mexican.' It's because I am, and if they weren't so Americanized ... like, I just won't put up with it anymore. It's too important, now. College is too important."

Profé's assistance in the organic work of college-going contributed to new possibilities for Cristina. With his assistance, she could complete more of the tasks more fully. The exceptional responsibility taken by faculty, such as Profé, clearly has the potential to make a huge impact on students' college-going. Higher education faculty have insider knowledge about the organic elements of college, and if they happen to be from backgrounds similar to those of the students who face marginalization, such as migrant students, they might also carry insider knowledge about how college-going can really happen for them. Also, the assumed legitimacy and cultural deference afforded to professors, especially professors with similar or empathetic backgrounds, cannot be understated as playing a major force in the nuance of their assistance.

Overall, higher education was a vastly vapid ecocultural group, yet students knew what the group was. Exceptional individuals who took responsibility outside of their institutionalized roles and practices contributed to substantial opportunities for students' literacy development. Generally, despite the fact that each of these students had spent time on college campuses in at least one outreach program (MSLI), and most had spent time on other campuses with other programs, the higher education ecocultural group remained elusive. The assistance provided by the higher education ecocultural group was less consequential than either the family or schooling groups. Yet, it appeared that the higher education group might have some of the strongest potential to assist students in the organic tasks of college-going.

Outreach

Outreach is an important sector of college access that has been under-researched and under theorized (Tierney, Corwin, & Colyar, 2004). Each of the participants in this study participated in outreach programs. As a baseline, all of them participated in the Migrant Student Leadership Institute, and this, in many ways, connects these students to each other, to me, and to some specific dimensions of common literacy practices. Nine of the 12 students in this study were also involved in other outreach programs funded by the California Migrant Education Program. Finally, nine of the 12 students in this study were also involved in some other forms of outreach programs that were not connected to Migrant Education Programs. Altogether, these outreach programs served crucial purposes in students' coming to know higher education opportunity. Outreach programs were seen as a regular event in students' lives—an additional dimension to their college-going community.

The members of the outreach ecocultural group are more disparate from each other than members of the other ecocultural groups. The three members that constitute outreach are only similar to each other in that they function outside of formal educational institutions, and they are not part of the social institution of the family. They are tied directly to educational institutions, but operate in supplemental, complementary, or subsidized relationship to schooling or higher education. Students participating in this study identified three types of outreach programs: the 2005 UCLA Statewide Migrant Student Leadership Institute, other Migrant Education Program initiatives, and a loosely grouped set of other outreach programs, such as Federal TRIO programs or GEAR UP. I have organized them in my conceptual model as three separate members, because students spoke very specifically about MSLI and more generally about other outreach programs. Migrant Education Programs were delineated from other supplemental educational programs by students, in part because of their specific, identity-based organization. Interestingly, students did not mention any California State sponsored programs, such as the UC Early Academic Outreach Programs, but rather spoke more generally of "this other program that I participated in."

Students spoke most articulately and most passionately about MSLI. This was unsurprising to me. MSLI is where my relationship to students began. It was a transformative experience for everyone involved. The immediate emotional impact was well documented in students' work during the Institute, and in the countless e-mails and MySpace messages that followed the closing of the Institute. The intellectual impact of MSLI was also documented in students' academic work from the Institute, as well as by follow-up research led by the Institute director.[2] Indeed, formal student evaluations of the program and my own ethnographic visits with students confirmed that, in students' own words, "MSLI was a life-changing experience," and it was "one of the most amazing experiences of my life." It was no surprise, then, that students shared openly, passionately, and extensively about how MSLI carried on in their lives after they left UCLA's campus in July 2005.

Table 7 presents the division of mechanical labor for which outreach, as an ecocultural group, took responsibility.

Table 7: Outreach Division of *Mechanical* Labor

	Course-work	Testing	Applications	Financial Aid	Resources
MSLI	X	X	X	X	
Migrant Education Program	X	X	X	X	
Other Outreach Programs	X		X		

Outreach in general took responsibility for assisting students in the greatest number of tasks. As a group, the constellation of outreach programs that students discussed appeared to serve as a catch-all group for as many college-going tasks as possible. Students overwhelmingly identified outreach programs as places where they learned the most about financial aid, preparing for and performing well on college entrance exams, figuring out what was required for admission and the differences between institutions (applications). Even students with older siblings who had attended college remarked that outreach programs made a difference in their senses of security around how they completed college-going tasks. For the undocumented students in this study, outreach programs were at times, their primary source of assistance for tasks that family members could not directly assist and schooling and higher education members ignored.

Eduardo said, "Yeah, I learned the most at MSLI. Like, we got help on how to do school, like the work and stuff, and we got all that college applications stuff and the SAT thing."

In a separate encounter, Carlitos added:

> I learned about AB540 from you. Your presentation was really good. And the SAT exam, and the UC application. That stuff was all new to me, but like, now, I know what people are talking about. And like, the work. It was

really important work. I'm better at school now. I can see what's wrong with things.

In a meeting at her *Abeula*'s house, Cristina told me:

> Without MSLI, I don't know what I would have done. Like, they say my school is college prep, but, I don't see it. I had just didn't really understand what people were talking about. That stuff [mechanics of college-going] didn't really even seem like MSLI, but when I got back to school, like, I knew how to figure it all out, I guess.

The comments of Eduardo, Carlitos, and Cristina highlight some important distinctions about MSLI in comparison to other outreach programs. Whereas some students definitely acknowledged other outreach programs as assisting them in understanding and completing mechanical tasks, MSLI was different. At MSLI, the mechanical tasks are not made the object of study or learning. Rather, the development of critical sense-making around the inequities in students' lives and ways to change them are made primary learning objects. Workshops around filling out applications and finding information about different colleges, financial aid policies, like AB540, and test-taking strategies all supplement the curriculum of MSLI. This sociocultural organization of learning that takes shape at MSLI allowed for Eduardo to count on the experience of filling out applications and preparing for the SAT. It allowed for Carlitos to interrogate financial aid policy in a way meaningful to his undocumented status. It assisted Cristina to decipher the coded practices of college-going assistance at her high school. Underlying all of these assistance strategies for mechanical college-going tasks was the assistance in coursework. MSLI was an intensive writing experience, which fostered students' learning through hybrid language practices,[3] instilling a sense of competence and desire in the students' academic identities.

Armando, an ELD student in his high school said, "I became a good boy. A good schoolboy because of MSLI. I could speak in English or Spanish, so I learned a lot better. I'm still doing better."

In a formal interview at her house in the Central Valley, Yaneth commented, "MSLI was so intense. It was good preparation for like, senior year with all the scholarships and applications on top of like, really tough courses."

Alex echoed Yaneth's sentiments, "Like, the writing was really good. It made me much more comfortable with wanting to write and write well."

Nené made the strongest impression on me, as a teacher, scholar, and friend when he said, "Man, Ryan. I never thought I was a writer until MSLI. Now, I'm a writer."

Outreach programs in general, and MSLI in particular, took responsibility for providing assistance to students in completing critical mechanical college-going tasks. The assistance provided by outreach programs was often one of—if not the primary—ecocultural groups from which students could draw support for tasks that were otherwise inefficiently or ineffectively supported on their own.

Outreach also took responsibility for more organic tasks than any other ecocultural group. This was especially pronounced in ideological work and making college more of a reality for students. Table 8 shows how many organic tasks the various members of the outreach ecocultural group assisted students in completing.

Table 8: Outreach Division of *Organic* Labor

	Ideologies	Aspiration Development	Politics	"Real"	Hidden Curriculum
MSLI	X	X	X	X	X
Migrant Education Program	X	X		X	
Other Outreach Programs	X	X		X	X

Ideological work assists students in understanding the guiding ideas that frame college access. Students' discussions of the various outreach programs in which they participated, as well as their ideological work with other community members, were combined with document analysis about the same outreach programs in order to understand the principles of the ideological work being done. Three ideologies emerged from this analysis: meritocratic, universal, and sociopolitical. A meritocratic college access ideology assumed that if students worked hard, earned good grades, and were good students, then they would be rewarded with college access, because they would have earned it. Meritocratic ideology expected students to matriculate into the institution they had earned the right to attend. A universal college access ideology assumed that all students could and should go to college. Universal ideology did not make a distinction between types of institutions (e.g., UC vs. community college). A sociopolitical ideology took a critical stance toward college access, assuming that there were multiple sites of privilege and marginalization throughout the process. Socio-political ideology claimed that college access needed to be deconstructed for students to make informed decisions about how and where to participate.

Most outreach programs, including the Migrant Education Program, assisted students in understanding college access from a meritocratic ideology—fostering belief in the meritocracy. This is the mainstream, dominant ideology that pervades college admissions conversations in the media. It is also the mainstream, dominant ideology that pervades public discourse around student achievement in K–12 education. Generally, members of other ecocultural groups (e.g., teachers) who assisted students in understanding college access ideology also supported the idea of the meritocracy.

Alex described the assistance he received through his participation in outreach programs other than MSLI:

> They're really good, because I don't know where else I might get some of that attention. They remind me that, like, I'm one of the bright kids, and I need to do something to stay that way. They help me maintain. They help my GPA. They teach me how to be my best, so, like, as a student, so, I'm just glad that's good enough to go to Cal State.

Alex's description illustrates how outreach programs generally sought to help students become the "best student" they could be, in order to get into the best college possible. Nené had an analysis of his own to explain why some students made it to college and others did not.

Nené told me:

> I think that, like, there's two kinds of Mexicans. Mexican families. Like, there's those that really care about education, and like, that's why they came here and all, like my family. But then, like, there's the Mexicans that just, like, sit around and don't really care. Like, maybe they don't know, but like, they just don't really care about education. That's what, like the migrant program up here looks like, at least. There's the ones who really care and they're in the migrant programs. The others, like, they're just not there.

Nené's analysis, based on his experiences with the Migrant Education Programs in his region, included racialized/ethnic-based elements to further complicate the meritocratic ideal. Access and educational opportunity were relegated to those who deserved it, based on their performance as good families that cared about education.

Assistance in understanding college access as a meritocracy enforced principles of competition and transactions of goods (e.g., good student is traded for a good college), as well as an assumption that everyone had equal opportunity to achieve (perform) the same accomplishments (signifiers) of being merit-worthy (the body of a good student). Dangerously, it made deficit ideologies readily accessible to be deployed into students' sense-making around what it meant to participate in college-going.

The universal ideology of college access was less popular in students' college-going. Outreach programs and migrant education programs that assisted students in learning ideologies of access as universal stressed the ability for anyone to get a college education in California.

Yaneth shared:

> Like, there was this one program, that I guess was helpful, but they told us that everyone could go to college. And like, I guess that's technically true, right? Like, they showed us how there were community colleges, and like, that's probably really good for people who don't really know and don't have other ways to find out, but, like, that's not what I want to do. And like, I worked really hard. I'm not saying I'm better than anyone else, but, I would be disappointed if I ended up at a community college. And not everyone can go to UCLA. That's just not how it works.

Yaneth resisted the ideology this specific outreach program tried to promote. In fact, she understood it, but her personal experience deemed it faulty. Although optimistic, the universal ideology failed to serve students who were trying to make sense of the process in which they were participating.

Finally, the socio-political ideology was the solitary domain of the MSLI. Congruent with the program's overall goal of fostering socio-critical literacy for students, MSLI took responsibility for assisting students in understanding college access ideology as a socio-political intersection of privilege and inequity. Taking a critical stance on college access, the sociopolitical ideology that MSLI worked to help students understand deconstructed the meritocratic and universal ideologies. Socio-political ideology accepted that the meritocracy was the dominant understanding of college access, but understood it as hegemonic social practice.

Carlitos explained how MSLI assisted him in understanding how college access ideology mattered. Over the series of our formal interviews, he said:

> After MSLI, I see it everywhere. My eyes are opened up. I can't not see it anymore. It is capitalism. The work. The competition. ... The manipulation of the demand or the supply. ... Even the grades that I get. I get good grades. But that means that someone isn't getting good grades. ... And they wouldn't let me in to the English class that I needed, because I speak Spanish. But I want to speak English. But they won't let me in, and that's like capitalism, too. Like, I just didn't have what they think deserves what I want. It gives me a headache, but ... I'm looking for the ways to get in. I, I want to be an astronomer, so MSLI helped me understand that I need to do more things than just study. I need to get the right classes. I need to ask questions. I need to do a lot, and I need to get support. Like you guys.

For Carlitos, deconstructing the meritocratic and hegemonic practices of educational opportunity in the U.S. was clearly connected to principles of capitalism. Understanding that nothing was guaranteed from this mainstream ideology enabled him to recognize additional actions he could take toward his goal of college access. Specifically, Carlitos recognized that there were further questions he needed to ask, and that he did not need to do it alone.

In addition to the ideologies that members in the outreach ecocultural group assisted students in understanding, there were ideologies that guided the practices of each outreach member. The students reported incredible variability as to how these disparate programs operated ideologically. There were three primary ideologies from which members of the outreach group provided assistance: complementary, subsidizing, and supplementary. Complementary assistance sought to extend students' repertoires of practice in order to take strategic action toward college access. Subsidizing assistance sought to make up for work that was not taken up by other ecocultural groups. This type of assistance was presented as a subsidy to make up for something students lacked in their lives. Supplementary assistance sought to support efforts of other ecocultural groups, without taking primary responsibility for assisting students with college-going tasks. MSLI served as complementary assistance, whereas Migrant Education Programs were generally discussed as trying to subsidize students' family ecocultural group assistance. They sought to fill a deficit in students' lives. The amalgam of other outreach programs generally vacillated between subsidizing students' families and supplementing assistance for which schooling members took responsibility.

Insights from Mapping the Community Division of Labor

From my conceptual model of the community's division of labor in migrant students' college-going practices, I have come to 11 themes that help explain some of the transformative opportunities in migrant students' college-going literacy development. These themes are empirically derived from the data that support both the preceding conceptual model and the assertions that follow. These interpretive analyses show some of the critical moments in students' literacy development. They point to substantive implications that I will address in the next chapter.

1. Parents provide assistance in relatively few tasks in comparison to other community members, but their support is crucial. Parents' labor enables much of the rest of the community to take responsibility for assisting students in all tasks.

2. Older siblings with college experience serve as pragmatic, efficient, and accessible members who can supplement the work that dominant groups in college-going (i.e., white middle and upper-middle-class families) reproduce culturally.
3. Students compensated for the work that is culturally reproduced in dominant social groups by employing the assistance of various other members of their community. This was most clearly exemplified in the following five tasks: completing coursework, funding college-going practices, understanding applications and financial aid, making college "real," and exploring the hidden curriculum.
4. Migrant students' aspirations were not only developed early, but were fostered throughout the community and over time. Supporting students' aspiration development was the task that more members of the community took as their responsibility most often. Notable exceptions to this division of labor were found solely in undocumented migrant students' experiences.
5. Other than peers and other pupils, school personnel by and large were not active participants in students' college-going literacy development outside their assistance in coursework. However, when school personnel do take responsibility for some labor, their influence can have tremendous impact on students' literacy, both in its positive development and in its harmful retraction.
6. The organic work of bringing college into a "real" rather than abstract artifact was a task that tended to happen later in students' development, and it was most comprehensively effected by older siblings who had attended college, relationships of *confianza* stemming from outreach programs, or, rarely, higher education faculty.
7. Faculty, like other higher education personnel were largely absent from students' experiences, but when they were present, their assistance often contributed to transformative learning moments. This was especially salient in the organic work.
8. Peers were present in almost every task, be it mechanical or organic, but rather than taking primary responsibility for any given task, their assistance was generally more supportive in nature.

9. The work of making college "real" and exposing the "hidden curriculum of college admission" seemed to go arm in arm for most participants and the corresponding members of the community that took responsibility for these tasks.
10. Ideological work is complicated. Different members of the community communicated and worked from competing ideologies of college access.
11. Regarding invisible actors, the rendering of highly consequential community members and their associated labor as invisible is consistent with the dominant ideology of college access, which posits higher education opportunity in a do-it-yourself framework founded in the merit-based rewards of a completely autonomous individual.

These last two themes were less apparent in the data. This might very well be an artifact of the research design, which did not account for the difference between student-centered labor and system- or institution-centered labor. Further exploration is required on these themes to examine how they might come to bear on students' college-going literacy development.

These eleven themes and the community division of labor model presented earlier ethnographically document that none of the transformative moments in students' college-going literacy came about from institutionalized practices. Rather, they were serendipitous and relied on the student happening to be in the right place at the right time with the right people around them and having the resources to take action. Public institutions vested with the authority and the responsibility to develop students' college-going literacies, plainly put, did not do so, except in the serendipitous happenstance.

Notes

[1] Significantly, the two students who did not discuss peer assistance as an important strategy for completing coursework were both undocumented migrants (two of four in this study) from working-poor families. They were also the two youngest students in this study. Each was a sophomore in high school during data collection. Their discussions of peers were generally around friends in

the neighborhood with whom they could speak Spanish outside of school. Schooling for these two students seemed to me to be a much more solitary affair than for the other students in the study. However, this analysis is based only on my personal interactions with them during MSLI and the course of this study. It is by no means exhaustive of their cultural practices with peers, as that was not the main focus of this study.

[2] A team of researchers has followed MSLI participants in a longitudinal research program that includes state data on individual, group, and comparison group academic achievement and educational trajectories. For further information, contact Kris D. Gutiérrez, 2005 MSLI Director. Also see Jaramillo & Nunez, 2005, referenced earlier in this manuscript.

[3] Hybrid language practices exist in classrooms where students can use whatever language they feel most confident in expressing the idea they are trying to communicate. These practices foster learning by using the students' entire linguistic toolkit. In an English-dominant environment, Spanish-dominant students remain legitimated as knowledge-creators and are free to use (and ask others to use) the language that will enable communication most clearly. See Gutiérrez, Asato, Santos, & Gotanda (2000).

Chapter Eight
Toward a College-going Pedagogy: Implications of Mapping a Fracture

My mapping of migrant students' college-going has outlined, in broad terms, how migrant students come to know college access by using tools that mediate their understanding of college access as an object of learning. Explicit and implicit rules regulate their use of these tools and mediate their participation in relationships with other individuals. These individuals belong to one of four primary ecocultural groups that provide assistance in college-going tasks: schools, family, higher education, and outreach. Mechanical and organic tasks constitute students' participation in the social practice of college access. This mapping represents a fracture in the master narrative, documenting ways that migrant students participate in college-going.

Recalling my main research questions:

1. How do migrant students come to know college access?
2. How do migrant students engage in college choice processes?
3. In what ways are migrant students constituted as subjects in college-going?

Altogether, the answers to these three questions constitute an understanding of what it means for the migrant students in this study to come to know college access. These answers have been presented in the metaphor of mapping a fracture, emphasizing the social practice of college access as an activity of learning and the optimism for social change afforded by this deeper understanding of college-going processes.

My map of this activity represents students' development of a college-going literacy. In detailed terms, I have discussed specific transformative learning opportunities as experienced by the migrant students participating in this study. These transformative learning opportunities were spatial moments in college access where and when their understandings of college access were re-imagined through the practices in which they were engaged toward college-going, or where and when their practices were re-negotiated through their understandings of college access as an object of learning. These recursive spatial moments were the moments in which development occurred. Central to the students' development was the way(s) in which they were constituted, through their participation, as human subjects in the social practice of college access.

My inquiry was based in critical ethnographic methodology (Trueba & McLaren, 2001; Kincheloe & McLaren, 2000) and informed by cultural-historical activity theory and New Literacy Studies (Gutiérrez & Rogoff, 2003; Gutiérrez, 2002; Engeström, 1998; New London Group, 1996), positioning college-going as a question of literacy, constituted by the cultural practices of the subjects (students) participating in it. College access became the object of learning.

My interpretive discussion of mapping students' college-going literacy development worked toward understanding the object of students' learning activity, as they experience it through their recursive practices of college-going. Thus, I submit a summary and discussion of the findings presented in the preceding chapters as a mapping of the object—the object of college access. Once this object is made known and visible, it can be taught and enacted. Hence, I argue later in this chapter for a college-going pedagogy.

Mapping the Object

Migrant students participated in college-going as a family project. They persisted through schooling practices, higher education expectations, outreach interventions and greater social activity as they engaged in a sociocultural nexus of family goals and responsibilities. They were not autonomous, individual agents free from influence of external forces. Rather, they were an interconnected product of their families' struggles for stability and sustainability. They were the hope of their family. They were the pride of their family. They were responsible to their families for labor that would yield the social mobility and political determination that their families struggled to achieve. Appropriating social mobility, as a historical act, meant achieving economic stability. Appropriating political determination, as a historical act, meant subverting the social inequities to which the family was subjected.

Externally, students were influenced by forces that racialized and classed them in ways that perpetuated racist discrimination, subjecting them to a litany of practices from other (dominant) subjects, and positioning them as objects to be policed and guarded against. These racializations also appeared to construct migrant students as bodies with inferior mental capacities, based on arbitrary indexes of intelligence. Most obvious among these racializations were the discriminations students faced based on their histories with (im)migration and their Spanish language practices.

Internally, the forces that motivated students to struggle through oppression influenced their construction as human subjects. Students' struggle for liberation was shaped by their acute, internal awareness of the inequities they faced. They subverted oppressive external forces through on-going, sophisticated mental and emotional analysis about the world around them, their goals, pathways, and (shared) histories.

Whereas external forces of discrimination politicized them in negative ways (e.g., illegal aliens) and attempted to shape their participation in college-going as individual beings, internal forces of liberation politicized them in ways that motivated the students in their on-going struggle (e.g., being college-bound) and supported their participation in college-going as social beings. The external forces work from and perpetuate the view of migrant students from a deficit orientation. The internal forces flow from a more complex understanding of discrimination as unequal exercises of power that dehumanize both individuals and groups.

A host of explicit rules governed the students' uses of tools to complete the mechanics of college-going. These rules can be summarized as a litany of regulations migrant students are subjected to in schooling and higher education that require specific behaviors, standards of achievement, bodily comportment, and language use. My study sought to uncover transformative moments in students' literacy development. The findings that emerged from the data did not lend themselves to deep understanding of these explicit rules, nor the tools that students used in addressing the mechanics of college-going. The absence of available data for analysis on these subjects suggests that these rules and tools might be such tacit experiences for students that their transformative potential is negligible.

The data *did* direct my analysis to two specific tools that mediated students' organic understandings of college access. These tools were the family's history with (im)migration and relationships of *confianza* that gave rise to transformative learning opportunities. (im)Migration was found to mediate the students' understanding of college access as the continuation of their family's migratory pathway. (im)Migration as a tool, was thought of as a dynamic experience that shapes and influences real-world consequences for migrant students. This understanding differs from traditional studies of (im)migration and its relation to education. Traditionally, (im)migration has been treated as a static signifier of students' social circumstances. Rather than thinking of (im)migration as a fixed artifact, my analysis illustrated that it was a dynamic process-oriented artifact that simultaneously influenced students' thinking and feeling, as well as their subsequent practices in college-going, while they continued to participate in their family's history of (im)migration.

College access was mediated by (im)migration in ways that directed students to make sense of higher education opportunity within a political framework. College-going became a political act that required students to engage in learning activity toward the goal of college access in order to subvert oppressive, dominant, ideological forces that structured their family's struggle for stability. In political, sociocultural terms, college access was connected to the liberation of humanization for migrant students. Participating in college-going was participation in *el movimiento.*

Sharing a commitment to the struggle for the liberation of humanization was central to relationships of *confianza* that students shared with more expert others in matters of college-going. *Confianza* was a space of possibility that students could use to explore potential re-negotiations of their college-going practices and possible re-imaginings of college access with someone who could assist them in making sense of their participation in the social practice of college access. *Confianza,* as a mediating artifact, or tool, was a mutually invested and beneficial cultural expression of trust. However, *confianza* should not be reduced to "trust" as if trust is all it takes to make a difference in students' college-going lives. As a cultural expression of trust, students engaged in projects of *confianza*, in which both members of the relationship invested in developing a shared system of belief related to their mutual struggles for humanization. It was a relationship that afforded students new potentialities in their college-going.

Looking across the constellations of *confianza* that students reported, six ecological characteristics were identified in the learning environments from which these relationships emerged. *Confianza* did not grade students' learning within the learning environment. Students' home languages were valued and legitimized as valuable tools for learning. Lived experience was an important medium through which to construct knowledge. Relationships with parents were permitted on the students' and parents' terms. Both individuals in the relationship were able to get to know each other and engage one another over time, without fear of penalty. Finally, students were assumed and expected to engage in learning as knowledge constructors and historical actors, rather than as deficient subjects who needed subsidies to their mental constitution. I call these six traits ecological because they were principles that constituted the environment proximal to the individual in specific learning activities.

Three implicit rules emerged in the analysis of data. These rules regulated how students' participation might yield transformative learning opportunities. Following these rules could mediate students' participation in some ways; while subverting them could mediate students' participation in others. The three rules were:

1. Migrant students should temper their aspirations;
2. Migrant students need to seek out financial aid; and
3. Migrant students have to work harder to get into college.

Each of these rules manifests from beliefs or folk knowledge about college-going that grew out of histories of participating or being excluded from participating in a set of official practices. Over time, these beliefs became instantiated and mediated students' college-going as rules.

The first rule reflects how migrant students were being prepared for post-secondary choices. Generally, institutional forces best prepared and encouraged students to attend community colleges, if students were encouraged to pursue higher education at all. The second rule directs attention to the class-consciousness of social forces that positioned higher education as a commodity for wealthy families—families in which the stability and sustainability sought by migrant students' families was socially or culturally reproduced. The third rule implied that reward structures for achievement and hard work ethics operated in drastically discriminatory power imbalances. Students with less at stake or less achievement were rewarded equally well or better than migrant students, whose achievement was often rendered invisible by the existing dominant structural indexes.

These tools and rules mediated students' literacy development as they worked to make sense, master, and perform two sets of college-going tasks: mechanical and organic. Mechanical tasks required students to do specific things in specific ways to specific expectations. These tasks can be summarized as completing college-preparatory coursework, performing adequately on standardized tests, preparing to apply and applying to colleges for admission, financing higher education, and acquiring the resources necessary for completing these aforementioned tasks (e.g., time and money).

Organic tasks were conceptual in nature. Students' organic labor moved college access from an abstract idea into a concrete social practice in which they could strategically participate. Organic tasks were summarized as deconstructing ideologies of college access, developing aspirations for post-secondary education, contextualizing college-going in socio-political terms, making college real, and exposing a hidden curriculum of college access. Together, these tasks constitute the labor that students had to take responsibility for in order to participate in college-going. My analysis adjoins these tasks with the other people (or institutional actors/positions) that took responsibility for providing assistance to students in completing their tasks. Other people and/or institutional actors were considered to be members of migrant students' college-going community. They were categorized into four ecocultural groups, based on the contexts in which they engaged students. The four groups were family, schooling, higher education, and outreach. These adjoining dimensions of college-going (college-going tasks and the people who assisted students in completing them) constituted a conceptual model of the community division of labor in students' literacy development.

I analyzed how migrant students' lives played out across the conceptual model of the community division of labor in students' literacy development and found 11 significant themes that illustrated how members in each ecocultural group participated in migrant students' literacy development. These themes explained both the normative and the subversive consequences to various members' participation. Student assistance for the organic work in college-going was overwhelmingly dominated by the family and outreach ecocultural groups. Assistance for mechanical work was the most popular type of labor appropriated across all groups. Most poignantly, these analyses cumulatively documented that transformative learning opportunities in migrant students' college-going literacy development were clearly serendipitous. None of the transformative moments in students' college-going came about from institutionalized efforts. This finding suggests that schools, colleges, and universities operate from a failed framework for preparing and matriculating students into higher education.

In sum, the object of college access for migrant students is a political act. It contributes to migrant families' sustainability in their struggle for liberatory humanization. Migrant students came to know college access through a complex nexus that was grounded in their lived histories and extended by the potential re-imaginings made available from transformative learning opportunities. The remainder of this concluding chapter presents specific implications that constituents who are invested in college access can incorporate into their research and practice.

The activity of migrant students' college-going reflects their participation in the system; it represents students' developing college-going literacy. The subheadings in Figure 2, below, are abbreviations of the major findings from this study. As depicted above, migrant students are constituted by external and internal forces that shape them in racialized, politicized, and classed ways, while also positioning them as subject to reinforcing investment from their families. Their college-going was mediated by at least two tools that I uncovered through ethnographic investigation and analysis: (im)migration and *confianza*. Their participation was regulated by a host of explicit and at least three implicit rules. Their participation in college-going demanded that they perform mechanical or organic tasks. These tasks were mandated by the explicit and implicit rules of college-going. Students were assisted in the completion of these tasks by members of four ecocultural groups: family, schooling, higher education, and outreach. Analysis of the division of labor between and across these groups led me to the 11 themes about migrant students' college-going labor that I presented in chapter seven.

Figure 2, below, is an empirically derived visual synthesis of how migrant students came to know college access. This figure updates the theoretical representation in chapter two (fig. 1).

Figure 2: Migrant Students' College-going Activity

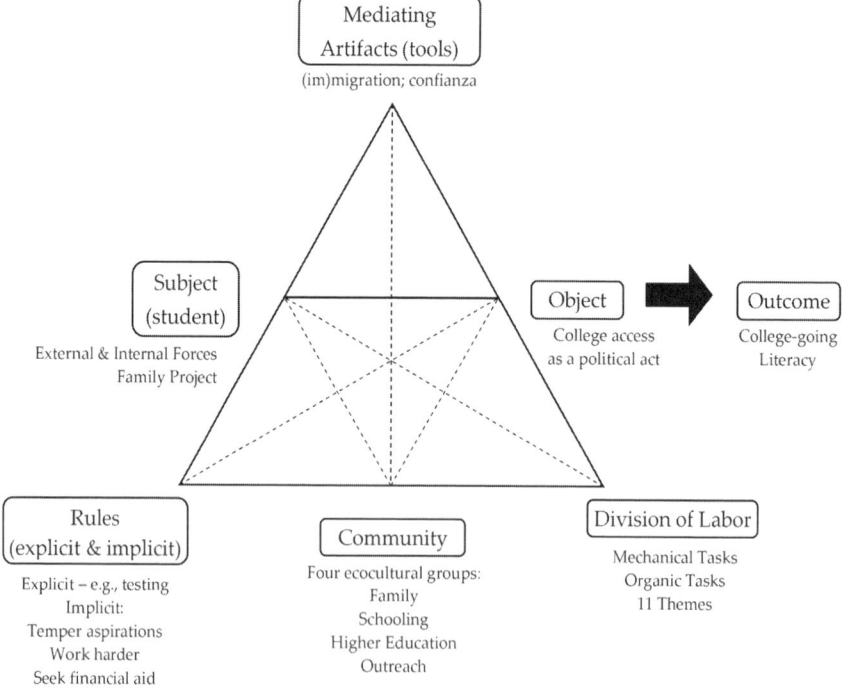

Toward a College-going Pedagogy

Students' traversed across, between, back and forth, and in line with these elements of their college-going activity. Specific moments, or points on their college-going map, were accounted for in this study. These points on the map were the transformative learning opportunities that my analysis sought to uncover. The moments when students' practices were extended in ways that changed their understanding of college access, or when their understanding of college access changed their practices, signify the development of a college-going literacy—the ability to read and write higher education opportunity toward the specific goal of going to college.

It is important to note that this system of migrant students' college-going activity is not a closed or fixed system. Rather, it intersects with multiple other dynamic systems. For example, in order to further illuminate the constraints imposed on migrant students' college-going by their pre-college experiences, a second triangle might be drawn from the institutional perspective, placing schools as the subject. The school system might interact with migrant students' college-going activity through the axes between the division of labor, community, rules, and subject. My data and analyses clearly link these two systems along these axes of interaction.

Conversely, the new potentialities afforded to students via their use of *confianza* could be mapped as an enabling activity system that might intersect with their college-going activity along the axes between the tools, object, division of labor, and community. As an enabling system of activity, *confianza* might interact with students' college-going activity and emerge in a specific relationship, as an outcome of that interaction. This discussion of *confianza* as an enabling system underscores the complexity embedded in *confianza* as a new conceptual tool for migrant students' college-going literacy development. It refutes any attempt to reduce *confianza* to a simple condition of trust.

Furthermore, the system of migrant students' college-going activity is historically contingent. The study presented here was certainly affected by the immigrant rights movement marches that emerged in the spring of 2006. This historical site is anchored by the 2005 MSLI, where students' college-going literacy development was transformed simultaneously with the onset of new analytical tools to interrogate dehumanizing practices in their social world, especially regarding their educational opportunity.

Implications for practice, policy, and research can be drawn from this representation of the mapping of students' college-going literacy. The contradictions of the map demonstrate potential sites for future re-mapping. These sites potentially will transform future learning opportunities toward the goal of college access.

Fracturing Inquiry: College-going Literacy as a Field Corrective for College Access

Early on in this book, I claimed to provide a field corrective that would contribute to reorganizing college access by integrating the four domains of higher education opportunity scholarship and examining access across the six major identified barriers. The college-going literacy development model, empirically represented in figure two, accomplished the goals of my field corrective. Treating college access as a social practice allowed me to organize an understanding of it based on the micro-practices that constitute the broader activity. Investigating the collective micro-practices that migrant students engaged in—which I then operationalized in my analysis to identify transformative learning opportunities—meant that I had to organize college access based on an integrated framework that accounted for the work that needed to be done by/for students (division of labor) and the people that were involved in that work (community), as well as the ways in which the work was done (tools and rules).

I began with the division of labor. I sought to understand the practices that students engaged in while working toward college access. From the documentation of students' practices, and the intuitive analysis of Cristina, I came to understand the work of college access in mechanical and organic ways, with 12 multifaceted college-going tasks. Thinking about college access as constituted in part by students' work (or labor) in the activity of college-going demands an understanding of the other political influences (community members) in their social practice of college access. The college-going literacy model of college access reorganizes the study and treatment of access into mechanical and organic dimensions of students' college-going, which incorporates all six barriers, seeking to understand how they interact. It breaks away from traditional understandings that contain "preparation" and "family involvement" as fixed categories. Rather, it looks to see how families might be involved in preparation, and how preparation might indeed have consequences for other dimensions of students' college-going, beyond satisfying higher education requisites for admission. "Preparation" itself is expanded across multiple tasks that students must perform in order to develop college-going literacy.

Parents, teachers, peers, and administrators are traditionally understood as influential actors in students' college-going. In the literacy development model, these agents are members of the activity's community. They are people involved in the work of college access. They emerged through my analysis as four distinct, yet related, ecocultural groups: family, schooling, higher education, and outreach. Thinking in a college-going literacy framework reorganizes the study and treatment of access into ecocultural groupings, because it explains how individuals and groups influence college access by their proximity to the student in a given context. Thus, families are understood to wield tremendous influence, yet parents only participate in a few college-going tasks.

The community assists students in college-going tasks in accordance (or resistance) to specific rules of the activity of college-going. These are the explicit and implicit ways that students and community members act with each other and in relation to the object at hand, college access. As discussed in chapter five, my study uncovered three implicit rules that were unsupportive of students' college-going. Traditionally, these rules might have been understood as part of students' aspiration development, without attention paid to the historic development and institution of these rules. For example, the rule that migrant students should temper their aspirations might be misrepresented in traditional studies of college access by suggesting that migrant students do not aspire beyond the community college. But by investigating the genealogy of the implicit rule, I documented how it plays out in students' everyday practices. These data did not support the notion that migrant students do not aspire beyond the community college. Rather, the social practice of college access has been organized in their proximal environments to usher them into community colleges rather than four-year institutions. In this sense, the college-going literacy model works across the four domains of access studies. Rather than reducing this rule to students' college choice aspiration, the analysis of the rule also implicates structural issues of how access is constructed by educational institutions, including the advising, preparation, and admissions practices of the K–12 and higher education sectors.

Another way in which the college-going tasks get performed is through the tools that students use in their practice of college access. As discussed in chapter six, tools mediate students' knowing of college access. Students learn through their use of college-going tools. My study uncovered two tools that were most salient to students and were related to transformative learning opportunities. These tools were (im)migration and *confianza*. Tools are artifacts in the social world that mediate understanding of specific objects of activity (Engeström, 1987; Wertsch, 1985). Tools can be both enabling and constraining, and they change over time. Traditionally, (im)migration has been understood as a fixed, finite process that might be a part of the students' past.

Traditional college access studies might treat (im)migration as a demographic variable, rather than as a tool for knowing college access. Likewise, dominant frameworks for understanding college access have sought to understand the influential relationships in students' lives based on the identity of those involved in the relationships. *Confianza* treats the relationship as a sociocultural mediator. The characteristics and principles of the relationship become paramount over who the relationship is with. Within the college-going literacy model, both (im)migration and *confianza* retain their dynamic influences on students' college-going practices. In the college-going literacy model, college access is reorganized to focus on how various artifacts mediate college access, rather than on who or what influences students' behavior. This shift allows analysis to cross fluidly over and between the four domains of access. *Confianza* informs understandings of how students obtain and use information about college (college choice) as well as the ways in which social forces shape higher education opportunities for students (college access).

Students in the college-going literacy model are understood as subjects in the social world. The subject, in sociocultural theory, develops socially. We, as human beings, are not solitary, wholly independent, autonomous individuals. Rather, we are agents of change within social and cultural constraints and affordances. In this study, I was able to document ways in which students were subjected to external and internal forces, which interacted to produce the college-going student as a project of the family. Traditional models might not make considerations for the forces to which students are subject, but rather assume or buy into the hegemonic ideologies around college access that construct the student as a solitary agent, wholly responsible for their knowledge and practice of college access. The college-going literacy model reorganizes college access to attune and attend to the ways in which students learn and develop as college-going subjects. This reorganization allows understandings of college access to work toward developing transformative practices that are responsive to students' lived experiences.

In sum, my reorganization of college access moves toward an understanding of college access as a social practice that gets performed over time. The college-going literacy model shifts understanding of college access into a process of learning that is based on the extension of cultural practices, rather than deficit models of cultural barriers. College-going literacy is a problem-based framework that seeks to promote transformative social change toward the goal of extending opportunity for the benefit of greater democratic participation in society within a more humanizing social sphere. Understanding college access as college-going literacy implicates all spheres of education in the development of such literacy for students. If college access is an activity of learning, and current practices and policies do not meet equitable standards across various social categories, then college access needs to be reorganized. That is, individuals and groups embedded within the social practice of college access must respond accordingly and revise the social organization of learning college access. This study is a call for a college-going pedagogy.

College-going Pedagogy

Putting the college-going literacy model of college access into practice, whether as researcher or practitioner, can take shape as college-going pedagogy. As pedagogy, college-going literacy must be theoretically congruent to its foundations. Any college-going pedagogy must account for the critical, sociocultural, and ecocultural principles from which the college-going literacy model was developed. Critical pedagogues contend that pedagogy is the social practice of teaching and learning toward emancipatory ends and that teaching and learning takes place across contexts (Duncan-Andrade & Morrell, 2008; McLaren & Kincheloe, 2007; Darder, et al., 2003; Giroux, 2001; McLaren, 1988, 1995). Pedagogy goes beyond the classroom teaching and learning practices, and it must critique the hegemonic practices that dominate institutions entrusted with students' learning and development. College-going pedagogy must interrogate the college-going ideologies of public higher education institutions.

Pedagogies that incorporate sociocultural theories of learning assert that the social organization of learning is of paramount concern in working toward emancipatory ends and using the cultural resources available to students (Gutiérrez, et al., *in press*; Gutiérrez, 2008; Rogoff, 2003). Hence, students' cultural practices can be made understandable as repertoires of practice that can be extended to address specific learning goals (Gutiérrez & Rogoff, 2003). College-going pedagogy focuses on assistance in students' learning, rather than subsidizing students' learning with other knowledge. Assistance retains and supports students' humanization by fostering transformative learning opportunities where and when students are co-constructors of knowledge. College-going pedagogy must work to unfix the seemingly rigid, dominant practices in the performance of college access. This work requires adjustments, concentrated effort, and intentional organization of learning from all ecocultural groups involved in college-going. College-going pedagogy would situate college-going learning in students' lives, recognizing that knowledge comes from students' lived experiences. As such, college-going pedagogy is a popular pedagogy—one that extends into all spheres of migrant students' social worlds, including but not limited to schools, higher education, community, and family.

Popular college-going pedagogy captures the constituent parts of the fracture in the master narrative re-presented in the college-going practices of the Mexican migrant students featured in this book. "Popular" signifies the critical and public nature of this pedagogy.

College-going literacies are developed across public and private spheres of schools, higher education, communities, and families. When each of these ecocultural groups commits to the success, rather than resigning to the failure, of Mexican migrant students, college-going literacies can develop and future fractures in the dominant master narrative that seeks to preclude migrant students can promote more social change. "College-going" signifies the need to understand college access as a question of literacy, rather than a problem of student ability, merit, and the accumulation of and achievement of a discrete set of tasks that students perform. This underscores the sense- and meaning-making processes that constitute college access, as well as the acknowledgement that college access is a social practice that students learn. "Pedagogy" puts the onus of teaching and learning college access on all those who involve themselves in the human development of Mexican migrant students. It emphasizes the fact that if college access is learned, then it can be taught. Cumulatively, it is incumbent upon educators, policy-makers, community workers, and researchers to actively disrupt, disengage, and ultimately destroy the master narrative that precludes Mexican migrant college-going. A popular college-going pedagogy comes from the workings and efforts of everyday people who choose to commit their energies to the academic success and social opportunities of Mexican migrant students. In this way, any college-going pedagogy must come from the grassroots and engage with key stakeholders to effect change. Ultimately, it must seek to provide a framework that is meaningful and practical for creating social change that supports Mexican migrant educational success.

Enacting College-going Pedagogy

The following sections suggest implications for the practice of college-going pedagogy. I have organized these implications by the ecocultural groups identified in migrant students' college-going. The practices I recommend should be understood as potential practices—but not an exhaustive prescription—that might constitute a college-going pedagogy. Rather, these are empirically derived suggestions for policy-makers and educators to consider if they commit to enacting a critical college-going pedagogy and contribute to the democratization of college access.

Fracturing Schools

Governing bodies of schools can organize curriculum and standards for all students to be college-prep. In tandem, teachers and curriculum developers can adjust their practices to assume that all students have the ability to learn college-preparatory material. College preparation in schools also can become more holistic in their approach. College preparation should include the deconstruction of dominant ideologies and hegemonic social practices, especially as related to college-going. High schools should institutionalize ecologies that might yield relationships of *confianza*. These ecologies demand a significant re-thinking of what high school classrooms might look like. A first step in helping high schools enact a college-going pedagogy could be to increase the personalization of learning, especially in the mechanics of college-going. This effort would provide institutionalized resources for students to draw from when performing critical tasks toward college-going. If effectively integrated with ecologies of *confianza*, the relations between teachers, administrators, and students could be reconfigured in more equitable ways, where power relations could be deconstructed to allow for students' to co-construct environments in which their college-going literacy development might thrive. Peer relations could also be utilized in conceiving the organization of learning in high schools within a college-going pedagogy. Peers could mutually support each other's processes of learning.

In its most radical analysis, college-going pedagogy asks to re-conceptualize the responsibilities of high school missions, including the job expectations for teachers, counselors, and administrators. The purpose of learning would be on its process, rather than its content. As seen from my analysis of the community division of labor, schooling members of the community were not particularly active in migrant students' college-going literacy development, yet when they did take responsibility for assisting students, their participation had tremendous potential for transforming students' learning. Poignantly, schooling has the opportunity to counteract and/or reconstitute the implicit rules in migrant students' college-going activity that were unsupportive of their college-going.

Specific Recommendations

Schools can support a college-preparatory curriculum for all students and incorporate more of the organic labor, such as exposing the hidden curriculum of college access into the day-to-day curriculum. Schools can build college-going workshops into their curriculum, expand college counseling services, and train teachers to incorporate college-going tasks into the everyday classroom experience. Teachers, counselors, administrators, and other schooling personnel should expect *all* students to attend college, and this expectation should guide their practices inside and outside of classrooms.

Fracturing Higher Education

Higher education, as a social institution, can reconfigure the meaning and operation of merit in admissions. Baez's (2006) analysis of merit suggests that merit indeed has been an exclusionary construct that works at odds with current social, cultural, and educational goals of developing and sustaining a democratic society that values pluralism. I recommend that merit be reconfigured to acknowledge non-dominant forms of merit, providing the opportunity for students to demonstrate merit for their own ecocultural niche (Weisner, 2002). Taken further, merit could be dismissed entirely, and the social institution of higher education could move to a universal ideology of access committed to educating as many people as enroll. These efforts will help ameliorate concerns and contestations over college access ideologies.

Individual institutions of higher education can begin to enact college-going pedagogy in two primary ways: personalization and resource allocation. As shown by my analysis of higher education's participation (or lack thereof) in students' college-going literacy development, and by the organic work of making college real and deconstructing the hidden curriculum of college access that other community members provide assistance for or various tools rely on to mediate the imagining of college access, personalizing efforts to individuals or small groups in relation to specific higher education actors shows great potential for developmental possibilities. Lorena suggested, "They [higher education members] could follow a student, like, assign someone to follow-up with me and answer my questions and check-in. If I say I want to go to a UC, why can't a UC person be assigned to me all through high school?" Lorena's suggestion requests that university admission offices take as much stake in her as she takes in them. She challenges the dominant paradigm that leaves power to be exercised by institutional forces, and asks for power to be redistributed. My recommendation is that institutions reorganize the work of enrollment management staff to carry specific caseloads of students, personalizing and contextualizing college-going from the institutional perspective. At a minimum, my ethnographic work serves as a clarion call for greater university involvement and presence in migrant communities.

The second way that individual higher education institutions can begin to enact college-going pedagogy is to commit the resources necessary to instantiate college-going as an institutional priority. These resources could take shape in the form of funding for migrant students' college-going. This funding might include additional personnel, the waiving of fees for testing, test-preparation, applications to colleges, and other miscellaneous and/or extraneous fees associated with college-going. Ultimately, providing free higher education to families who cannot afford tuition, fees, and associated expenditures would do much for migrant students' college-going.

Finally, both the social institution and individual institutions can assist in the deconstruction of college access ideologies by making them more transparent, or indeed, engaging the public sphere in debate over what values and principles should guide college access as a social practice.

Specific Recommendations

College applications can ask students to document their achievement in context of their own lives, seeking a localized, culturally relevant conception of merit. Admission offices can embed themselves in migrant students' communities, providing on-going assistance throughout college-going processes. The goal of this involvement should focus on being more hands-on with the mechanical work of college-going and more explicit or transparent in the organic work of ideology, politics, and the hidden curriculum. Faculty should participate more often, and more fully in future students' college-going.

Fracturing Outreach

Outreach organizations can partner with schooling and higher education to institutionalize the practices that serendipitously emerge from their assistance, especially the much-needed organic work of unveiling the hidden curriculum, and deconstructing ideologies of college access. Engaging in college-going pedagogy would require outreach to further its current influence and become part of the fabric of migrant communities. Embedding outreach in communities would foster more rigorous and vigilant co-constructions of knowledge from migrant students' lives.

Outreach efforts can recruit more faculty members from higher education institutions to participate and contribute. As discussed in chapter seven, faculty are rarely involved in students' college-going, but when they are, the potential for transformative learning increases greatly. Of course, recruiting faculty requires the institution of higher education to adjust its promotion and rewards structure so as not to punish faculty members for taking the time away from their other responsibilities (i.e., research). However, there is a tremendous opportunity for mutual benefit here. Outreach organizations and higher education institutions can partner to create structures for faculty to participate in outreach in ways that foster their involvement in students' college-going and their careers. For example, faculty who are passionate and committed to college access could participate meaningfully in outreach programming, while also generating new resources for their research agendas. Specifically, outreach programs can be designed in collaboration with institutions of higher education to include a sponsored research component that faculty could use to sustain their own research activity. Such initiatives could directly benefit the outreach program itself by providing evaluative/assessment data while also encouraging faculty involvement in students' college-going.

Finally, outreach is poised to make a huge impact on the college-going literacy development of migrant students. Outreach is not yet bound as tightly in the longstanding hegemonic practices in which the social institutions of schooling and higher education find themselves. Outreach has far greater autonomy over its organization than its institutional counterparts. For outreach to enact college-going pedagogy, it must take advantage of this comparative autonomy and demonstrate how learning can be ecologically organized around new principles that have college-going embedded as a core value. I recommend that outreach design itself in ways that elicit ecologies associated with developing relationships of *confianza*, and value the non-dominant frameworks of merit that are at stake in migrant students' lives.

Specific Recommendations

Programs should take advantage of their relative autonomy and reconfigure learning within students' lived experiences, co-constructing their services based on migrant communities' needs and desires. These programs can improve dramatically by incorporating resource allocation into their missions, working to provide economic assistance in migrant student's college-going.

These three ecocultural groups in migrant students' college-going have unique opportunities to respond to the under-representation of migrant students in higher education. I have tried to provide some specific ways in which each ecocultural group might begin to enact college-going pedagogy. I reiterate that these recommendations are not prescriptive for college-going literacy development, but might be first steps in translating research into praxis. Additional considerations include questions about aspiration development and resource allocation. These were the two tasks that members of the community took responsibility for most and least often, respectively. Are there better places to invest resources across the ecocultural groups, rather than focusing on aspiration development? Are there ways to alleviate the resource allocation assistance provided solely by families? Can institutions develop programs, policies, and practices that might assist students in building the economic (and time) capacity required to develop college-going literacy? To further the goal of praxis, I continue my discussion of implications by centering the act of inquiry. I present future maps that might be investigated and co-constructed with migrant and other under-represented students.

Future Mapping: Scholarly Implications for Theory, Method, and Enduring Questions

The college-going literacy model affords scholars the ability to understand multiple pathways to college, with multiple intersections with competing activities. It refutes conceptual models of college choice that seek to understand students' behavior in sequential steps, and it challenges some interpretations of college access that position it as a fixed pipeline in which students either persist or get flushed out. Positioning college access as a project of literacy allows scholars to investigate multiple sites of intervention simultaneously. The college-going literacy framework is extremely useful in exposing the competing ideologies involved in college access, an area of inquiry that has not received much attention.

Methodologically, the college-going literacy model suggests three contributions to the study of college access. First, the college-going literacy model focuses inquiry on the cultural practices of communities, rather than the cultural differences between dominant and marginalized communities. Focusing on cultural practices reworks dominant and hegemonic notions of culture, which can often equate culture with race in static and deficit notions. Cultural practices form repertoires of practice that are shared and performed by cultural communities. Repertoires of practice allow for dynamic yet sustainable concepts of culture. Analysis of repertoires of practice then provide insights into moments, conditions, and opportunities for these practices to be extended toward specific learning goals. I call these moments transformative learning opportunities in college-going literacy.

Vygotsky's genetic approach (1978) accompanies the shift to cultural practices as a unit of analysis. The genetic approach analyzes activity from its historical development, illustrating the process of how practices get instituted. Engeström (1987) contributed to this method with his activity theory, in which human activity is analyzed by the practices that constitute it. Future research can build on the activity analysis of migrant students' college-going that I have presented by incorporating third-generation activity theory (Engeström, 2006). Third-generation activity theory looks at the interaction of multiple activity systems as they relate to specific learning objects. Specifically, future research should investigate the various dimensions to migrant student college-going that I have presented here. Research should seek to understand the production of (im)migration and *confianza* as cultural tools, the production of migrant students as college-going subjects, the production of the explicit and implicit rules that govern college-going, and the production of the object of college access. The fracture mapped herein has done the preliminary work and opened up new space from which future studies can design more nuanced investigations into the specific productions of each of these dimensions.

Further activity analysis will hopefully yield descriptions and interpretations of additional tools that migrant students use in coming to know college access. I have already indicated that talk should be chief among these tools for further inquiry. Future research should also ask questions about the various relationships embedded within migrant students' college-going. These questions should focus on the principles and characteristics of such relationships, rather than limiting inquiry to naming the specific people involved in the relationships. The invisible actors in college-going need to be explored in greater detail. The college-going literacy model should be used to uncover the participation of these invisible actors by focusing on the contradictions in the division of labor. Future inquiry should begin to investigate invisible actors by shifting the unit of analysis from students' participation to the participation of other members or ecocultural groups in the activity of college-going.

Finally, in context of the college-going literacy model and the praxis of college-going pedagogy, I call for on-going debate, contestation and inquiry about the social change regarding the object of college access. My study examined how students come to know college access. Future work must explore how society wants to know college access. Future work must call into question: What do we want college access to mean? How does college access impact democratic participation in society? How does college access reflect democratic practices? How can college access be a requisite literacy that fosters democratic participation? From these questions, educators will be able to moderate public debate with an informed perspective on the social change needed for the further humanization of society.

Reflections on a Fracture

The aforementioned implications for engaging in college-going pedagogy and understanding college access inquiry as a question of literacy move the fracture from a space of disruption, to a space of possibility—and very intentionally so. The fracturing of the master narrative that this book sought to achieve opens up the opportunity for a popular college-going pedagogy to work toward transformation. Enacting college-going pedagogy holds promise for effecting social change for a more democratic organization of educational opportunity.

Afterword
On Method and Coming to Know

"El tiempo de Ser"

Una poema de Nené

Mi padre y mi madre me apoyan muy bien desde pequeño me
Dice mi madre mijo ve a la escuela. Sonriendo le digo si mami, mi sueno es el tuyo yo quiero aprender
Un día un Diploma de la Universidad usted va tener.
¡Que bueno Mijito quiero que recuerde que el querer es poder!
A mí, a Ti y a El también
El vino y se fue pero no sin Volver. Tú eres un Niño
Que esta por crecer, me invitas contigo pa mejor comprender?
¡A si! Vente conmigo compartiré mi vida con usted.
Me encanta tu vida pero que es crecer? Poquito a poquito pensado
Y luchando pa poder aprender llegaste a mi vida en UCLA un padre Segundo que me tiene fe. Contento y seguro cada que nos ves, me hiciste reír y
Pensur todo bien. Me abriste los ojos al mundo que fue.
No se que paso pero aun no termine me falta la escuela que tanto planeé.
Me dicen que puedo
Pero eso ya se, solo necesitó el Apoyo de usted!

For the *gueros*:

"The time of being"

A poem by Nené

My Dad and my mom support me real good since I was small my mom tells me son go to school.

Smiling I tell her yes "*Mami,*" my dream is yours too I want to learn

One day you will have a university diploma of mine

Good my son! I want you to remember that wanting to is being able to!

To me, to you, and Him also *(Something she always told me! And I still remember all the time!)*

He came and he left but not without returning *(That's you).*

You're a kid that's about to grow up? *(You asking a question. I thought about this because like we are all pretty much of coming age so yeah),* will you invite me with you to better understand? *(You asking another question like you want to learn about us, which is what you were doing man.)*

Ah yes! Come with me I will share my life with you.

I love your life but what is growing up? *(That's another question.)*

Little by little thinking and fighting to be able to learn ... you came into my life at UCLA, a second father to me that has faith in me.

Happy and sure/secure every time you see us *("Us" meaning migrant students.)*

You made me laugh and think everything's right.

You opened my eyes to the world that was *(I was thinking of all the stuff we ever talked about, like when I first talked to you and I told you "I never really talked to anyone about this" the whole parent thing ... things that you made me see ... also like, stuff we talked about in UCLA 'bout how the system is set up and stuff like that.)*

I don't know what happened *(Meaning like, Where did time go, or like what the shit just happened?),* but I'm still not done. I still need all that schooling that I planned out so much.

They tell me I can, but I already know that, I only need your support.

I cannot pinpoint the moment that this project began for me. Claiming my preliminary orals would not do justice to the work I did before that academic meeting. Claiming the day I met with Kris D.

Gutiérrez about studying access with migrant students would undercut their influence in my life before that conversation. Claiming the days in which I met *los estudiantes migrantes* would unfairly assume that the project began with me at its center, in authoritarian control. I am uncomfortable with that—especially because it was within the earliest voices of migrant students that I heard the direction to consider studying their educational experiences. They saw and recognized a need for change in the study of educational opportunity in order to help address the inequities they faced. I witnessed that recognition and took advantage of the privilege to take action toward it. This project began over many moments in my life and the lives of each of the other participants. Although I cannot pinpoint *the* moment that this project began for me, I can state with confidence what it has become for me.

This project has become a process of my own coming to know ... coming to know what it means to live more fully human. As Nené states in his *poema* above, "*A mí, a Ti y a El también / El vino y se fue pero no sin Volver ... ¡A si! Vente conmigo compartiré mi vida con usted.*" Living more fully human includes more than just myself. From the idea and its initial questions, to the work itself, to making sense of things, to producing something that might be of value to someone, the process of coming to know in this project has been an interdependent one. It has taken shape over time, with the process of coming to know taking shape as knowing to come back. Recognizing the remaining emptiness that perpetuates our desire to know became an integral principle by which to work and live. Finally, engaging in any knowledge-process toward humanization carries a weight of responsibility. I solicited invitations into people's lives. I was invited into people's lives. I did not know into what I was invited. I did not know many things. And now, I have the responsibility to share my process of coming to know.

As Nené concludes, "*Me dicen que puedo / Pero eso ya se, solo necesitó el Apoyo de usted!*" I know that I can share, but coming to know requires the involvement of others. As I write, others must be willing to read, and read their own writing onto my words, which are words that I have come to from *mi campañeros y campañeras, los estudiantes migrantes.*

The goal of this appendix is to analyze my reflections throughout the production of this inquiry. However, I aim to do so in a reflexive manner, providing critique and making insights into the process of performing critical sociocultural inquiry. To this end, I offer a somewhat autoethnographic (Ellis & Bochner, 2000) account of my participation in this study.

On Performing Sociocritical Inquiry

After stopping by the grocery store to pick up a new supply of frozen diet dinners, I searched my neighborhood for about ten minutes until I found a parking spot. I opened the trunk of my car and loaded up. The backpack with my laptop in it first. I slung it over both of my shoulders. Then my sports-duffle bag. I draped the shoulder strap across my chest. My file box with transcripts, notes, and release forms. I picked it up with my left hand, squeezing my car keys between my thumb and the box handle. Finally, the paper-handled double-stuffed grocery bag. I grabbed it with my right hand, hoisted it above the trunk and let gravity slam it all shut. I clicked the remote-control alarm to lock my car, while peeking into the drivers' window to double-check I hadn't forgotten the residential parking permit. I walked the block and a half back to my apartment building, stepped up into the open courtyard and found my front door. I set down the groceries and the file box, grabbed my house keys from my back pocket, checked my mailbox next to my front door before unlocking and entering my apartment. I kicked in the file box. I dumped the two bags on my sofa. I returned for the groceries, pulling out the orange juice and drinking directly from the carton before I reached the kitchen.

I was exhausted.

I packed away my groceries as quickly as possible. I didn't unpack my duffle bag. I cleaned-up, changed my clothes, and crawled into my bed. It was 10:30 p.m., and I had been driving for hours after a full day of interviewing across the northern side of the Baja—California border. All I wanted to do was get a good night's sleep before hopping on the #2 bus down Sunset Boulevard in nine hours.

I couldn't sleep.

I was exhilarated.

I grabbed my laptop, sat up in bed, and began to write. I had just returned from my first visit to students, and my mind was racing! There were far more questions than insights. There were far more doubts than assertions. I wrote them all down. I had to get them out so as not to sleep them away. I felt so purposeful, like participation in my work could really matter. I felt a huge weight of responsibility. Students were eager to share with me. They were eager to spend time with me. They were sweet to me. Renaldo, Jesus, Lorena, and Butterfly made me feel like I was doing them a favor by spending time with them. I tried my best to express how thankful I was for their willingness to spend time with me.

My writing was circuitous. I went around and around feelings of inadequacy to thoughts of confidence to questions of method to insights about what I had heard, back and forth, in between, like my mind was firing off ideas faster than my fingers could keep up. I paused, looked at the clock. Suddenly, I'd been writing for an hour and a half. I reread the randomness that appeared on my screen. The only conclusion I came to was that I needed to move beyond interactions that were based in the rejuvenating feelings of reunion. I wanted to honor our reunions, but move into a space of mutual engagement about the larger project that we were engaging in. I wanted to return to our work in MSLI—becoming more fully human.

On Expectations

I did not expect to get as many students as eager to volunteer as I received. The 12 participants represented in this study each contacted me within a week of receiving the formal invitation. There were two additional students that initially agreed to participate with me, but for different sets of circumstances, scheduling encounters together became too difficult for each of us, and they left the study early on. Something else struck me, though. Of the 45 invitations to participate in the research that I sent out, at least fifteen were returned to me by the post office as undeliverable. Students had moved within the previous six months. As I followed up with some students who did contact me, whether they participated or not, personal updates revealed that some students had struggled with homelessness, abuse, and the extreme housing instability that often accompanies poverty.

Each time an envelope came to my door that was marked, "RETURN TO SENDER," I felt sad and confused. How might those of us wanting to engage in the struggle for a more humanized democracy together keep better care for each other? How might we support each other better so as not to lose (quite literally) each other? I am still looking for an answer.

On Fieldwork

One sunny southern California morning, I set out from my cozy studio apartment in West Hollywood to drive a few hours on the California highways and meet up with some students I had met months earlier during MSLI. I planned to spend some time with them in their hometowns, but the goal of my visit was made explicit—I wanted to interview students about their experiences in and around college access.

This plan worked.

This plan did not work.

Students were more than willing to be interviewed. I asked questions. They responded. I followed up with more questions based on students' responses. They, in turn, elaborated on their initial response or gave more examples to further illustrate their point. Two things nagged at me. First, I suspected there was more to students' lives in relation to what they were sharing with me, that the interviews alone were not affording us the possibility to address. Second, we wanted to spend more time with each other.

After an initial first-round of interviews with each participant, I made the conscious decision to move the interviews into a more conversational encounter. I achieved this by sharing the main topics I hoped to address with students before any formal interviewing or recording of conversation began. We talked about what topics seemed important to them, and why I thought certain topics might be important or helpful for me. We then dove into conversations about the topics. Rather than sitting quietly and listening attentively to what students were reporting, I engaged in the conversation with students, mostly by asking further questions, but also asserting my own thoughts and experiences when I felt I had something substantive to add. These conversations seemed to flow much more easily than the open-ended interviews. They also provided a more natural way for me to check back with students to make sure I understood what they were saying over time.

Transitioning from recorded conversations into recreational time hanging out together also seemed much less strange than shifting from a formal interview into hang out time. Eventually, our recorded conversations melded into unplanned encounters, in which students and I planned time in our schedules to spend with each other during my visits to their homes and communities. We took turns with the digital recording device, each indicating moments when we thought it appropriate to turn the device on or off. These unplanned encounters afforded me the ability to interview, observe, and participate with students in ways that simple interview visits could not. I consistently wrote analytic field notes and memos to myself during and after each visit with students.

The unplanned encounters also allowed me to break down one of the arbitrary and in many ways, artificial barriers between the students and me. I have often felt uncomfortable with the strict dichotomy between roles as researcher and participant. Since when did the researcher stop participating in the research process? Unplanned encounters helped me view myself as a participant, which also helped me view students as primary knowledge constructors in this inquiry. We each retained different responsibilities within our roles, but our roles as participants brought us much closer and allowed for more intimacy to be fostered between us.

Early in my fieldwork, my notes often reflected my awareness of my surroundings. When I entered students' homes, I wrote about the characteristics of their dwellings. As the study continued, I took less notice of where we were and more notice of what we were doing. I noted the where as much as I felt necessary to explain the what, but as a participant, I became much more comfortable with my discomforts. That is to say, I am often uncomfortable in other people's houses, especially when I do not know the owner (e.g., parents) as intimately as I do the resident (e.g., students) who invited me inside. I felt much more authentic and genuine during my unplanned encounters than during my formal interviews.

Before ever entering the field, I made the decision that I would always pay for any activities in which I participated with students. I thought that if I expected them to include me, they should expect me to pay. They had not signed-on to a project with explicit costs associated with it. As much as possible, I tried to suggest ways for us to interact that would not require money. These encounters usually relied on access to students' homes, city parks, or school facilities. However, some students were reluctant to meet in their homes. Weather did not always permit us to meet outdoors. Schools were rarely accessible for a non-school sanctioned activity. Many of my encounters occurred in coffee shops, diners, and other usual hangout spots that students frequented. Even though these were places that students regularly hung out, I still felt the responsibility to pay. If I were not there, would they have spent money on that activity? There was no way to really judge, so I assumed financial responsibility.

I learned to temper my monetary sponsorship, though. Generally, if I were sharing coffee with students, I would purchase the first drink. If students wanted more, I would not make a fuss over paying. If we went to the movies after meeting over dinner because a student really wanted to see the latest teen heartthrob on screen (one of my own guilty pleasures), I usually only purchased a ticket for myself. Slowly, as our encounters became more and more like regular hang out activities, I found myself abiding by our own set of implicit rules. If we did something that was student initiated, like inviting me to a football game, I took care of my own costs only. If we did something that I initiated, such as going out to dinner in order to get face time together, I made an effort to pay for each of us.

There were cultural dimensions to my funding practices with students as well. Six students graduated from high school over the course of the study. I gave each of them a graduation card and a $15 gift card to merchants that I thought might be useful for first-year college students (e.g., local coffee shops). I visited the Imperial Valley one week after Renaldo's graduation. This was a huge accomplishment that he and other students I was working with in the area recognized. I wanted to recognize Renaldo's achievement, and I offered to take everyone out for dinner to celebrate. When I asked where to go, I was met with blank stares and silenced voices. I was confused.

In my family, going out to dinner was a regular practice. It was no big deal. It was expected behavior. Celebrating major achievements and milestones by paying other people to plan, prepare, and serve us food was the normal thing to do. As the blank stares and silences grew longer, I prodded a bit. Then, I made some suggestions of my own. They agreed with every restaurant I named, even though they had never eaten in any of them.

We decided on an Italian restaurant similar to a number of national chains with sit-down service. What ensued was unsettling for me. Students were taken aback by the offering of complimentary bread and free beverage refills. I suggested an appetizer for the table to share. When the unused plates in front of us were removed for newer plates that would be used for our forthcoming calamari, students awkwardly rearranged themselves to make the server's job easier. Students were confused by some of the items on the menu. When the entrees came, the food was not what students expected. The whole experience seemed unfamiliar. When the bill came I got it, both literally (I paid.) and figuratively—these were white, middle-class practices of dining out.

I cannot say that students were uncomfortable. We had a very lovely dinner, and everyone agreed that it was a very nice time. I was unsettled, because I had orchestrated an event that positioned students as ignorant, simple, and less-than-me. This event, which had been intended to bring us all together, forcibly highlighted the ways in which society keeps us apart. I was responsible for tipping the power balance unequivocally in my favor. Students needed me to make sense of the practices to which they were subjected.

I felt like an idiot. Why did I think this would be a treat for them? Why would my family's version of celebrating translate into celebration for them? If I wanted to acknowledge Renaldo's academic achievement, why did I fail to inquire how he might want that event to be constructed? I had made a huge assumption that my values universally transferred into their lives. After all, I had celebrated several academic achievements in my lifetime. Then again, so had they.

The evening was an astute lesson in event planning. Later, while hanging out at Jesus' parents' house, we were laughing about the whole experience. Jesus even said, "Didn't you notice that everyone was white there? It's like, the only place in El Centro where there's more white people than Mexicans." Indeed, I had recognized the racialized components to the evening when we walked inside the restaurant. Still, it did not make me question my ideas of what celebrating Renaldo's graduation should be like.

The conversations at Jesus' house reminded me about all of the celebrations that students had already invited me to participate with them. Jesus and Renaldo both reminisced about other celebratory events, such as *quinceañeras* and family members' birthdays. I remembered being at Alex's graduation party just one week earlier. Two common characteristics across all of these events were that they included the entire family, and they took place at home. I am not trying to reduce migrant families' celebratory practices to these two characteristics. My reflection on this experience aims to highlight one dimension of how complicated fieldwork can be, especially when all participants are committed to mutual social justice goals.

Furthermore, as an event within an ethnographic study, this dinner was in many ways, a complete failure. In no way was I engaged in the students' normative practices. At the same time, I was engaged in their normative practices—their practices of negotiating and navigating social environments that perpetuated dominance over their cultural communities. In this sense, failure in ethnography can also mean success. Even so, the potential for harm in this situation could easily outweigh any construction of "success" in the field.

On rare occasions, I would hang out with students in my hotel room. Most students seemed terribly interested to know where I stayed when I visited them. I had strict rules for myself when this occurred. The hotel was used only as a last resort as a place to hang out. I would always prop the door open by opening the deadbolt lock and resting it against the doorframe. I would only invite students into the hotel on weekend visits, and only if they indicated that their parents knew where they were and who was with them. Still, these were some of my most uncomfortable encounters.

Part of my social history includes an overriding, hegemonic, and ideological public concern about adult gay men and unethical sexual indiscretions. Explaining my sexuality by claiming a gay male identity is one of the easiest ways to express my same-sex desires. Within the dominant discourse of U.S. society, "gay male" invokes caution for many, especially when young people are involved. This discriminatory myth plagues me in my work with youth. I am acutely aware of threats that plague gay men who work with youth. These threats circle around innuendo of sexual misconduct by gay men. At the same time, I cannot say that this myth has ever played out in tangible, explicit, and/or direct threats or disabling actions against me.

My relationships with youth, and the youth who participated in this study in particular, stand as a testament that my ethics are not in conflict with my sexuality. In addition to the pervasive false presumptions that gay men are sexual predators, I also carry a social history that has pitted communities of color against gay identities. "Gay men" is assumed to mean "white." Queers of color are subject to a triple-threat of marginalization. Dominant white communities marginalize queers of color for their racialized ethnicity. White queers marginalize them in similar ways. Communities of color marginalize them for their queerness. Beyond that, "gay men" is assumed to indicate a middle-class privilege that may or may not always transfer into social relations. Society has tried to teach me that communities of color and white queers, such as myself, do not get along. I have found that to be a vicious fiction that is simply not true.

In spite of these dominant social myths, the students and I challenged ourselves to relate as humanly as possible to each other. I am proud of the ways in which we defy normative social relations. Latina/os and queers are not mutually exclusive social identifiers, nor are we endangerments to each other's cultural communities. In fact, we came to know a very rich, complicated, and dialogically complex world together. Ours was a space of interrogation and support that I have rarely found in educational practices. The hotel room became a less scary space after time, and its utility extended into other spaces, which did not carry the same potential risks, and indeed provided different conveniences, of which I was thrilled to partake.

Still, some of my richest moments in getting to know students occurred in my hotel rooms. It was in my hotel room that I learned about how Renaldo would earn money for his educational expenses by helping out church elders. He didn't think of it as work, because it was through his church, but it was a clear example of his contribution to the family economy. It was in my hotel room that I learned about

Renaldo's struggle to make his goals clearer to his father, who thought that going to college was strictly in order to get a higher paying job and could not understand Renaldo's desire to become an underpaid high school counselor. It was in my hotel room that Nené setup my MySpace page, which unleashed a transformation in my fieldwork practices. It was in my hotel room where I first felt like I was just hanging out with students.

The influence of Nené's setting up my MySpace page was incredible. Until then, I relied primarily on e-mail and telephone calls in order to communicate with students when I was not visiting with them. Generally, e-mail and telephone worked pretty well. However, compared to MySpace, e-mail and telephone were simple supplements to a new primary interface for high school students. On MySpace, I could message students instantly, or leave a message for them to find the next time they visited their MySpace page. I could post a public announcement about them, explaining how cool I thought they were, or editorialize on their latest improvements to their personal pages. On my own page, I could blog about the study or any other topics that seemed pressing to me. Students responded at least twice as fast and usually with longer, more in-depth writing. MySpace was a way to continue my interaction and participation with students beyond the confines of my face-to-face visits with them. In a sense, for students who were active on MySpace, we were always visiting each other, rather than once every four weeks.

I restricted my personal MySpace page to only be accessible to students participating in the study or other students from MSLI. I did not want to risk sacrificing students' confidentiality outside a known safe group. MySpace constrained the study in one significant way; not everyone has a MySpace account. For students who were not active on MySpace, I continued using e-mail and telephone. However, in reviewing my records of my interactions with students, I ended up consistently spending more time with students who remained in more constant contact, using more media. The influence, affordances, and constraints of media such as MySpace present a new methodological quandary that I am eager to explore further.

Afterword

On Relationships

I feel very close to the students participating in this study. They are important to me, and I will continue to do everything that I can to assist them in working toward their own, and our collective, goals of humanization. I have tried to be as explicit as possible throughout my presentation of this inquiry process about my relationships with students. I made the conscious decision not to shy away from implicating my own participation within and throughout this study. However, there were constraining consequences to the relationships that students and I fostered together. First and foremost, I found myself feeling anxious and stressed about spending as much time as possible with as many students as possible. If I had a free day in the week or an unexpectedly free weekend during the month, my first consideration was to see if any students might be free for a visit. These considerations not only took a minor toll on my other relationships, but also on my physical well-being, which in turn seemed to diminish my participation when I could visit students. Reaching balance was a struggle for me.

More poignantly, the strength of my developing relationships with students made it very difficult for me to share my future plans with them. Over the course of this study, I was offered and accepted a faculty position at Iowa State University, to begin in January 2007. I did not share this news with students until very near the end of the formal study. I made the decision to keep this information from students, not with the intention of deceiving them, but rather, because I wanted to continue fostering our relationships as we had begun, and I did not want to explain how our relationships could be sustained after I left California. That explanation seemed too difficult for me, in part because I had not figured it out for myself. I knew that I was committed to sustaining our relationships, but I had not thoroughly explored how I could do so. I felt it was incumbent on me, as the person with more resources and as the departing party to figure these things out before engaging in any conversations about them. I regret not sharing with students sooner.

The first time I shared my future plans with a student, his eyes sank into his lap for a moment before he returned my gaze and asked, "You're still going to come back, right?" This was followed by congratulations and questions about what I would be doing in my new job. That first response stuck with me. I tried to explain that I will definitely be back in California in the future, for all sorts of different reasons, and that keeping in touch with them was a top priority for me. These conversations did not get easier, and I quickly recognized that I had indeed deceived students on some level, even though my sentiment around the sustainability of our relationship remained intact. To those ends, some students have suggested continuing the inquiry project and volunteered to work with me so that I may follow their educational experiences through college. I am very excited to have the opportunity to collaborate with them.

My relationships with students were friendly, intimate, and filled with hope. I was pleasantly surprised when these traits were carried over into my relationships with students' families. As a middle-class, attractive, queer twenty-something, racialized as white, able-bodied graduate student, I expected more tension between students' families and myself. I was also really worried that students' parents would not like me, putting students in an awkward position. I found that families' trusted their students' judgment in who they brought into their homes and that my earnest desire to get to know the family on their terms were met with encouraging, inviting, and caring efforts to share. Language often became an irrelevant barrier as we worked together to communicate across our linguistic strengths and limitations. I am proud of the relationships that parents, siblings, cousins, and friends fostered with me. I am proud of the relationships that I fostered with them.

On Analysis

Cultural practices are the everyday things that humans do while going about their everyday lives. They are the practices that most readily make intuitive sense to us, but that we might not be able to explain or isolate without rigorous documentation and analysis. As they are so embedded in daily life, they also lose some value when isolated and treated independently. Rather, examining the repertoires of practice that individuals and groups put forth toward specific goals provides a richer understanding of what is really going on (Gutiérrez & Rogoff, 2003). A repertoire can be thought of as a sort of rotating set of things that I might do in any given situation. These things emerge from my shared history with others like me. Repertoires of practice connect people in cultural groups, even though, and perhaps in spite or because of the differentiation of practice across individuals in any given group. Hence, students' repertoires of practice could be examined by my ethnographic encounters with them and my activity-based analysis.

When I began working with data, I initially thought I was going to find a collection of themes that jumped out from some codes I imported from my cultural-historical activity theory framework. I thought that I had gathered data that spoke to students' repertoires of practice and that I would be able to nicely document their college pathways. The problem was that I was not looking to document their college pathways in any reduced or simple way. I was seeking to understand a complex recursive process between imagining college access and practicing it, back and forth and in between. After forming lists and lists of what students did, and how students thought about college access, I made an important leap in my analysis. I realized that in order to explain access as a learning activity, as a social practice, as literacy, I needed to understand how this literacy developed.

From my theoretical framework, I recognized that learning and development happened when students' repertoires of practice were extended toward the object of college access. These were moments when assistance was provided to students so that they could work within their actual levels of development to reach and participate from their potential levels of development. I was looking to identify what Vygotsky (1978) called, "zones of proximal development" (p. 84). In order to express them in a way familiar to scholars of higher education opportunity, I called them transformative learning opportunities.

This shift emblazoned my analysis. Suddenly, I had more things to explain, and a more cohesive framework in which to explain them than I had ever anticipated. It also moved my analysis from static to dynamic process. Looking at transformative learning opportunities meant I was mapping students' development in the recursive way that they expressed it to me. Thinking of transformative learning opportunities corresponded to the problem-based theoretical framework of CHAT and led me to the hope-filled concept of a college-going pedagogy.

On Writing

Generally, I do not struggle with writing. Writing is an enjoyable, creative, and meaningfully challenging process for me. I write daily. However, writing in order to represent and to re-present real peoples' experiences provides its own unique challenges. Questions of fairness and completeness shape concerns about the quality, integrity, and impact of the writing when real peoples' lives are at the center of expression. I struggled with finding answers to questions about how to represent and re-present my analysis of participants' lived experiences.

I sought advice from three sources: literature, colleagues, and participants. Specifically, I was looking for non-traditional ways in which to treat what I had learned through my fieldwork and analysis in my writing. The traditional practice of substantiating analytic claims through short quotes (Maxwell, 1996; Merriam, 2001) directly from the data did not seem to meet my own standards for some of the findings I was trying to explain. The emotional impact of what I experienced through my fieldwork and analysis often seemed lost. Erickson's (1986) narrative vignettes were helpful in pushing my writing toward a more holistic re-presentation of what and how I had learned, and I incorporated this strategy in some cases.

Still, for some of the most dramatic findings, I felt like I was losing the corporeality of students' meaning-making experiences. I also felt that my own participation was being ignored or rendered as omnisciently absent from the representations of my analysis. I felt trapped in (and out of) my writing. In speaking with colleagues, both within and outside the academy, I was encouraged to look at writing that excited me most in my own reading. I took this to heart, and I extended the advice to include reading outside of the scholarship in my own field. I examined research articles that I found most convincing and enjoyable. I explored essays from political pundits that I rely on for deft analysis of current events. I revisited some of my favorite authors of fiction: Alice Walker, Carlos Fuentes, Arundhati Roy, and David Mitchell. These re-readings of texts that previously had moved me as a writer encouraged me that there were other ways to treat data and analysis that might indeed recapture some of what I feared I might be losing. Looking outside the social sciences also returned me to my previous passions in the humanities, specifically in theater.

As a theater major in my undergraduate education, I found drama afforded an acute social analysis that was intertwined between the production (including actors, directors, and designers) and the audience. Theater, for me, was the presentation of social realities that emerged from the exchange of expression between the production and the audience. I asked myself how I might apply my experience and expertise in the dramatic arts to my work as a social scientist. How could I put myself back into my work and retain the integrity of students' experiences from this research study?

After my reconnaissance into the humanities, I returned to the social sciences and (re)read further into the latest developments of writing in qualitative inquiry. I found texts on performance ethnography (e.g., Jones, 2002; Pelias, 2002), queer ethnography (e.g., De Castell & Bryson, 1998; Talburt, 2000), and autoethnography (e.g., Creef, 2002; Travisano, 2002) to be most informative. They sought to address some of my fundamental concerns about how I was treating my analysis in my writing. These methodologies encouraged me to retain the corporeal elements of experience and to make explicit my own involvement in the research process. I knew that I did not want to write a purely performance ethnography, nor was my study designed as queer, and my autoethnographic components were far from central to the concerns of my inquiry. Still, I returned, refreshed and energized, to my own writing.

I figured that I wanted to explain my findings in ways that captured the participation in the activity. I wanted to re-present data in action. Hence, I structured each finding differently, based on the participatory experiences of students and myself within the findings. The writing that came as a result of these efforts eventually took form as the context-rich narratives of Carlitos' migration story, Cristina's migration speech, and the elaborated field notes that constitute my substantiation of *confianza* between Nené and me. These are examples of some of my riskiest and most daring expressions of what I learned about migrant students' college-going. In order to feel most secure in them, I felt it was incumbent upon me to share these writings with the students who I felt were truly co-authors of the material. Their insights were immeasurably helpful. They provided corrective feedback as well as new ideas of other moments from our encounters to include. I believe the result is a collection of very moving portraits that help explain some of the dilemmas and imaginable remedies of college access for migrant students.

On Learning

My methodological training equipped me well for this project. I confidently made adjustments through thoughtful and informed deliberations throughout the inquiry. However, I found myself struggling through something that most methodological texts ignore—feelings. Specifically, I struggled with feelings of unworthiness and guilt. I rarely feel either of these emotions in my life. Their creeping presence in this project was not necessarily unanticipated, yet still surprising. I felt unworthy to hear students' stories, especially some of the most horrifying and dehumanizing tales of interactions with U.S. institutions, such as Homeland Security. I felt guilty that my encounters with students seemed to benefit me more than them. Feelings are difficult to capture. Feelings are challenging to admit. Feelings are uncomfortable to deal with. I did not want my feelings to penetrate my work.

I learned, however, that my feelings were an integral part of my own participation in the inquiry. In attempts to capture my feelings, I challenged myself to write them, as best I could, in my analytic memos. I then shared these memos with some colleagues and other participants. These practices assisted me in working through my guilt and developing efficacy around my involvement in students' lives. My colleagues pointed out ways in which my own reflections evidenced honest concern and integrity in my relationships to students and in my work. Students shared their own feelings with me about participating in the study. Students' reflections oftentimes were similar to my own. Some of them felt unworthy to be asked the questions I was asking and guilty about putting me in the position to know and understand their lives more deeply. We took these opportunities to deconstruct our feelings in ways that made sense for our own relationships. We talked through our feelings. Talking reassured me that my feelings were an important lens through which I made sense of my encounters with students. In the end, I welcomed these feelings and their effects on the study, and I sought to both alleviate and understand them via my writing and conversations with students.

The truth behind incorporating my feelings into my work was evidenced to me most poignantly when I spoke about my work with friends outside of the academic world. My final reflection about performing critical sociocultural inquiry is a reassertion that the researcher must be conceived as a primary participant in the inquiry. The necessity of deconstructing the researcher-participant dichotomy was reinforced for me through the stories created by my conversations with neighborhood friends.

Friends in my neighborhood primarily work in corporate environments. The processes and demands of educational research are not part of their everyday experiences. These friends predominantly live lives of privilege in terms of their socioeconomic status. Their social views range across a wide spectrum of political ideologies. Still, there is general consensus that my work matters, and we provide each other with much needed support and respect outside of our specific fields. Two questions around this project became especially helpful to me in making sense of my own process of coming to know. The first is a question I asked my friends about their views on class in the U.S. After sharing a story from one of my visits, a friend told me that the students I was working with "couldn't really be that poor if they drove you around in a nice new truck." My first reaction was to be infuriated. My friendship with this man helped me refrain from getting upset, and instead I responded with, "What? Poor people don't deserve nice things?" This question, for me, has come to represent the multifaceted, hegemonic, and hypocritical narratives around class and poverty in the U.S. It simultaneously questions the inherent judgment of private economic management practices embedded in my friend's statement, while also questioning the assumptions around the ways that poor people live—a social condition about which my friends had absolutely no first-hand knowledge.

The second question was asked of me by another friend who accompanied me on a visit to a student while I was in the midst of writing this manuscript. The student had introduced me to a number of his friends, and we were both eager for him to meet one of mine. After spending the day together, my friend commented that he had enjoyed getting to know this student, but questioned, "It was just so weird, 'cause, like, is it just me, or is he like, a little version of you?" His question implied that my relationship with the student included some sort of ideological training. My reply was that perhaps my friend needed to shift the gaze and consider that I might be becoming a bigger version of him.

This second question represents the hybridity inherent in critical sociocultural work, where I was constructed as much as a learner, or novice, as the student participant, and that he was constructed as much as a teacher, or expert, as I. We mutually engaged in the work of understanding how migrant students came to know college access, together. The principled assumption is that all participants in the research process co-construct knowledge through the inquiry. There is no doubt that my relationship with them influenced the students' lives. More importantly, the influence of the students' relationship to me must not be ignored or cloaked by the dominant gaze that would situate me as a more powerful mediator in coming to know social phenomena.

These two questions strike at the heart of who migrant students are and who they are not. They are everyday instances of how my third research question about the constitution of migrant students as subjects gets taken up in dominant discourse. Deliberating over and deconstructing these questions became essential in my process of coming to know during this project. Through these questions, my performance of critical sociocultural inquiry permeated my life beyond my academic endeavors. For me, my process of coming to know through inquiry informed not only my academic career, but also my daily practices, an insight that will guide my future performances of critical sociocultural inquiry.

Bibliography

Adelman, C. (1999). *Answers in the tool box: Academic intensity, attendance patterns, and bachelor's degree attainment.* Washington, DC: U.S. Department of Education.

Apple, M.W. (1990). *Ideology and curriculum,* 2nd edition. New York: Routledge.

——— (2006). *Educating the "right" way: Markets, standards, God, and inequality.* New York: Routledge.

Auerbach, S. (2004). Engaging Latino parents in supporting college pathways: Lessons from a college access program. *Journal of Hispanic higher education, 3*(2): 125–145.

Avery, C., Fairbanks, A. & Zeckhauser, R. (2003). *The early admissions game: Joining the elite.* Cambridge, MA: Harvard University Press.

Baez, B. (2006). Merit and difference. *Teachers college record, 108* (6), 996–1016.

Barton, D., & Hamilton, M. (1998) *Local literacies: Reading and writing in one community.* London: Routledge.

Barton, D., Hamilton, M. & Ivanic, R. (2000) *Situated literacies: Reading and writing in context.* London: Routledge.

Barton, D. & Tustin, K. (2005). *Beyond communities of practice: Language, power, and social context.* Cambridge, UK: Cambridge University Press.

Baum, S. & Ma, J. (2007). *Education pays 2007: The benefits of higher education for individuals and society.* Washington, DC: The College Board.

Berkner, L. & Chavez, L. (1997) *Access to postsecondary education for the 1992 high school graduates.* Statistical analysis report from the National Center for Education Statistics.

Bloom, L.R. (1998). *Under the sign of hope: Feminist methodology and narrative interpretation.* Albany, NY: SUNY Press.

Breland, H., Maxey, J., Gernand, R., Cumming, T. & Trapani, C. (2002). *Trends in college admissions: A report of a survey of undergraduate admissions policies, practices, and procedures.* Tallahassee, FL: Association for Institutional Research.

Brown, S.K. & Hirschman, C. (2006). The end of affirmative action in Washington State and its impact on the transition from high school to college. *Sociology of education, 79*(2), 106–130.

Bureau of Labor Statistics (2007). *Volunteering in the United States, 2006.*

Cabrera, A. & La Nasa, S. (Eds.). (2000). Understanding the college choice of disadvantaged students. In A. Cabrera, & S. La Nasa, (Eds.), *New directions for institutional research,* No. 107. San Francisco: Jossey-Bass.

California Department of Education (2005). Educational Statistics [Data file]. Available from California Department of Education Website, http://data1.cde.ca.gov/dataquest/.

——— (2007). *California migrant education program: comprehensive needs assessment.* Sacramento, CA: Author.

Chaiklin, S. (2003). The zone of proximal development in Vygotsky's analysis of learning and instruction. In A. Kozulin, B. Gindis, V. Ageyev, & S. Miller (Eds.), *Vygotsky's educational theory in cultural context* (pp. 39–64). New York: Cambridge University Press.

Choy, S. (2002). *Access and persistence: Findings from 10 years of longitudinal research on students.* Washington, DC: American Council on Education.

Cole, M. (1996). *Cultural psychology: A once and future discipline.* Cambridge, MA: Harvard University Press.

Conchas, G.Q. (2006). *The color of success: Race and high-achieving urban youth.* New York: Teachers College Press.

Contreras, F.E. (2005). The reconstruction of merit post-proposition 209. *Educational policy, 19*(2), 371–395.

Creswell, J.W. (2008). *Research design: Qualitative, quantitative, and mixed methods approaches.* Thousand Oaks, CA: Sage Press.

Darder, A., Baltodano, M. & Torres, R.D. (2003). *The critical pedagogy reader.* New York: Routledge Farmer.

DeWelque, D. (2004). *Education, information, and smoking decisions: Evidence from smoking histories, 1940–2000* (Policy Research Working Paper No. 3362) Washington, DC: World Bank.

Dixson, A.D. & Rousseau, C.K. (2007). And we are still not saved: Critical Race Theory in education ten years later. In A.D. Dixson & C.K. Rousseau (Eds.), *Critical race theory in education: All God's children got a song.* New York: Routledge.

Duncan-Andrade, J. & Morrell, E. (2008). *The art of critical pedagogy: Possibilities for moving from theory to practice in urban schools.* New York: Peter Lang Publishing.

Ellis, C. & Bochner, A. (Eds.) (1996). *Composing ethnography: Alternative forms of qualitative writing.* Lanham, MD: AltaMira Press.

Engeström, Y. (1987). *Learning by expanding.* Helsinki, Finland: Orinta-Konsultit Oy.

——— (1993). Developmental studies of work as a testbench of activity theory: The case of primary care medical practice. In S. Chaiklin & J. Lave (Eds.), *Understanding practice: Perspective on activity and context* (pp. 64–103). Cambridge, UK: Cambridge University Press.

——— (1999). Activity theory and individual and social transformation. In Y. Engeström, R. Miettinen, & R-L. Punamaki (Eds.), *Perspectives on activity theory* (pp. 19–38). Cambridge, UK: Cambridge University Press.

——— (2006). *The activity system.* Retrieved November 1, 2006, from University of Helsinki, Department of Education: Center for Activity Theory and Developmental Work Research Web site: http://www.edu.helsinki.fi/activity/pages/chatanddwr/activitysystem/.

Fann, A. (2005). "Forgotten students: Native American high school students' narratives on college going." Revised 01/05 for the American Educational Research Association Annual Meeting, Montreal, Canada. First presented as "Native college pathways in California: A look at college access for American Indian high school students." Paper presented at the Association for the Study of Higher Education Annual Meeting, Sacramento, CA, 2002.

Faulstich Orellana, M. (2001). The work kids do: Mexican and Central American immigrant children's contributions to households and schools in California. *Harvard educational review, 71*(3), 366–389.

Flint, T. (1992). Parental and planning influences on the formation of student college choice sets. *Research in higher education, 21*(2), 21–32.

Gándara, P. (2002). A study of high school Puente: What we have learned about preparing Latino youth for post-secondary education. *Educational policy, 16*(4), 474–495.

Gándara, P. & Bial, D. (1999). *Paving the way to higher education: K–12 interventions for under-represented students*. Washington, DC: National Center for Education Statistics.

Gándara, P., Orfield, G. & Horn, C.L. (Eds.). (2006). *Expanding opportunity in higher education*. Albany, NY: SUNY Press.

Gee, J. (1991). *Social Linguistics: Ideology in discourses*. London: Falmer Press.

Gibson, M.A. (2003). "Improving graduation outcomes for migrant students." *ERIC Clearinghouse on rural education and small schools*. (ERIC Document Reproduction Service No. ED478061).

Gibson, M.A. & Bejinez, L.F. (2002). Dropout prevention: How migrant education supports Mexican youth. *Journal of Latinos and education, 1*(3), 155–175.

Gildersleeve, R.E. (2006). *Toward a college-going literacy: Voices of migrant students coming to know college access*, Unpublished doctoral dissertation, University of California Los Angeles.

——— (2009). Organizing learning for transformation in college outreach programmes. *Pedagogies: An international journal, 4*(1).

Gladieux, L. & Swail, W.S. (1999). Financial aid is not enough: Improving the odds for minority and low-income students. In J.E. King (Ed.), *Financing a college education: How it works and how it's changing* (pp. 177–197). Phoenix, AZ: Oryx Press.

Gonzalez, G.G. & Fernandez, R.A. (2003). *A century of Chicano history: Empire, nations, and migration*. New York: Routledge.

González, N., Moll, L.C. & Amanti, C. (Eds.). (2005). *Funds of knowledge: Theorizing practices in households, communities, and classrooms*. Mahwah, NJ: Lawrence Erlbaum Associates.

Gutiérrez, K.D. (1995). Unpackaging academic discourse. *Discourse processes, 19*(1), 21–37.

——— (2002). Studying cultural practices in urban learning communities. *Human development, 45*, 312–321.

——— (2004, April). "Intersubjectivity and grammar in the third space." Paper presented at the annual meeting of the American Educational Research Association, Montreal, Canada.

——— (2006). White innocence: A framework and methodology for rethinking educational discourse. *International journal of learning, 12*, 1–11.

——— (2007a). Commentary on a sociocritical approach to literacy. In C. Lewis, P. Enciso, & E. Moje. (Eds.), *Identity, agency, and power: Reframing sociocultural research on literacy* (pp. 115–120). Mahwah, NJ: Lawrence Erlbaum Associates.

——— (2007b). Historicizing literacy. In M. Blackburn & C. Clark (Eds.), *Literacy research for political action* (pp. ix-xiii). New York: Peter Lang Publishing.

——— (2008a). Developing sociocritical literacies in the third space. *Reading research quarterly, 43*(2), 148–164.

——— (2008b). Language and literacies as civil rights. In S. Greene (Ed.) *Literacy as a civil right: Reclaiming social justice in literacy teaching and learning* (pp. 169–184). New York: Peter Lang Publishing.

Gutiérrez, K.D. Hunter, J.D. & Arzubiaga, A. (2009). Re-mediating the university: Learning through sociocritical literacies. *Pedagogies: An international journal, 4*(1).

Gutiérrez, K.D. & Jaramillo, N. (2006). Looking for educational equity: The consequences of relying on *Brown*. In A. Ball (Ed.), *With more deliberate speed: Achieving equity and excellence in education—Realizing the full potential of* Brown v. Board of Education (Yearbook of the National Society for the Study of Education, Vol. 105, Issue 2, pp. 173–189). Malden, MA: Blackwell.

Gutiérrez, K.D., Morales, P.Z., & Martinez, D.C. (2009). Remediating literacy: Culture, difference, and learning for students from non-dominant communities. *Review of research in education, 33,* 212–245.

Gutiérrez, K.D. & Rogoff, B. (2003). Cultural ways of learning: Individual traits or repertoires of practice. *Educational researcher, 32*(5), 19–25.

Harding, S. (1995). "Strong objectivity": A response to the new objectivity question. *Synthese, 104,* 331–349.

Heller, D.E. (2002). *Conditions of access: Higher education for lower-income students.* Westport, CT: American Council on Education/Praeger Series on Higher Education.

Horn, C.L., Flores, S.M. & Orfield, G. (Eds.) (2006). Latino educational opportunity. *New directions for community colleges, 133,* 1–84.

Hossler, D., Braxton, J. & Coopersmith, G. (1989). Understanding student college choice. In J.C. Smart (Ed.) *Higher education: Handbook of theory and research* (pp. 231–288), New York: Agathon Press.

Hossler, D., Schmit, J. & Vesper, N. (1999). *Going to college: How social, economic, and educational factors influence the decisions students make.* Baltimore: John Hopkins University Press.

Ikenberry, S., & Hartle, T. (1998). *Too little knowledge is a dangerous thing, what the public knows and thinks about paying for college.* Washington, DC: American Council on Education.

Jackson, G. (1982). Public efficiency and private choice in higher education. *Educational evaluation and policy analysis, 4,* 237–247.

Justice for Immigrants (2007). *Take action alert.* Retrieved November 19, 2007, from http://www.justiceforimmigrants.org/action.html.

Kincheloe, J.L. & McLaren, P. (2000). Rethinking critical theory and qualitative research. In N.K. Denzin & Y.S. Lincoln (Eds.). *Handbook of qualitative research,* 2nd ed. (pp. 279–313). Thousand Oaks, CA: Sage.

―――― (2005). Rethinking critical theory and qualitative research. In N.K. Denzin & Y.S. Lincoln (Eds.). *Handbook of qualitative research,* 3rd ed. (pp. 303– 342). Thousand Oaks, CA: Sage.

King, J.E. (1996). *The decision to go to college: Attitudes and experiences associated with college attendance among low-income students.* New York: The College Board.

―――― (Ed.) (1999). *Financing a college education: How it works and how it's changing.* Phoenix, AZ: Oryx Press.

Kirst, M.W. & Venezia, A. (Eds.). (2004). *From high school to college: Improving opportunities for success in postsecondary education.* San Francisco: Jossey-Bass.

Lather, P. (1986). Issues of validity in openly ideological research: Between a rock and a soft place. *Interchange, 17*(4), 63–84.

―――― (1993). Fertile obsession: Validity after post–structuralism. *The sociological quarterly, 34*(4), 673–693.

Lave, J. (1988). *Cognition in practice.* Cambridge, UK: Cambridge University Press.

―――― (1996). Teaching, as learning, in practice. *Mind, culture, and activity: An international journal, 3,* 149–164.

Lave, J. & Wenger, E. (1991). *Situated learning: Legitimate peripheral participation.* Cambridge, MA: Cambridge University Press.

Lewis, C. (2001). *Literacy practices as social acts: Power, status, and cultural norms in the classroom.* Mahwah, NJ: Lawrence Erlbaum Press.

Lincoln, Y.S. & Denzin, N.K. (2005). Epilogue: The eighth and ninth moments— Qualitative research in/and the fractured future. In N.K. Denzin & Y.S. Lincoln (Eds.) *The handbook of qualitative research* (pp. 1115–1126). Thousand Oaks, CA: Sage Press.

Linehan, C. & McCarthy, J. (2001). Reviewing the 'community of practice' metaphor: An analysis of control relations in a primary school classroom. *Mind, culture, and activity, 8,* 129–147.

Litten, L. (1979). Market structure and institutional position in geographic market segments. *Research in higher education, 11,* 59–83.

Long, B.T. (2003). The connection between government aid and college pricing. *Journal of student financial aid, 33*(2).

Lopez, G.R. (2001). The value of hard work: Lessons on parent involvement from an (im)migrant household. *Harvard educational review, 71*(3), 416–437.

―――― (2004). Bringing the mountain to Mohammed: Parent involvement in migrant-impacted schools. In C. Salinas, & M.E. Franquiz (Eds.), *Scholars in the field: The challenges of migrant education* (pp. 135–146). Charleston, WV: AEL.

Lopez, G.R., Scribner, J.D. & Mahitivanichcha, K. (2001). Redefining parental involvement: Lessons from high-performing migrant-impacted schools. *American educational research journal, 38*(2), 253–288.

Maxwell, J. (2004). *Qualitative research design: An interactive approach.* Thousand Oaks, CA: Sage Press.

McDonough, P.M. (1997). *Choosing colleges: How social class and schools structure opportunity.* Albany, NY: SUNY Press.

———— (1999, April) "Race-based or conflict-based college admissions?" Paper presented at the annual meeting of the American Educational Research Association, Montreal, Canada.

———— (2004). *The school to college transition: Challenges and prospects.* Washington, DC: American Council on Education, Informed Practice: Syntheses of Higher Education Research For Campus Leaders.

———— (2005). Counseling matters: Knowledge, assistance, and organizational commitment in college preparation. In W.G. Tierney. Z.B. Corwin, J.E. Colyar (Eds.), *Preparing for college: Nine propositions relating to the effectiveness of college preparation programs* (pp. 69–88). Albany, NY: SUNY Press.

McDonough, P.M. & Gildersleeve, R.E. (2006). All else is never equal: Opportunity lost and found along the K-16 pathway to college access. In C.F. Conrad & R.C. Serlin (Eds.) *The SAGE handbook of education research* (pp. 59–78). Thousand Oaks, CA: Sage Press.

McDonough, P.M., Ventresca, M. & Outcalt, C. (2000). Field of dreams: Organizational field approaches to understanding the transformation of college access, 1965-1995. In J.C. Smart (Ed.), *Higher education: Handbook of theory and research.* Vol. 14, 317–405.

McLaren, P. (1988). On ideology and education: Critical pedagogy and the politics of education. *Social text, 19/20,* 153–185.

———— (1995). *Critical pedagogy and predatory culture: Oppositional politics in a postmodern era.* New York: Routledge.

———— (1998). *Life in schools: An introduction to critical pedagogy in the foundations of education, fifth edition.* New York: Pearson Education, Inc.

McLaren, P. & Kincheloe, J.L. (Eds.) (2007). *Critical pedagogy: Where are we now?* New York: Peter Lang Publishing. New London Group (1996).

Mishel, L., Bernstein, J. & Allegretto, S. (2007). *The state of working America, 2006–2007.* Economic Policy Institute.

National Center for Health Statistics (2005). *National health interview survey.*

New London Group (1996). A pedagogy of multiliteracies: Designing social futures. *Harvard educational review, 66*(1), 60–92.

———— (2000). A pedagogy of multiliteracies designing social futures. In B. Cope & M. Kalantzis (Eds.), *Multiliteracies: Literacy learning and the design of social futures* (pp. 9–38). New York: Routledge.

Nicolopolou, A. & Cole, M. (1993). Generation and transmission of shared knowledge in the culture of collaborative learning: The fifth dimension, its play-world, and its instrumental context. In E.A. Forman, N. Minick, & C.A. Stone (Eds.). *Contexts for learning sociocultural dynamics in children's development* (pp. 283–314). New York: Oxford University Press.

Noblit, G.W., Flores, S.Y. & Murillo, E.G., Jr. (Eds.). (2004). *Postcritical ethnography: Reinscribing critique.* Creskill, NJ: Hampton Press.

Nuñez, A-M. (2009). Migrant students' college access: Emerging evidence from the Migrant Student Leadership Institute. *Journal of Latinos and education 8*(3), 1-18.

Nuñez, A-M. & Jaramillo, N. (2005, November). *Migrant students' college pathways*. Paper presented at the annual meeting of the Association for the Study of Higher Education, Philadelphia, PA.

Oakes, J. (1985). *Keeping track: How schools structure inequality*. New Haven, CT: Yale University.

——— (2003). "Critical conditions for equity and diversity in college access: Informing policy and monitoring results. UC All Campus Consortium for Research on Diversity. Retrieved July 1, 2008 from
http://repositories.cdlib.org/ucaccord/papers/acrd-rr001-0203.

——— (2004). Investigating the claims in *Williams v. State of California*: An unconstitutional denial of education's basic tools? *Teachers college record 106*(10), 1889–1906.

Oakes, J., Rogers, J., Lipton, M. & Morrell, E. (2002). The social construction of college access: Confronting the technical, cultural, and political barriers to low-income students of color. In W.G. Tierney & L.S. Hagedorn (Eds.), *Increasing access to college: Extending possibilities for all students* (pp. 81–104). Albany, NY: SUNY Press.

Oakes, J., Rogers, J., Silver, D., Valladares, S., Terriquez, V., McDonough, P., Renee, M. & Lipton, M. (2006). "Removing the roadblocks: Fair college opportunities for all California students." Los Angeles: UC All Campus Consortium for Research on Diversity and UCLA Institute for Democracy, Education, and Access.

Olson, L. & Rosenfeld, R.A. (1984). Parents and the process of gaining access to student financial aid. *Journal of higher education, 55*, 455–480.

Perna, L. (2005a). The key to college access: Rigorous academic preparation. In W.G. Tierney, Z.B. Corwin, & J.E. Colyar (Eds.), *Preparing for college: Nine elements of effective outreach* (pp. 113–144). Albany, NY: SUNY Press.

——— (2005b). A gap in the literature: The influence of the design, operations, and marketing of student aid programs on college-going plans and behaviors. *Journal of student financial aid, 35*(1), 7–15.

——— (2006). Studying college access and choice: A proposed conceptual model. In J.C. Smart (Ed.), *Higher education: Handbook of theory and research, XXI*, 99–158.

Piirto, J. (2002). The unreliable narrator, or the difference between writing prose in literature and in social science: A commentary on Tierney's article. *International journal of qualitative studies in education 15*(4), 407–415.

Price, D.V. (2004). Educational debt burden among student borrowers: An analysis of the Baccalaureate & Beyond Panel, 1997 Follow-up. *Research in higher education, 45*(7), 701–737.

Ream, R.K. (2005). *Uprooting children: Mobility, social capital, and Mexican American underachievement*. New York: LFB Scholarly Publishing.

Rhoads, R.A. (1998). *Freedom's web: Student activism in an age of cultural diversity*. Baltimore, MD: Johns Hopkins University Press.

Rhoads, R.A., Saenz, V. & Carducci, R. (2005). Higher education reform as a social movement: The case of affirmative action. *Review of higher education, 28*(2), 191–220.

Rogers, R. & Fuller, C. (2007). As if you heard it from your momma: Redesigning histories of participation with literacy education in an adult education class. In C. Lewis, P. Enciso, & E.B. Moje (Eds.). *Reframing sociocultural research on literacy: Identity, agency, and power*, (pp. 75–114). Mahwah, NJ: Lawrence Erlbaum Associates.

Rogoff, B. (1995). Sociocultural activity on three planes. In J.V. Wertsch, P. Del Rio, & A. Alvarez (Eds.), *Sociocultural studies of mind* (pp. 139–164). New York: Cambridge University Press.

—— (2003). *The cultural nature of human development.* New York: Oxford University Press.

—— (2009, November). "Learning by observing and pitching in: Generational and community shifts." Paper presented at the annual meeting for the American Anthropological Association in San Francisco, CA.

Rogoff, B., Matusov, E. & White, C. (1996). Models of teaching and learning: Participation in a community of learners. In D.R. Olson & N. Torrance (Eds.), *The handbook of education and human development* (pp. 388–414). Oxford, UK: Blackwell.

Roth, W-F & Lee, Y-J. (2007). Vygotsky's neglected legacy: Cultural-historical activity theory. *Review of Educational Research, 77*(2), 186–232.

Rothenberg, D. (1998). *With these hands: The hidden world of migrant farmworkers today.* Berkeley, CA: UC Press.

Salinas, C. & Franquiz, M. (Eds.) (2004). *Scholars from the field: The challenges of migrant education.* Charleston, WV: AEL.

Salinas, C. & Reyes, R. (2004). Creating successful academic programs for Chicana/o high school migrant students: The role of advocate educators. *High school journal, 87*, 54–65.

Solórzano, D.G. & Delgado Bernal, D. (2001). Critical race theory, transformational resistance, and social justice: Chicana and Chicano students in an urban context. *Urban education, 36*(1), 308–342.

Solórzano, D.G. & Ornelas, A. (2002). A critical race analysis of advanced placement classes: A case of educational inequality. *Journal of Latinos in education, 1*(4), 215–229.

Solórzano, D.G. & Yosso, T.Y. (2001). Critical race and LatCrit theory and method: Counter storytelling Chicana and Chicano graduate school experiences. *International Journal of qualitative studies in education, 14*(4), 471–495.

St. John, E. (2002). *The access challenge: Rethinking the causes of the opportunity gap* (Policy Issue Report No. 2002–1). Bloomington: Indiana Educational Policy Center.

—— (2003). *Refinancing the college dream: Access, opportunity, and justice for taxpayers.* Baltimore: Johns Hopkins University Press.

Street, B. (1995) *Social literacies.* London: Longman.

Suarez-Orozco, C. & Suarez-Orozco, M. (2001). *Children of immigration.* Cambridge, MA: Harvard University Press.

Tejeda, C. (2000). Spatialized understandings of the Chicana(o)/Latina(o) educational experience: Theorizations of space and the mapping of educational outcomes in

Los Angeles. In C. Tejeda, C. Maritnez, & Z. Leonardo (Eds.) *Charting new terrains of Chicana(o)/Latina(o) education.* (pp. 131–160). Cresskill, NJ: Hampton Press, Inc.

Tienda, M., Cortes, K. & Niu, S. (2003). "College attendance and the Texas top 10 percent law: Permanent contagion or transitory promise?" Paper presented at the Conference on Expanding Opportunity in Higher Education, the Harvard Civil Rights Project, Sacramento, CA.

Tierney, W.G. (2002). Get real: Representing reality. *International journal of qualitative studies in education* 15(4), 385–398.

———— (2009). Applying to college. *Qualitative inquiry, 15*(1), 71–95.

Tierney, W.G. & Auerbach, S. (2005). Toward developing an untapped resource: The role of families in college preparation. In W.G. Tierney, Z.B. Corwin, & J.E. Colyar (Eds.) *Preparing for college: Nine elements of effective outreach* (pp. 29–48). Albany, NY: SUNY Press.

Tierney, W.G. & Colyar, J.E. (Eds.) (2006). *Urban high school students and the challenge of access: Many routes, difficult paths.* New York: Peter Lang Publishing.

Tierney, W.G., Corwin, Z.B. & Colyar, J.E. (Eds.) (2004). *Preparing for college: Nine elements of effective outreach.* Albany, NY: SUNY Press.

Tierney, W.G. & Hagedorn, L.S., (Eds.) (2002). *Increasing access to college.* Albany, NY: SUNY Press.

Tierney, W.G. & Lincoln, Y.S. (1997). *Representation and the text: Re-framing the narrative voice.* Albany, NY: SUNY Press.

Trueba, E.T. (1990). The role of culture in literacy acquisition: An interdisciplinary approach to qualitative research. *International journal of qualitative studies in education, 3*(1), 1–13.

Trueba, E.T. & McLaren, P. (2000). Critical ethnography for the study of immigrants. In E.T. Trueba & L.I. Bartolomé (Eds.), *Immigrant voices: In search of educational equity* (pp. 37–83). New York: Rowman & Littlefield Publishers.

U.S. Census Bureau (2004). *Voting and registration in the election of November 2002.*

———— (2006). *Current population survey, Annual social and economic supplement, Current population reports.*

———— (2007). *Statistical abstract of the United States.* Washington, DC: U.S. Department of Commerce.

U.S. Department of Education (2005). Office of migrant education. Retrieved December 1, 2005 from http://www.ed.gov/programs/mep/funding.html.

Valencia, R.R. & Black, M.S. (2002). "Mexican-Americans don't value education!": On the basis of the myth, mythmaking, and debunking. *Journal of Latinos and education, 1*, 81–103.

Villalpando, O. & Solórzano, D.G. (2005). The role of culture in college preparation programs: A review of the research literature. In W.G. Tierney, Z.B. Corwin, & J.E. Colyar (Eds.), *Preparing for college: Nine elements of effective outreach* (pp. 13–28). Albany, NY: State University of New York Press.

Vygotsky, L.S. (1978). *Mind in society: The development of higher psychological processes.* M. Cole, V. John-Steiner, S. Scribner, & E. Souberman (Trans.). Cambridge, MA: Harvard University Press.

Weis, L. & Fine, M. (2004). Compositional studies in four parts: Critical theorizing and analysis on social (in)justice. In L. Weis & M. Fine (Eds.), *Working method: Research and social justice.* New York: Routledge.

Weisner, T.S. (2002). Ecocultural understanding of children's developmental pathways. *Human development 45*(4), 275–281.

Wenger, E. (1998). *Communities of practice.* New York: Cambridge University Press.

Wertsch, J.V. (1985). *Vygotsky and the social formation of the mind.* Cambridge, MA. Harvard University Press.

Yosso, T.Y. (2006) *Critical race counterstories along the Chicana/Chicano educational pipeline.* New York: Routledge.

Zallaquett, C.P., McHatton, P.A. & Cranston-Gringas, A. (2007). Characteristics of Latina/o migrant farmworker students attending a large metropolitan university. *Journal of Hispanic higher education, 6*(2), 135–156.

Studies in the Postmodern Theory of Education

General Editors
Joe L. Kincheloe & Shirley R. Steinberg

Counterpoints publishes the most compelling and imaginative books being written in education today. Grounded on the theoretical advances in criticism, feminism, and postmodernism in the last two decades of the twentieth century, Counterpoints engages the meaning of these innovations in various forms of educational expression. Committed to the proposition that theoretical literature should be accessible to a variety of audiences, the series insists that its authors avoid esoteric and jargonistic languages that transform educational scholarship into an elite discourse for the initiated. Scholarly work matters only to the degree it affects consciousness and practice at multiple sites. Counterpoints' editorial policy is based on these principles and the ability of scholars to break new ground, to open new conversations, to go where educators have never gone before.

For additional information about this series or for the submission of manuscripts, please contact:

> Joe L. Kincheloe & Shirley R. Steinberg
> c/o Peter Lang Publishing, Inc.
> 29 Broadway, 18th floor
> New York, New York 10006

To order other books in this series, please contact our Customer Service Department:
> (800) 770-LANG (within the U.S.)
> (212) 647-7706 (outside the U.S.)
> (212) 647-7707 FAX

Or browse online by series:
> www.peterlang.com